SOUL

TRANSCENDANTS

Stories on the Path Home to GOD

Compiled by
Jackie Peterson

Living Light Press
Los Angeles, California

SOUL Transcendants
Stories on the Path Home to GOD

Published by
Living Light Press
Los Angeles, CA

First Paperback Edition 2022

ISBN's:
979-8-9861702-0-6 (Paperback)
979-8-9861702-1-3 (Adobe PDF)
979-8-9861702-2-0 (Ebook)

Library of Congress Control Number: 2022909941

Cover & Interior Design: Diane Rigoli
Cover Photo: Ray Rakozy
Interior Photo: David Sand ©MSIA

Printed in the United States of America

This book is dedicated to the Traveler Consciousness in all of us as we practice Soul Transcendence, which is becoming aware of yourself as a soul and as one with God.

John-Roger and John Morton

There is a difference in people who are following the oneness on the upward path, because there's a bright Light that comes out of them. There is a truth that speaks through their voice. You hear something in their words—not the vocabulary they use, but in the energy of their words. It touches that place inside of you that is open to inspiration.

– JOHN-ROGER
Loving Each Day
(www.msia.org/quotes)

TABLE OF CONTENTS

ACKNOWLEDGMENTS

First of all, I want to thank John-Roger. There are no words to express my eternal gratitude to him for his guidance, his friendship, and most of all his loving. I also want to thank John Morton, who early on caught the vision of this book and has supported it consistently along with the MSIA Presidency—Paul Kaye, Vincent Dupont, and Mark Lurie.

I especially want to thank the storytellers, without whom this book would not exist. Every book is a collaboration, and this one is probably more so than most. All the contributions were valuable, even though it was impossible to include every story or even something from every storyteller. So, whether your story is included or not, I'm sending you a heartfelt "Thank you!" All the stories, in their original form, are now part of the archives of the Movement of Spiritual Inner Awareness (MSIA).

Acknowledgments are also due to Kate Ferrick and Lori Matson, who met with me monthly to keep the energy moving forward, and for their work conducting and transcribing interviews and for initial editing. Sue Dolan assisted with editing the interviews into stories and then after I compiled the stories into chapters, she continued to edit and organize the stories and chapters. Ardyth Phillips assisted with the next round of editing followed later by Penelope Bright. Tannis Benedict spent weeks going through the detail of line editing. Laren Bright oversaw the entire process and was a constant consultant, editor, hand holder and supporter throughout the years as this book took form. Thank you all.

I want to add a special thank you to Chuck Millar. He worked to organize and pull all the parts of the book together into a coherent whole. Despite severe health issues, Chuck kept going until he was literally unable to go any further. This would not be the book it is today without Chuck's skill and dedication.

Also, thanks are due to our wonderful transcribers—Valerie Rambo, Matthew Van Fossen, Leslie Fabian, Merry Parrish, Juliana Rose, Penelope Towle, Barbara Weiland, and Lena Perrotta.

To get this book to publication, we needed to have everyone sign a release and this became a project by itself. My thanks to Michael Kamen, who got it started, and Kate Ferrick, who brought it over the finish line.

J-R used to be very hesitant to acknowledge people on projects because, he said, you're always going to forget someone. If I've left out anyone, I sincerely apologize and my only consolation is that I know your work has been acknowledged in Spirit.

This book has been a labor of love and devotion to John-Roger, our Traveler John Morton, our church, MSIA, and the Spirit in all of us.

— Jackie Peterson

INTRODUCTION

I wandered into an MSIA meeting near the end of 1969 and somehow found myself at home in a small family of people looking for a connection to something greater than the physical "reality" going on around us. Today there are thousands of people worldwide currently studying in The Movement of Spiritual Inner Awareness (MSIA), which was founded by John-Roger and is now under the spiritual directorship of John Morton.

This book is a compilation of the recollections of some of the people who were there at the very beginnings of MSIA. It's their remembrances of some of the events that shaped what MSIA was to become.

The work of John-Roger (J-R to most people), seen from the inside, is profound and, in fact, world changing. But it's focused on transforming the "inner worlds" of each person, not making a splash in the headlines. For nearly 60 years, MSIA has quietly gone about its business of presenting the precepts of Soul Transcendence: Knowing yourself as a Soul, and even more, as one with God, not as simply a theory, but as a living reality.

While this book may be interesting to anyone pursuing spiritual teachings, it is primarily aimed at those who do know about MSIA and want to know more about the extraordinary people who brought forward its teachings and guided its students for over half a century. It provides some personal glimpses into Roger Hinkins, the regular guy, and reveals some of the earliest days as he was evolving into John-Roger, the wayshower. It also reveals some insights into John Morton and his work of continuing the teachings of John-Roger.

These sharings might be considered love stories dedicated to John-Roger and John Morton. It is hoped that you catch the Spirit from their words.

– Laren Bright

CHAPTER ONE

THE BEGINNING (1965-1967)

We begin with an engaging account of a warm friendship between John-Roger and Lee Clausen. Lee was only sixteen when he met J-R and his story takes place before 1967 when J-R was teaching at Rosemead High and before he started to offer regular meetings/classes called home seminars held in people's living rooms. Lee's story is unusual in that he was drawn to J-R as a friend and only gradually became convinced that J-R was much more than what he appeared to be on the surface.

CALIFORNIA

LEE CLAUSEN
I Knew That J-R Was Something Special

The year before I met J-R, I was fifteen and had very little interest in "spiritual things." I was living with my family in Palo Alto, California, and was involved in my family's Methodist Church. My parents eventually drifted away from the Methodist Church, however, and started dabbling in non-traditional forms of spirituality.

They became followers of a woman named Neva Dell Hunter, who was well known in the sixties and early seventies, mostly in the Southwest. She billed herself as a medium who channeled higher spiritual beings, and she gave talks from these spiritual beings to audiences while in trance. She also claimed she could "read" past lifetimes in one-on-one counseling sessions.

I never felt a connection spiritually with Neva Dell Hunter, but my parents did. So, in the summer of 1964, they took the whole family on a car trip to Phoenix, Arizona, to attend a weeklong conference put on by Neva Dell and her group. I wasn't interested at all in Neva Dell Hunter or the spiritual/psychic things, but I met a girl there who was the daughter of another couple who were followers of Neva Dell, and I was smitten by her.

All the next year, I wrote to her. I literally wrote once a week and she hardly ever wrote back, but that didn't deter me at all. So, the following year—in 1965—I was anticipating we would go to the Neva Dell conference in Albuquerque as a family again. But that was the year my parents were in the middle of their divorce and were not interested in going to it. When they told me this, it was like, "How can this be? I have to see that girl!" I guess I complained a lot, so they approached some of their friends who were planning to attend the conference, and the people said, "Hey, you can come with us." So, I traveled with them, and they allowed me to stay in their hotel room at the conference and sleep on the floor. I don't think it cost them anything.

When I got to the conference, it was apparent from day one that the girl of my dreams didn't want anything to do with me—and I was crushed. I had never experienced that much of a broken heart, and this was just the first day, with still a week to go. But I met some other people who were friendly to me, and I hung out with them and ended up having a nice time. One of the guys I hung out with, who was in his early twenties, was named Ellis. One day, I was walking through the lobby and some distance away, I could see Ellis at a table talking with someone I had never seen before but was immediately drawn to. When Ellis looked up and motioned to me, I came right over and he introduced me to the man he was talking to, who turned out to be J-R. (J-R told me later that he had asked Ellis to call me over, because we had been together in past lives, and he knew he was going to meet me at the conference.)

When I was introduced to J-R—he was known as Roger Hinkins back then—there was something about him from the first moment that just lit up inside of me, and I couldn't explain it except that he seemed like the neatest guy I had ever met. And so, throughout the week, I would run into Roger from time to time. One time, we sat at the breakfast counter, had breakfast together, and just chit-chatted.

The last day of the conference was a formal dinner which I wanted to go to, but I didn't have a tie to wear. The family I was with had left the day before, but they paid for an extra day so I could stay and attend this last dinner. I had to come up with a tie at the last minute, and I just had a feeling that Roger would have some extra ties. So, I thought, "Well, that gives me an excuse. I'll ask him." And so, about an hour before the dinner, I knocked on his door and asked, "Can I borrow a tie?" He said, "Oh yeah, come on in. Take whatever you want. Just take your pick." So, I thanked him, picked out a tie, and left. And then at the farewell dinner, it just so happened that I was sitting directly across from J-R, and I was very happy to chat with him again over dinner. And during dinner, he said, "So Lee, how are you planning to get home?" Up until then, I hadn't even given any thought to how I was going to get home, so I just kind of mumbled the first thought that came to my mind, "I guess I'll take a bus. I've taken a bus before. I can take a bus." And he said, "Where do you live?" And I told him, "The Bay Area—Palo Alto." And he said, "Well, I live in L.A. I need to go back to L.A. first for a couple of days, but then I have to go up to the Bay Area. So, if you don't mind staying at my place for a couple of days, I'll be happy to take you back to your house afterward."

Mind? I was ecstatic! Not only was he the coolest guy I had ever met, but he had a brand-new car, an electric blue 1965 Mustang. And he didn't want to drive; he wanted me to drive! I was in heaven. I mean, what can I say?

So, we drove from Albuquerque to Phoenix on that first day. It was a long drive, and during that time, we got to know each other. One of the things I remember the most about the first few hours was that I felt such trust that no matter what I said, it wouldn't matter to him, he'd still care for me. I remember laughing so hard at his dirty jokes. Then he said, "Well, do you have any?" I'm not very good at telling jokes, but the only one I could think of was one I'd heard from my high school friends that I considered almost embarrassingly dirty to tell anyone other than boys my own age.

So, I told him, "I'm kind of embarrassed about telling you this joke." And he said, "There's nothing you can tell me that I haven't already heard many times before." And that just seemed to cement the relationship that I felt with him. It was like, "This is my best friend now. And I've only known him for a couple of days," but I didn't know anybody else like him. You know, he was a little older than I was—maybe fourteen years older than me—not quite old enough to be my father, but almost too old to be my brother, so he was kind of in-between. He was like an adult figure who related to me like a brother and in some ways, like a father, so he was both.

I remember we stopped in Phoenix and spent the night with a friend of J-R's and then continued on to L.A., where J-R lived in a small two-bedroom, one-bath house with a roommate. I don't remember who his roommate was, but I have a feeling J-R and he might have been buddies growing up. I didn't ask a lot of questions. Being in J-R's energy—as anyone who's ever been with him can probably relate to—it's like nothing else really matters when you're with him, except just being with him. All the questions seem to drain away. They seem so pitifully small and a distraction from actually just being with him.

One of the more significant events that happened while I was there was when we were enjoying a barbeque in the afternoon—hamburgers in the backyard—and I was still feeling quite brokenhearted over the girl who rejected me. J-R and his roommate were both sitting across from me at a table and I must have been looking down in the mouth because his roommate said, "Lee, what's wrong?" And I tried to brighten up and brush it off, you know like nothing was wrong. But then within seconds, I just let the depression kind of overtake me again. And they both laughed, both of them, and said, "We can tell something's wrong you know. Tell us what's bothering you."

So, I came clean. I said, "I am still feeling brokenhearted." I don't know the exact words, but something like that. So, J-R asked a few questions about who she was. He asked, "Does she live around here?" And I knew she lived in L.A., but it was way across town. And so, J-R said, "Well, do you have her address?" And of course, I had her address—I wrote to her every week. (She had written to me once, but only after her mother felt sorry for me and made her.) And he said, "Why don't we drive over there tomorrow and take a look?"

The next day, all three of us got in the Mustang. J-R was driving, his roommate was in the shotgun seat, and I was in the backseat. It took most of the day to get there, but finally, we were driving up the street where she lived. I was checking the addresses on the houses and just making sure it was the right one, and pretty soon we drove up to the house. J-R was driving about five miles an hour, real slow. As we were driving by the house, he asked, "Is that the house?" I said, "Yeah, that's it." And I just watched the house go by. And when we got past the house, my heartache had completely vanished! It was like the karma or whatever was taken out. It wasn't that I noticed this change later on—I was aware of it right then because I had been feeling so depressed and yet the next moment it was totally gone. It was like she didn't exist. That's when I knew that J-R was something special. But I didn't know how special. And it took me a few years to figure that out.

A day or two later, J-R drove me up to my home in Palo Alto, dropped me off, and then went on to San Francisco. What followed for me was probably the darkest period in my life—darkest in the sense that I felt like I didn't have parents because they were divorcing. They didn't have time for me, either one of them. My father was an alcoholic, and he just left, and my mother had to get a job and support four kids, so she didn't have time to really interact much with me.

But I did have J-R, and there were times when I was just so depressed that I had to talk to somebody. And so, there were times when I called J-R. And one time, I remember talking to him about the stuff that was going on, and I started feeling really good over the phone. And I mentioned it to him: "You know, when I called you, I was feeling down, and now all that's gone and I feel really good." And he goes, "Yeah, I've been known to have that effect on people." That was another inkling that something was going on here, but I still didn't know what.

Another weird thing happened during that period when I was hitchhiking to school. During my senior year in high school, my father left and my mother moved us from our home in Palo Alto to an apartment in Sunnyvale. I had to hitchhike to school every morning, which was about seven miles down El Camino Real. One day, I got into a conversation with a guy who picked me up, and he said, "People are generally interested in three main categories: people, information, and things." This is something J-R had told me, this exact same wording. And I'm kind of like, "Yeah, I've heard that before." And he said, "Somebody named J-R told me that." The driver said that to me! And the funny thing was, I didn't tell him I knew J-R. I don't know why. He probably thought I was crazy. And I was wondering if this was one of those Twilight Zone moments, you know—wondering, "Is this really happening? How could it be that out of the millions of people in the Bay Area, this guy picks me up and mentions J-R to me?"

During the same dark period, when I was coming home from school one day, I walked around the corner and saw J-R's Mustang parked in front of our house. And I go, "What's that?" And then I looked and J-R was standing on the steps. I guess he had just knocked on the door or something. And, you know, I was so glad to see him! He said he had business in San Francisco and he thought he'd just stop by since my house was on the way.

I invited him into the house, and while we were chatting, there was a book on the kitchen counter that was upside down and facing away from him. J-R, who was at the far end of the kitchen, just pointed to the book and said, "Oh, I see you're reading blah, blah, blah"—the name of the title. I looked at him and thought, "Huh? How did you know that? You didn't go look." I flipped it over and that was the title of the book. I said, "How did you do that?" He looked at me and said, "Come on, Lee, don't you know by now?" And I said—I don't know what I said, but I was skeptical. It's like, "How did you know that?" So, he said, "Okay, open up the cover." And on the inside of the cover were these images, different images. And J-R's standing about ten feet away, and he goes, "Okay," he says, "Just look at one of those images." And while I was looking at it, he told me which one it was. And then he said, "Okay, look at another one." So, we did this two or three times, and I must have looked at him with my mouth open because I'm thinking, "I know you can't see this. All I'm doing is looking at it. I'm not giving you any clues, and you're calling out in detail what it is." This was running through my head.

So that was another mind-blowing experience. At that point, I realized that J-R was somebody special, but I still didn't know how that specialness could relate to me on a more personal level. I wasn't looking for that. I wasn't looking for a spiritual person or for enlightenment. I just loved J-R because he was so real, he was so present. And everything was okay, no matter what I said, no matter what I did—it was okay.

Around this time, I had an interesting experience with David Spangler, a spiritual teacher I knew about from a Neva Dell Hunter conference in 1964, the year before I met J-R. My brother Darrell had pointed him out to me at that conference and said, "He's supposed to be a really spiritual guy." Then, the following year, I attended a seminar in the Bay Area that was led by David Spangler. My mother was involved with a lot of different spiritual groups at that time, and so my brother Darrell and I went with her to that seminar. It was held in a living room in Redwood City, and there were about seven of us who sat around on chairs with David Spangler at the head of the room. I remember he talked about the Cosmic Christ during the seminar.

David Spangler wasn't at the Neva Dell Hunter conference in 1965 when I met J-R, but I later discovered that J-R knew him. I don't remember how his name came up, but J-R said, "People who can see auras often remark when David and I shake hands because the auras just go wild." The way he described David to me was like he was a very close friend, almost like a brother, maybe in another lifetime, but they were super close.

David was a few years younger than J-R—I'm not sure exactly how old he was. At any rate, one day in Palo Alto, where I lived with my mom and family, we were having a family picnic in one of the parks out in the rural part of the foothills. At one point, Darrell and I were walking down a long hill, about a hundred yards away from the picnic area. We were in the middle of a conversation when, all of a sudden, I hear my mother's voice calling, "Lee!" And I'm going, "What?" And I look up the hill. "Lee! David Spangler's here to see you!"

And then I see David, and he's jogging down the hill, and I'm jogging up the hill to meet him. Now, okay, I knew who David Spangler was, and I'd been to one of his seminars, but I didn't really know him. It was like, "David Spangler's here to see me?" And I'm away from home at a park, and it's like, "He sought me out?" He had to go out of his way to find me, and so I'm thinking, "Well, this must be important." So, I'm running up the hill, he's running down the hill, and when we meet, he's got the biggest smile on his face. We shake hands, and he goes, "Lee, Lee! Oh

God, I'm glad I caught up with you! J-R wanted me to tell you something." The background was that J-R and I had been planning to meet somewhere at a certain time. And it turned out that J-R wouldn't be able to make it and wanted to let me know. He knew David was going to be up where I was, and so he asked him to tell me that he wouldn't be able to make it.

That was the message on the surface. But the real message was far deeper than that for me. First of all, J-R went to a lot of trouble to get me that message. And secondly, David Spangler greeted me like he was an old family friend—he was so open and smiling—and I just wondered, "What's really going on here? Why am I getting such special treatment?" The deeper message I was getting from this was that J-R must really care for me. It's like that expression, "The medium is the message." The fact that he went to so much trouble to tell me that simple thing was much deeper than the actual message. The real message was, "I want you to know that I care for you."

So, I continued my relationship with J-R over the phone for a while, and then I asked if I could come to visit him in L.A. He said, "We're having a New Year's Eve party. Why don't you come down for New Year's Eve for the weekend?" So, I flew down there—the first time I'd ever flown. He met me at the airport, and we had a little New Year's Eve party. It was him and his roommate, and they had dates. It was the five of us. It sounds kind of boring, but it was fun. They played music, and we all danced. I mean, I actually danced with their dates—me, a sixteen-year-old kid, dancing with women who were in their mid-twenties.

So that started a series of weekends where every couple of months or so I'd fly down to L.A. and J-R would meet me at the airport. We also kept in touch through letters and phone calls. In one of the letters, he said, "I've been going through so many changes, I don't know if you're going to like me anymore." And I thought to myself, "What? No, how can that be? That can't be." And so, on one trip, I remember he picked me up at the airport, and he was talking about all the changes he was going through. He talked about something called "transmutation," and I didn't know what that was. But he wanted to demonstrate something to me. So, we went into one of the side rooms of his house, where there were a lot of books in the bookcases. He shut the curtains, dimmed the lights, and lit some candles. His roommate wasn't around, so we had the house to ourselves. We sat in chairs about six or eight feet apart, facing each other, and there was enough light so I could see his face and everything, but it was dim. As we sat there and looked at each other, his face started to change. I wasn't sure if I was imagining this or what, but the energy in the room started swirling around him, and his face moved—it morphed into other faces. I'm getting chills thinking about this now. I didn't know what to make of it, and he didn't really explain it. I remarked about seeing the changes in his face, but he didn't say much about it.

Another trip happened when I was between my junior and senior year of high school in 1966, and summer vacation had just begun. My brother Darrell and I and a friend were looking for some adventure, so I piped up that we could hitchhike to L.A. and see my friend J-R. The idea was to hitchhike to J-R's house, stay one night, and hitchhike back the next day. J-R had an apartment in Rosemead then, and we showed up on his doorstep late one weekend night. He let us in, and we slept in our sleeping bags on the floor. J-R was teaching summer school at Rosemead High at that time, and the next morning he was correcting papers at the kitchen table. I sat across from him and just sat there for maybe five minutes without saying a word, watching him. And he didn't say a word either. But then I just kind of blurted out, "Would you mind if I stayed with you this summer?"

He just looked at me for a minute. You know how he does sometimes when he looks at you and then looks up above your head and then to the side—and I don't know if he was talking to somebody or what he's looking at—and he said, "Well, there's two conditions. First, it has to be okay with your mother. Number two, you have to support yourself, because I will not support you financially. So, you'd have to get a job." I said, "Okay." At that point, I would do anything for the chance to spend the entire summer with him, so even though I had no job experience except bussing tables at my father's hamburger restaurant, I agreed.

There was no problem getting my mom's permission because it meant one less mouth to feed, and I was hoping to find a job in a restaurant.

We arranged for a time a week or so later when he would be in the Bay Area and could pick me up at our Sunnyvale apartment. I remember waiting for him out on the street and getting really excited to see him drive up in his blue Mustang. He didn't want to drive, so I got to drive his very cool car all the way to his apartment in Rosemead.

The next morning, we were having breakfast at a favorite café of his, and the owner came around to say hello. I was somewhat shy in those days, so J-R introduced me and said, "He's looking for a job—could you use a busboy for the summer?" This was a 24-hour café, and the owner said, "Well, the only position we have for him is the graveyard shift, from 12:00 midnight to 8:30 in the morning, five days a week." I jumped at the chance to fulfill my agreement and have a job to support myself. J-R never ate at his apartment; we always went out somewhere for our meals, so I would now have the money to do that.

So, I settled into a routine. The apartment was a mile or two away from the café, so I would hitchhike to work around 11:30 p.m. If I didn't get a ride, I could still get there on time if I walked. And then, after my shift was over at 8:30 a.m., it was the same thing. I usually got back around 9:00. By then, J-R would have already left to teach summer school, so I would be able to crash and get some sleep. But he made it clear that I had to be up and ready to go by 12:30 because he was going to swing by and pick me up, and then we would go to the beach. He emphasized that he didn't want to wait for me. So, I made it a point to be up and ready, and we'd go down to Huntington Beach, which is a long drive from Rosemead. We did this almost every day.

Phillip Anthony was one of J-R's special students, and he was almost always in the car with J-R when he came home to pick me up. Phil and I were the same age, but we were very different people with different backgrounds. We really liked each other and had a close relationship, like brothers. I still hold a very dear place in my heart for Phil. He was a big surfer dude, and he taught me a bit about surfing that summer. Meanwhile, J-R would park himself on the sand with a beach chair and just read books the whole time. He never went in the water that I knew of; he'd just set up his space and say, "Okay, you guys get out of here." Phil and I would take off, we'd just run—we ran everywhere we went, and we would swim and body surf until it was time to move on.

In the evenings, if we weren't going out somewhere, I'd usually go to bed early and try to get a few hours' sleep before getting up to be at work by midnight. But sometimes we'd go out to do things in the evening.

On Saturday evenings, we would drive down to Long Beach to see a preacher who gave psychic readings. Usually, Phil went with us, and once Candy Shanklin (now Candace Semigran), who was also one of J-R's students at Rosemead High, joined us. One time, J-R took a date along—she was a good-looking woman who was a neighbor in the building where J-R had his apartment.

When you entered this preacher's church, you had the opportunity to write a question on a small piece of paper that was then folded tightly and put into a wicker basket. After the preacher gave a sermon, an aide would approach him in his pulpit with the wicker basket. The preacher would reach into the basket, pull out one of the folded pieces of paper, and without unfolding it, hold it up to his forehead with his eyes closed. Using his psychic ability, he would then say the name of the person who wrote the question and attempt to give a helpful answer. He may have had some psychic ability, but I know he wasn't right all the time. J-R just seemed like he was interested in unusual people who had unusual abilities. It was entertaining, though, and it was fun. We always went out for dessert and coffee afterward to talk about the events of the evening, and we usually laughed a lot.

I remember one time when J-R had a date and he took Phil and me with him. I don't remember where we had gone that evening, but Phil and I were in the backseat of the car, and he and his date were in the front as he was driving her home to her place in Hollywood. She was really pretty. I remember that. And so, Phil and I were just kind of along for the ride. Phil and I would crack each other up—you know, it's like brothers and sisters who are close together; all they have to say is two words and they're just in stitches. Phil and I were like that. So, we were knocking around in the back seat, just laughing the whole way. And she kind of looked back and made a comment to J-R, but I didn't hear what it was. We got to her place, and J-R took her to the door, then came back to the car. One of the first things he said—which we thought was kind of cool—was, "She wants to know when we're going to go to bed," because obviously, it wasn't going to happen that night. We thought that was pretty funny. But J-R was like that, you know, he just said stuff. It was like he was just one of the guys—one of us. We were fifteen years younger than him, but he didn't act like he was superior or anything. I mean, we knew he was superior. But that is just one of the things that has made him so beloved to everybody who knew him.

I remember driving to Lake Arrowhead two or three times because one of J-R's students used to have a summer job up there. It was just J-R and me on those two-hour trips, and that's when I started asking questions. J-R would answer all my questions on those trips, and he would give seminars to me—like literally forty-five-minute seminars—where he was just talking the whole time telling me about spiritual things. But for me personally, I'm still not feeling like this is what I need to do for the rest of my life, that I need to study Spirit and grow inwardly. I wasn't thinking that at all. But I was interested. And J-R spoke from a position of authority, which made an impression on me.

One time, we were having breakfast at a restaurant where Phil was busing tables, and Phil came over to our table to talk with us for a short time. As he walked away, I turned to watch him go and J-R said something. I only heard about half of what J-R said, so I turned to him and asked, "What did you say?" He looked at me like, "I didn't say anything." And I said, "I heard you say something." He said, "I didn't say anything." So, I told him what I heard and he said, "I was thinking that." And he filled in the blanks that I didn't quite hear. Then we talked about how it's possible to hear people's thoughts out loud. He said, "You're starting to tune in. People do that around me. But I know how to turn it off so they can't tune in to my thoughts." And that was the only time I had that experience with him where I could actually hear his voice speaking words and yet he didn't speak those words. All this stuff was starting to add up for me, like, "What's going on?" I wanted to know how I could relate to Spirit more.

One of the higher spirits that Neva Dell Hunter channeled was this spirit who called himself Doctor Joseph Miles, and he was considered by her followers as the "high guy"—you know, the one who comes from way up there in Spirit. One time, I was in the room with Phil and J-R, and I was asking who J-R was in relation to some other reference point I had in Spirit, and Joseph Miles was a reference point of a really high guy. And when I asked J-R how he compared to Joseph Miles, he didn't say anything—he just looked at me. But Phil was standing behind him, and Phil said, "There's nobody that compares to J-R." And when he said that, I knew it was true—it went home. And that's when I started really seeing J-R in a different light, in a different frame of reference, because I knew it was true.

Towards the end of the summer of 1966, Neva Dell had another conference—in Flagstaff, I believe it was. And I was thinking, "All right, let's go." And J-R said, "You're not going." I said, "Come on!" And he said, "No, you're not going. You're going to have to stay here. I'm going there to meet a New Ager." "What's a New Ager?" I asked, He said, "Well, you know, just somebody who believes in the New Age that's coming forth." That's the way he described it. I said, "How come I can't go?" And he said, "You just can't." He didn't explain why. So, I stayed at his apartment and just worked for the whole week.

I found out later that it was Jack Reed he was going to meet. Years later, I told Jack about this, and Jack said, "He went there to meet me?" I said, "Yep, he told me he was going to meet you. I didn't know your name then, but you were the one." And that's when I asked J-R if he had gone the year before to meet me, and he admitted that he had. He said, "I knew you would be there."

***

One day, J-R was talking to me about traveling in the higher realms, and he said, "The reason you don't travel in those high realms—at least you don't bring back memory of it—is because you'd slit your throat when you came back. It's so beautiful there, and you wouldn't be able to stand living here." So, I took that as kind of a challenge. I said, "Well, I think I could handle it." He said, "You won't be able to." And I said, "I think I could. You know, I'd like to try." And he said, "Okay, come here." So, he was sitting in a chair, and I walked up and stood in front of him. He holds out his hands, palms up, and says, "Put your hands on mine." So, I put my hands' palms down on his, and he says, "Just look in my eyes." So, I looked into his eyes, and he started bringing up the energy. And what it felt like to me was, first of all, just the loving in his eyes was almost overwhelming. But the main thing was that it felt like electricity tingling through my hands, through my palms. And it began creeping up my forearms and into my shoulders. It felt like it was on a dimmer switch, where you're gradually turning up the wattage. This whole process probably took only fifteen or twenty seconds, but it got to the point where it was so powerful it hurt. The energy hurt so much that I jerked my hands away. It felt like I was going to get burned—I mean, really burned. And he said, "That's what I'm talking about." He says, "You're not ready to handle the energy yet."

So that was a big lesson for me about what I could handle. And it was also a big lesson about my relationship with J-R and how I thought of him. There was never any doubt in my mind that he was my best friend and that I wanted to be around him the rest of my life. It's just that at that time I hadn't consciously acknowledged that I wanted to be on a spiritual path. That came later.

* * *

In the summer of 1967, which was the summer after the one I spent with J-R, I hitchhiked to Minnesota. I had an uncle who was in construction who lived there, and he gave me a summer job and a place to stay so I could save money for college. J-R sent me a couple of postcards during the summer saying he was going to be in that area around the end of August and that we could drive back together. So, he showed up at my uncle's place one day, and we spent five days driving back, the two of us. We went to Mount Rushmore, and we went to Yellowstone where he used to work as a summer intern. He told me about some of the experiences he had there when he was starting to see auras and that kind of thing.

After I got home, I hitchhiked to visit J-R every couple of months. Several months later, he started doing seminars on a regular basis, and I thought, "Oh, what's this? Seminars? Wow, cool!" So, if I was with him, I would go. We'd travel in the car—usually just him and me—and so I attended several seminars.

From the very first day that I met J-R, he presented himself to me as Roger—Roger Hinkins—and as I became more and more aware of the Spirit that he represented, I became a little confused about calling him Roger because I knew that he worked with the John energy and John consciousness (a spiritual consciousness related to Jesus's disciple, John the Beloved). So, one time—it felt kind of awkward, though—but I asked him, "Should I call you John from now on?" And he said, "You can call me whatever you want to call me." But it still felt odd to call him Roger. And then one day—this was early on, around when seminars first started—Phil was at the apartment with Roger, and I hadn't seen either one of them for maybe a month or two, and Phil was calling him J-R. That was the first time I heard that term. And it seemed like a great blending of John and Roger. John just didn't seem appropriate enough and Roger didn't seem appropriate either, but the name J-R seemed to fit. And I remember I just started calling him J-R.

So, in addition to doing the seminars, he began to put out the Discourses. Pauli McGarry (now Pauli Sanderson)—who taught with J-R at Rosemead High—was working diligently during this time transcribing seminar tapes into Discourses. She had a mimeograph machine that printed them out on 8.5 x 11 paper, and I remember when the very first Discourse came out. I still have those early Discourses.

Around this time, J-R began talking about the concept of the "Mystical Traveler." The way he explained it to me is that the term Mystical Traveler is kind of a made-up term. He said that it's really the Christ that he's bringing forward, but he told me, "If I say I'm the Christ, who's going to believe it? People will block that right away. So, you have to come at the whole concept with something where there are no reference points—something where they can't say, 'Oh, it's this,' and pigeonhole it, and then lock themselves into that." So, the idea of the Mystical Traveler was something new, something where there is no reference point so that people wouldn't block themselves who would normally be open to it. But it really was and is the Christ Consciousness.

*　*　*

One time, J-R and I were driving somewhere in his Mustang—J-R was driving—and I think I might have asked him a question. Either that or, you know, sometimes he would be talking out loud to the "boys upstairs," spiritual beings that worked with J-R, and it was like a one-way conversation as far as I was concerned because I couldn't hear what they were saying. Whenever he was doing that, I would just be a little mouse in the corner, and not cause any distraction. But he's driving and talking—this is the way I remember it—and he's saying like he's talking to somebody, "So what do we call this thing?" And there's kind of a pause of five or ten seconds, and he goes, "Oh, of course. M-S-I-A—Messiah—because we're all going to save ourselves." So that's how I recall the name of MSIA coming into J-R, but I'm not absolutely sure whether it happened in the moment when I was sitting there with him or if it happened earlier and he was relating to me how it happened.

I moved down to L.A. in the fall of 1969 to continue college and also so I could be near J-R and MSIA people. It was around this time that I heard people talking about initiation—being connected to the sacred names of God. And I'm thinking, "What's with initiation? What is that?" I had to ask J-R because he had never told me about initiation. We were in the living room at J-R's house in Baldwin Park. He had these two big armchairs for watching TV, and I was in one, he was in the other. I asked him about initiation, and he talked about the whole spiritual promise, that once you're initiated, you don't have to reincarnate anymore. It'll all be finished up. If you don't make it to Soul, it will be finished up on the inside. And I said, "I want to do that!" He said, "Okay. Why don't you come in next week and we'll get you initiated?"

It was during this same conversation that I said, "You know, this is too much for me. I never thought of myself as a spiritual person. And yet, you are the most spiritual person I've ever met, and the power you have is incomprehensible to me. Why am I sitting next to you? Why did you meet me four years ago in Albuquerque, and we've had, you know, a lot of good times together, a lot of laughing and wonderful teaching moments? Who am I? I don't get it." J-R didn't really answer this question, and I still wonder about it. I only know that I would die for him, as many of us would, and I love him with all my heart.

I remember hearing J-R talk about the "boys upstairs," and he'd talk about the "guardian angel society." And one day, he told me the name of my first guide in Spirit, so you could say I was on the path at that point. But it wasn't until December 1969 that something happened that made me realize that J-R is not just my best friend and a very, very spiritual guy, but he's also inside of me. We were driving back from the second MSIA conference—the Conference of Cooperation—J-R and Pauli in the front seat, and Phil and me in the back. I was talking to Phil about my experiences at the conference, and he looked at me and said, "Well, you know, Lee, J-R is the Inner Master (an inner guide and teacher)." Phil told me this. J-R didn't tell me this. But it was sort of like, "Bong!" And it was at that very moment that I accepted J-R as my inner teacher as well as my outer teacher. And, you know, it took me all that time to get to that point.

***

J-R used to get all kinds of pamphlets and books on different psychic stuff and what he called phenomena and lower-level stuff. At that time, I didn't know the difference between a higher level and a lower level, but it was all kind of interesting. For example, he had a booklet about a civilization that lives in the middle of the earth. And when I read it, I was trying to figure out how there could be an entrance to the middle of the earth and nobody knows about it. He said, "Well, it's really in the psychic realms. That's where it exists. But it doesn't make it any less real. It's just that it's not physically visible." So, it was stuff like that, different things.

J-R was always one to make sure my ego didn't get too big. During the late '70s—'78 or '79—there was a plant in South-Central L.A. where a guy named John Eversole was heading up a project to build smooth hemispherical domes out of thick polyurethane foam. J-R was involved with this project, as well as some other MSIA people who contributed money. The idea was to sell these domes to be used as homes or barns. Each dome was a complete hemisphere with a 44-foot diameter and a 22-foot-high ceiling, which was the radius of the dome. They only paid us minimum wage, but what appealed to me was being part of something greater than myself—something on the cutting edge of technology. At some point, they decided to make a small-scale model of the domes, about twelve inches in diameter, that could be used in marketing. They needed miniature furniture to go inside these models, and I volunteered to make it. I don't remember exactly how I did it now, but it came out really cute, these little pieces of furniture, which I made out of plastic in different colors. I spent a lot of time and care making this furniture, but J-R never said anything about it, and this went on for several weeks.

One day, I was in the lower level of Prana, and J-R came down the stairs and there was nobody else around. And I said, "Hey," you know, blah, blah, blah, just kind of making conversation, and I thought, "This would be a good time." So, I said, "So what do you think of that furniture, that dome furniture?" And he paused, and he goes, "You did a really good job on that." And then it was like he caught himself, and he said, "You know, I wouldn't have told you that if you hadn't asked me." And I said, "I know—that's why I went fishing for the compliment." And then we both just cracked up at the humor of it. I'm not sure why he rarely said anything complimentary to me, but maybe it's just so I would keep my head down and keep working. One of my biggest fears in life is that I let my ego misrepresent me. And I think that's one of the reasons J-R would always seem to put a lid on me. He was very sparse with his compliments, and I know he did it to protect me from myself because I can get a big head pretty easily.

After more than a decade of my having a lot of access to J-R, there came a time when he was not as available to me—it was right around the time when Insight[1] started and things really took off in 1978. Everybody was so busy creating Insight, creating all the different workshops, that it just became impossible to hang out with J-R the way I used to. But my point is, I was relying on his physical proximity to fulfill me, and I hadn't gone inside to cultivate the inner experience, the inner relationship, as much as I could have. I hadn't needed to.

For the next six or seven years, it was very difficult for me—the separation. I couldn't go see him or call him on the phone the way I used to, and he didn't call me anymore. So, I was more or less forced to go inside. And as I began to cultivate that more and more through spiritual exercises (we call them S.E.'s for short) and experiences on the other side through the dream state—things like that—I realized that the inner relationship was far more fulfilling than the outer relationship. I mean, there's no comparison. And that's what J-R always told us—that it's all inside of us. It's not out here.

CHAPTER TWO

THE EARLY YEARS (1968-1973)

John-Roger visited the Quimby Center in New Mexico just a few months after he began offering home seminars in Santa Barbara, California. Word spread, and as the months and years unfolded, seminars were offered in the Los Angeles area, Northern California, and on the East Coast of the United States in places like Pennsylvania, New York, and Florida.

During these years, MSIA (the Movement of Spiritual Inner Awareness—often referred to as "the Movement")—was incorporated as a formal organization and began offering an annual conference and "Soul Awareness Discourses," printed pamphlets that were mailed each month for students to study. The stories in this chapter reflect the refreshing simplicity and camaraderie of those early years.

NEW MEXICO

ELLAVIVIAN POWER
The New Age Teacher

At a conference I attended prior to 1968, I had a feeling that the new-age teacher was there. I could feel his presence. I even wrote a letter to a friend saying, "He's here. I know he's here. I can feel his presence." But I couldn't identify the energy with any particular person. (It was later confirmed that J R was indeed present at that conference.)

It was August 1968 when J R first came to the Quimby Center, a training school for spiritual teachers in Alamogordo, New Mexico, founded by Dr. Neva Dell Hunter. J R did some Light readings (a form of spiritual counseling) and gave classes in personology, the study of a person's personality traits and the shape of their face, the way their eyes are set in their head, their nose, their ears, their lips and mouth, and body language. I attended the classes. We had a great time and laughed a lot.

I was writing a book on aura balancing, a form of clearing the energy field around the physical body called The Auric Mirror. Periodically, I would write chapters and bring them to the Quimby Center to discuss the contents. One night, after a group of us, including J-R, had been sitting around talking, Dr. Hunter said, "We need to work on the last chapter of Ellavivian's book." J-R looked up at me and sent me the Light and a wonderful burst of unconditional love. I could just feel it flood through me. Dr. Hunter continued, "It would be wonderful if you would include something about John-Roger's work in your book." I replied, "Well, you figure out what you'd like to say and we'll put it in there." Which we did.

Years later, the Quimby Center was involved in bringing forward Southwestern College, whose mission was to provide innovative and holistic education. We were working with Robert Waterman and Ron Hulnick, researching personal growth as an educational process. I believe it was the first time on the planet this had ever been taught exactly in that way. The psychological process of releasing blocks and formulating them into an educational process was a new concept. The aura balancing work was the foundation and the instrument of doing that. John-Roger took that work and magnified it, glorified it, exemplified it, and refined it to what it is today.

Years before, we had learned that the new age teacher would be taking groups of people—up to three hundred—and balancing them all at once. This was really mind-boggling at that time. We tried to figure out how he was going to do it. We were working one-to-one, and he was going to do three hundred at once? When Insight Seminars and the Peace Awareness Trainings came forward, it was tremendously rewarding and exciting to see it evolve into that. The transformation that came about in people—to be able to attend those classes of fifty to one hundred or more at one time—just seemed fantastic. From the minute J-R started the whole thing, I knew who he was.

In January of 1979, I took Insight I in Colorado and recognized the Insight training as a culmination of the prophecy that the new-age teacher would be balancing people in groups of hundreds. Six months later I took Insight II in California, where I saw J-R for the first time since 1969. It was a wonderful reunion.

The cosmic plan is unfolding, and as time is accelerated, various structures in the outer world are collapsing very fast. The intention of the aura balancing and the seminars was to prepare people with a consciousness so they would be able to handle the changes that are happening in the days that are now upon us.

CALIFORNIA

JACK REED & MURIEL ENGLE
Time Stands Still

The following is an excerpt from Jack Reed's excellent book, Linchpin, about the founding of MSIA. What led up to where the story starts was that Jack had arranged with a woman in Santa Barbara, Muriel Engel, to host John-Roger and a group of others for a talk by him. After the meeting, Muriel invited a small group for a spaghetti dinner at her home:

The evening continued with the kind of rapport and joy that people experience who've known each other for years. Toward the end of our spaghetti dinner, Muriel asked J-R about the meal.

Muriel recounted,

We shared so much more that evening, but what dimmed everything else for me was J-R's response to my comment that I hoped the spaghetti meal I had prepared was not imbalanced in starch for someone as sensitive as he. Casually remarking, "We will now have a demonstration of what the pendulum can do to change the chemical action of whatever…" He opened his shirt collar and removed a golden chain over his head, then proceeded to use his medallion like a pendulum.

The medallion was a golden disc with praying hands on a gold chain. He held it over the wine and told us he was transmuting the wine so that it would have no negative effect on him. Muriel noted:

Suspended for one flashing moment—I froze. I didn't need the sound of trumpets! Every nerve in my body rang in chords. For a few moments, nobody said a thing. We just looked around at each other, and I knew that if I began to speak, the music would stop. It was like the music of the spheres. Then John-Roger said, "You have a story to tell," so I had to break in and share.

In the process of her metaphysical explorations, Muriel had met many psychics and had been asking inwardly and outwardly to find a spiritual teacher. In Muriel's own words from a 1970's *Movement Newspaper* interview,

Two years prior to August of 1967 (the night of our dinner), when I first met John-Roger in the physical, it had been predicted by George Daisley, a well-known psychic, that I would, within two years, meet a young man (J-R was 32 at that time) who would be a great and lasting influence on my sojourn here and with whom I would work closely. No elaboration was given at that time. I was to abide quietly and be patient, for this meeting was to precede important changes in my life. Patience has never been my forte, but I did keep this counsel to myself. If it were to be such an important milestone, I was reluctant to permit any opportunity for a "set up." However, I had been given a sign, and the clue was (that the person would have) "the Praying Hands on a golden disc on a golden chain."

Although I had never heard Muriel's praying hands story, when J-R pulled the chain with the praying hands from around his neck, a whoosh of energy circled around the room like a wave that swept us into a different plane of existence. It was something I'd never before experienced, and it seemed like we were all caught up in it. I thought, "What's going on here?" Time seemed to stand still in the several seconds of silence that ensued. The energy whirling around the room was overwhelming—like a wind of Spirit, making the kitchen seem like it was shimmering into another realm. However, whatever was going on, I felt like it did not directly concern me—it was more with Muriel—but we were all involved in it. When the music stopped for Muriel, she asked J-R how they were to work together, to which he replied that he didn't know but would let her know as soon as he knew.

YVONNE MOCHEL
But the Christ Was There!

I came into MSIA through the North American Consolidated Flying Saucer Club. The people who ran it called my husband and me one night and said they were going to see a psychic named John-Roger. They often received invitations that they didn't accept, but they decided they'd like to go see this psychic—and did we want to go? I didn't know what a psychic was, but I said, "Sure, let's go." So, we drove from the Hollywood Hills to Thousand Oaks, which seemed like a very long drive. In the course of J-R's seminar, it was clear to me the Christ was present. It was really beautiful to me.

My first impression of J-R was that of a very ordinary man. I didn't know anything about him. He began the seminar with verbal sharings from those present, which he called "contributions." Then he began talking, and at some point, I was aware that "the Christ is here." It didn't make me put him on a pedestal, but it drew me into the Christ. If you've ever experienced the Christ, you probably understand that it's not a casual thing. You don't just say, "See you later," and go on about your life. After that first seminar, I could not get enough of hearing J-R speak.

As we were driving home, the only thing my husband and the couple who invited us could talk about was his sniffing. When J-R first started doing seminars, he had a condition that caused him to sniff a lot as he was presenting the seminar. They were talking about sniffing, and I was sitting in the back seat saying, "But the Christ was there! The Christ was there!"

SARA NAHMIAS
Enough Love for a Thousand Years

In 1963, my young husband, thirty-one years old, had a heart attack, and I was absolutely devastated. Five years later, he had a second heart attack, and he died a few months after that. I was young and in disbelief that he was gone.

When the mourning period was over and everyone left, I completely collapsed and sobbed at the reality of him being gone. My cousin, Reuben Paris, said, "I know a man—we met at a flying saucer convention—and he's starting seminars." And I simply said, "Reuben, I'm so glad you found something. It's not for me. I'm not interested."

This went on for a while. But the pain of grief was so excruciating that I eventually told Reuben, "Okay, I'll go to a seminar." And so, we drove to the Hollywood Hills. I didn't know what was going to take place. Then this young man—a very handsome-looking man—came in, and I thought, "I didn't picture him that way." At the end of the seminar, there were people in a line waiting to talk to J-R. And Reuben said, "You know, you can talk to him and just see what happens." And I said, "Oh, I wouldn't even know what to say." But I found myself at the end of the line anyway.

J-R leaned over and looked, then said, "If you'll all excuse me, I want to talk to that woman right there." I sat down next to him and I said, "I don't know what to say." And he said, "Well, you lost someone who was very dear to you, and you are dealing with this now." I looked into his eyes and said, "I let go. I let go." He said, "It was time for you to let go. He had to go."

What I did not explain was that I had been praying for almost six years to God, "Please save him. Take me instead of him." It went on and on and on. And then I said, "God, I leave him in your hands." Then he died. So, there was this guilt that I let go, and there I was talking to J-R, telling him, "I let go." He said, "Yes, yes. Let go." I went home and I was so lifted. A lot of that heavy pain was just leaving me. And this went on every Friday night. I would go to the seminar and I would feel better. My commitment was so extreme that no matter where J-R's seminars were held, even though I didn't know how to get there, I was going. I was going to be there. I had to be there.

Then it was Thanksgiving of 1969, my husband's favorite holiday. He had always loved Thanksgiving dinner—the turkey and everything that went with it. I was so despondent at my first Thanksgiving dinner without him that I decided to attend a seminar J-R was offering. At the seminar, J-R said, "We're going to do a different seminar today. We're going to do a love feast. We usually have a focal point of someone sitting in this chair. Sara, would you like to come and sit in this chair?"

Then he put his hands over me and said, "The Christ in me salutes the Christ in you." He unfolded all the beautiful blessings and loving that anyone could bestow upon anyone. And each person was to come up and bestow their blessings in a similar way. By the end of the love feast, J-R said, "You have enough love for a thousand years." It was a beautiful experience, very uplifting, and it got me through a terribly difficult time.

GREG SMITH
He Had My Back Right from the Start

I was freshly back from Sweden, where I'd been living for the past 6 months, back in Isla Vista, where I'd lived during my last year of college at UC Santa Barbara. My trip to Sweden had not been an attempt to avoid the draft; my mind wasn't that focused in those days, quite possibly because of a residual haze from the marijuana that I'd inhaled during those last couple of years.

The wake-up call came in the form of a letter from my father forwarding my draft notice to me and suggesting I'd better get back to the states and deal with it. I had a short spell of considering that one way of dealing with it would be to ignore it altogether, but then I remembered I had a lot of family and friends in the states I'd like to visit outside of the confines of a penal institute. The one thing I was sure of was that I was not going to fight in that insane Vietnamese war. So, I found myself back in Isla Vista, crashing on my cousin's couch, pondering how I would resolve the draft issue.

About this time, sentiments against the war were rising. Rallies were devolving into riots, and the local police were joined by regiments of the National Guard. A hoard of protestors formed a sit-in on the steps of UCSB's administrative offices, completely blocking access to the buildings. Finally, University Chancellor Vernon Cheadle invited the protest leaders to meet with him to address their concerns and demands.

One key issue was that, although the university center (UCEN) was a marvelous multipurpose facility, the students had no say in how it was used. Our reps were therefore petitioning that we be able to apply some of our own agendas to its future use. Why not let students reserve one of the many meeting rooms to offer a class of their own interest and choose to fellow students at no charge? This was part of the free university movement that emerged at various colleges throughout the country. To our amazement, the Chancellor agreed. He told us that we could submit our proposals to his office, naming our topic and booking our desired time. The university would attempt to accommodate all reasonable requests.

When postings of these new free classes appeared, several caught my attention. I enrolled in a pottery class, a skydiving course, and a class in mysticism. I was somewhat familiar with the first two but was clueless about the last, which turned out to be a seminal experience in my life. This class was taught by Matt Stiling, a fellow of prodigious energy and enthusiasm, who told the class our course text would be the book "In My Soul I Am Free," written by the leader of Eckankar, Paul Twitchell. It was my introduction to the concept of Soul Travel. I read the book in one day.

In our second class, Matt casually mentioned that he knew a guy in Los Angeles who had God Consciousness. It was probably the first time I'd heard those words used back-to-back in a sentence, and although I had no idea what that meant, I knew it was big. A couple of us began badgering Matt to get us an introduction to this dude named John-Roger. At first, he said it wasn't possible; J-R had been working for some time with a small select group and the class was closed. We continued to badger him. I told Matt that at least he could ask the dude, right? He acquiesced, and when we convened for the next class, he announced we had been invited to attend the next John-Roger seminar (whatever that was).

Apparently, when Matt had told J-R about us, J-R had said, "Oh, those guys in Santa Barbara; yeah, you can bring them down." And so, he did.

In that first seminar, I had no idea what was going on, but I knew without a doubt I wanted more. In the second seminar, after my verbal contribution, J-R said, "Greg, can I talk to you after the seminar?" I said something like, "Sure, why not?" We were standing there and J-R was looking at me and then up above my head, up and down, up and down, like he used to do. Then he said, "You know, Greg, I think if it was me, I wouldn't do any more drugs." I was pretty sure he wasn't talking about Tylenol or Sudafed, and I also knew I had a stash in my apartment of the stuff he was talking about. His gentle suggestion went deep, and when I got back to the apartment, I flushed my remaining supply down the toilet. I was 22 years old, and I never looked back. I have never had an illicit drug since.

Years later, when I went on a 6-month tour with a famous musical group, there were ample opportunities to have all kinds of illegal substances, and I have no doubt that J-R's gentle suggestion saved me from a lot of wear and tear and unwanted experiences. Thank you, J-R, you had my back right from the start.

KAY TURBAK
The Love Man

When you start exploring the inner Spirit that
allows each person to exist as a special individual,
you start finding a treasure chest of love.

– John-Roger, *The Way Out Book,*
c. 1980 (first edition), page 62

I met that beautiful Being called John-Roger on April 8, 1969, the night of my first MSIA seminar, where John-Roger appeared in person at the home of Wanda Mansbach in Thousand Oaks, California. Although I had been invited to meet him before by my university mentor and spiritual "mother," Muriel Engle, this was the date that was set up in Spirit for me to be physically present, go up after the seminar ended, shake his hand, and be shaken to the core by the strongest force I had ever encountered.

The night before the event, at exactly midnight, I awoke, got out of bed, and flushed the last vestiges of my marijuana stash down the toilet. I was instantly aware that this drug pattern, although short-lived, had ended. Other karmic patterns took longer to overcome. My sense of wanting to be loved and not loving myself was pervasive. This took the form of promiscuity, seeking a false sense of validation and connection in sexual encounters. In the lyrics of the great country singer, Johnny Lee, I was "looking for love in all the wrong places. I was looking for love on too many faces."

The Love Man, as I affectionately called John-Roger, taught me many lessons about being accountable and responsible for all my actions in all areas of my life. So eventually, I did fall in love (responsibly, I thought) with a man in MSIA, and J-R performed the wedding ceremony. For years, we struggled to work out our karma together. And when this gentleman left me after meeting another woman one weekend--and marrying her within a very short time--I was at first heartbroken. However, I used this experience as a stepping stone to greater unfoldment and, within weeks, was approved for another initiation.

In one of my three Light Studies (Light Studies with J-R were offered in the early days of MSIA and were like a combination counseling session, past life reading, and Light booster), John-Roger told me specifically, "You will have reached the apex of spirituality when you can love no matter what."

As a student in MSIA, I discovered what J-R called the "treasure chest of love"—eternally given, free, and full of precious gold. Steadfast in my growth, I began to uncover the inner, divine loving that was always available to me as I practiced acceptance and unconditional loving of whatever was placed before me.

As a Bringer of Love, a Way-Shower, and Love-Shower, John-Roger was extraordinary in the ways he could demonstrate loving in action, loving in being. In INSIGHT II (a personal transformation seminar), he shared a personal affirmation: "I am communicating Living Love." This communication was more than just words; it was pure, unconditioned energy from the Source (the Godhead) which enfolded and embraced all things and all people, lifting everything and everyone into a higher vibration.

The Love Man brought me many experiences of loving, which were varied and sometimes very challenging. He would often ignore me (especially when I wanted attention or recognition) and would even scold me (which seemed harsh at the time—even though I probably needed it).

However, he could also touch me tenderly, using kind words and sweet gestures. I recall one exchange of supreme Loving that took place at my PTS Masters of Spiritual Science graduation in 2001. John-Roger was on stage congratulating each of us as we received our diplomas. When it was my turn, he hugged me and kissed me on the lips, whispering the words "forever and ever." Stunned and almost speechless, I replied that I would love him forever.

Although the Love Man no longer embodies a physical form, he lives forever in my Heart of Hearts and in the Heart of God.

MONICA VALDEZ
Not One Soul Will Be Lost

When I met J-R, I was living at a drug rehabilitation center. I was fairly new, but I had become friends with others who had been at the rehab center for a lot longer. One was a guy named Rene. When Rene was in Santa Monica at a shopping mall, he got into a conversation with someone named Reuben. During this conversation, Reuben told him about a man named J-R who gave seminars about spiritual topics. Rene told a few of us about this, and we all agreed that we wanted to go with him to a seminar. The others had to sneak me out of the rehab center because I wasn't allowed off the premises at that point—I was eighteen and had only been there a few months.

We went to this seminar at someone's house, and it was amazing. It was 1969, or maybe early 1970. In those days, everybody would do a sharing and then J-R would give a seminar. He was just an everyday guy. Nothing stood out about him. He was a regular-looking, regular-sounding guy, and he wasn't overbearing. Everything about him was so gentle, so loving, and he just talked extemporaneously. He didn't have notes or anything. It was amazing.

The things he said in that first seminar have always stuck with me. He said, "Not one Soul will be lost," and he talked about unconditional love and how there's really no right or wrong. People do what they have to do, and there's no point in getting into judgments because, well, what's the point?

Before that, I had been searching for something that could answer the questions I had. I really wanted answers. I had been abused as a child, experiencing terrible things, and I wanted to know why. In every religion where I went to find answers, there was a good and there was a bad—a right and a wrong.

J-R didn't say anything like that. He just said, "You're on your own path, and all paths lead back to God," which had always been what I had thought. I was always thinking that if we were created by God, how could he lose a part of himself? How could he lose us? The things that J-R said were what I had always thought. I always knew there was a teacher somewhere, but I just didn't know who it was. When I left that seminar, I knew I had found my teacher.

DAVID REED
That's the Light

My mother started going to J-R's seminars in 1969 or 1970, and she kept raving about him, saying how great it was. At the time, I was about nine years old, and I asked if I could go with her. She said, "Sure, I think kids can go."

So, we went to a seminar with my uncle, and we all sat in chairs in a row. Each person had to stand up and say their name, then say who brought them there or why they were there. I was getting nervous because I could see that I was going to have to stand up and say my name. J-R was sitting in a chair at the front of the room. When it was my turn, I stood up, said my name, and mentioned that my mom had brought me. Then, as I sat back down, I felt a sensation like cold chills over my whole body. My mom later told me, "That's the Light."

At the end of the seminar, I waited in line with my mom and got to ask him a question, which was, "How could I be better at school?" He looked at me and said, "Well, first off, you're a very old Soul and you are going to be fine. You don't need to worry about it; you're going to make it." Back then, I thought he was talking about school, but years later, I realized he wasn't referring to grammar school at all.

My mom and I started going to seminars every week, and each time, J-R would tell me to sit up near him on the couch, which was next to his chair. He was super nice and always smiling—a very nice person. It always felt really good to be around him.

Many years later, at a book signing J-R was doing in San Francisco, he came up to me and said, "I want you to know that you need to take care of yourself. Be careful, and I love you." Right after that, I went through a lot of changes in my life—so I realized that he was totally aware of what I was going through.

GAILA CORRIE
You Have Finally Come Home

In 1970, I was being what you might call a "metaphysical tramp." My friend Barbara said to me, "You're going from spiritual teacher to spiritual teacher, spiritual organization to spiritual organization, just one after the other. Why don't you come and meet John-Roger and give it a go?" And I said, "But I don't need one more." She said, "Believe me. Do me a favor—please give it a try. At least go five times. I'm getting that you should come five times, and then you're going to recognize the greatness of this teacher."

So, when I went with her the first time, it was funny, because my impression of a spiritual teacher was of an Indian guru with a long beard and a white robe, that type of thing. And here I see this good-looking man with a turtleneck—very interesting, unusual, and extremely self-confident. I thought, "Oh my God, this guy really has got an ego." Of course, that's where I was at that stage of my life, in total judgment.

So, I stayed and listened. I really didn't understand where he was coming from. I kept falling asleep, and I thought, "I must be bored. I keep falling asleep." Well, at the end of the seminar, Barbara said to me, "Go and at least acknowledge him, and say hello." He was sitting on a platform someone had built for that purpose at their home. During the whole seminar, when I was awake, I had done nothing but judge him: "Who does he think he is? What an ego, blah blah blah. What a quack." On and on.

So, I went up to the stage and said to him, "Nice to meet you. I've heard nice things about you. You were interesting from what I can remember, but I kept falling asleep, so I missed a lot of it. I'll be back some time." All of a sudden, a powerful energy pushed me and forced me to look straight into his eyes. And at that moment, this Light just went totally through me. It was amazing, absolutely amazing. And it shook me. It was an incredible Light. J-R just smiled and said, "You have finally come home."

What got to me was that phrase, "You've really come home," because I had always said that I would know my true teacher because he'll tell me, "You've truly come home." I was flabbergasted and in shock. But I'm a bit of a "doubting Thomas." So, it actually took five visits before it really sank in. Barbara was right. And every time I went, I'd fall asleep. When I'd wake up, I knew something had been going on but, I didn't know what. I still didn't quite understand what he was saying.

By the fifth visit, I knew I had a contract with him—that we had been connected through other lifetimes, and that somehow, he was working with me and I was meant to meet him and be part of the Movement. I thank God that occurred because J-R totally turned my life around for the better.

CAROLINE HERNDON
Where's My Throne?

In 1967–1968, I began to experience a feeling of depersonalization. There were times when I felt I was not there. I would sometimes become aware that I was sitting on my bed rocking, and I had no idea how long I had been there. I was very depressed. It became harder and harder to function at the university I was attending. I eventually quit school and came home to my parents' house in California.

For the next year, I was severely depressed. I lay on my bed and wanted to die. Even though I had no previous understanding of the out-of-the-body experience, I thought that if I could cut the connection to my body, I might die. I would lie there and try to get as far from my body as I could, and then try to disconnect. When I got to that point, I would hear a voice call my name. It would simply say, "Caroline," and I would jolt back into my body. One day, I suddenly got up, got a job, and got on with my life.

A year or so later, a friend came over and told me that he had met a "Mystical Traveler" and wanted me to meet him. The next night, I went with my friend to someone's house to meet this "Mystical Traveler." There was a raised platform with a chair on it, and John-Roger came in and sat down. He looked like a used car salesman to me. He began to speak. I noticed how beautiful and happy everyone in the room was.

As I watched, questions would pop into my mind. And every question I thought, he answered. It frightened me a bit, and I began to think, "You charlatan!" I could suddenly see my negative energy hurl across the room and hit him. It bounced off him and came right back at me. I got a headache and a stiff neck. When the seminar was over, I headed to the door. J-R came up to me and touched my arm. Suddenly, the headache and stiff neck were gone. He said, "Come back." I then knew something was happening; I still was not sure what it was.

I came home and told my roommate what had happened. We decided to go to J-R's seminar the next night. When we arrived, there was no platform for his chair to sit on. We took a seat on the couch. When he came in, I thought, "Ha! Where's your throne?" He said out loud, "Ha! Where's my throne?" Then I knew. He could see and hear everything. He could see my Soul. As he began to speak, the Light came all through me. I drifted off and came out of my body. A beautiful fountain of lights went off, and a voice said, "Caroline, who are you?" I was startled to awareness and looked at J-R; he continued to talk to the group, but looked at me and winked. That question has been my journey ever since.

In the early '70s, J-R was doing Light Studies, a form of spiritual counseling. In my first Light Reading, he said, "I want to talk to you about what you called your nervous breakdown in 1967–68. That was not a nervous breakdown. It was a spiritual confrontation. You experienced it as a death and tried to die, so I called your name out through the day and night to keep you anchored to your body." I began to cry and asked him how long he had been working with me. He told me he began to work with me in 1965, five years before I met him physically. I asked him how he found me. He said he could see my light on the other side.

CANDACE HUGHES MACNAIR
Memories of J-R and Muriel Engle

I lived in Santa Barbara with Muriel Engle for about two years from 1971 to 1973. During that time, J-R would sometimes come up, spontaneously, to stay for a few days.

Early in my time staying with Muriel, I remember coming home from work one day and Muriel saying that J-R and Michael Sun would be coming up the next day. I had come into the Movement in May 1969 and was still in some awe of J-R—the idea that he would be staying in the same house as me for a few days was thrilling and nerve-wracking for me.

Arriving home from work the next day, I saw J-R and Michael sitting at the small Formica table in the kitchen, Muriel at the stove cooking, and all of them laughing. I smiled and said hello, then headed to my room. At dinner, we sat together and J-R regaled us with stories, jokes, and insights. Suddenly, he began talking about other universes and planets. He turned to Michael and me and said, "You both spent time in the devic realm, but Michael came through Venus, and you, pointing a hand at me, came through another planet" (he didn't say which). Someone asked how we could be human and devic and J-R explained the evolution differences. Michael and I kept looking at each other, with figurative mouths hanging open and eyes wide. All this over dessert.

The next afternoon, we were all in Muriel's living room in her house on La Coronilla, which was at the top of the hill of the Mesa, overlooking the ocean. Muriel was a devotee of Satya Sai Baba and had a special altar for him in her home. Muriel was telling stories of her experiences with Sai Baba, and in the middle of a sentence, J-R got up and went to his bedroom—no word, no explanation.

Throughout the rest of the afternoon, Michael told us that when J-R was "out of his body," it was important to check on him and keep him warm. When J-R got up and came back into the living room, he shared that the Spirit had called him at that moment, and when called, he responded, no matter what was going on. It was a deep moment of awareness for me that, even in the middle of a conversation, if called by Spirit, he responded, no delay. I have remembered that moment all my life.

SHARON SOELLER
This Is Your Way Back to God

In December 1970, I was a student at California State College in Fullerton and taking a psychology class. To celebrate the end of the semester, our professor invited the whole class to a party at his apartment. When I arrived at the party, I joined one of the female students, Caroline Herndon, and her friend, Jacquelyn Rone. They were seated on the floor in a circle visiting with a few of the other students. You have to remember this was the early '70s when people sat on the floor at parties!

Caroline was telling the group about some seminars she'd been attending where a man shared about things like auras and colors and Light. I had just moved out of my parents' home into my own apartment, having been raised in a very fundamentalist Christian religion, so this was very unfamiliar to me. She invited us to go along with her to one of the seminars where this man, who spoke about spiritual things, would be sharing. I didn't answer Caroline right away, because I began to feel a little bit strange and woozy. I excused myself from the group and went into the bathroom and sat down on the closed toilet lid, hanging my head down because I was feeling so strange. No, I wasn't drinking or doing drugs!

I began seeing bluish-colored light all around me and heard a man's voice say, "This is your way back to God." I was quite surprised to hear a man's voice in the bathroom. I pulled back the shower curtain to see if someone was hiding behind the curtain. There was no one. I climbed up on the edge of the tub and looked out the window above the tub. Again, no one was there.

Prior to this incident, I had never heard voices. I had never seen blue light shining except from an electrical light source. I was confused by all of it, yet there was a compelling feeling in it for me. I had a sense this was somehow connected to what my friend Caroline had been talking about. Not quite sure why I returned to the student group and told Caroline I would go with her to the next seminar.

So, one evening after work in January 1971, I attended my first seminar in my waitress uniform, with tips rattling in my apron pockets. I joined the group of people who came to listen to this man. I don't remember much of the seminar or who was there, but I do remember John-Roger. By the time I left the seminar that night, I had experienced a very deep level of loving by being around this man. This ordinary man, John-Roger, spoke of loving and kindness and did so with humor. Most of all, I remember the loving and the goodness that exuded from him. I did not understand it, yet I wanted to have what was present in that room. I wanted to know love within myself and be able to have that experience more in my life.

Since that first seminar, I knew that my path was to experience more of that loving, which was present every time I attended a

John-Roger seminar. Every moment I have spent with John-Roger since then—learning how to hold in the higher consciousness and in the loving—has been a blessing beyond measure.

RANDY GARVER
The Preceptor Consciousness*

In terms of the Preceptor Consciousness, I don't remember J-R saying, "Hey, looky here, this thing is here," but he certainly started referencing it. When calling in the Light, he would call that presence forward. I can't say what the interplay was between the Mystical Traveler Consciousness and the Preceptor Consciousness, but I noticed that it was a powerful key.

With the Preceptor Consciousness, things started shifting. More and more people started coming into the Movement, like the Philadelphia contingent and people from Northern California and Florida. This was right around 1970–1971. It was a powerful, expansive time. A lot of people came in through that opening, that window. It was a real revolution in terms of the Movement.

Right around 1972, J-R started ordaining people into the MSIA ministry. That was a big shift. People started seeing the Movement as something more than what it was before.

* Note: In addition to holding the keys to the Mystical Traveler Consciousness, J-R also anchored the Preceptor Consciousness, an energy from the highest source that comes physically present on the planet every 25,000 years.

ASHTAR-ATHENA
Please Come and Take Me Home

I "met" the Traveler in Fort Lauderdale, Florida, when I was around twelve years old. On a hot evening, I went out and looked up at the stars and said, "You know, I can't stay on this planet anymore. There's not enough love." I was crying. And I said, "Whoever up there brought me here, would you please come and take me home?" That night, a young blond man appeared in my dreams, and that was John-Roger. I didn't know he existed on the physical plane. I had no idea who or what he was, but he was always by my side and would teach me, sometimes vocally but usually telepathically, and I didn't think twice about it.

Over the next twenty years, I lived many and varied life-times—I joined the circus, I was a member of a dance company, I went to college, I married, and I had a daughter. In 1970, my husband and I moved to Santa Barbara, California, which had one of the first Sai Baba centers. There I met Muriel Engle, who was this glowing woman full of love and Light. I noticed her right away. She was always talking about John-Roger. I didn't know anything about John-Roger, other than this woman glowed, and whatever she had, it had to be great. And we were very close.

Meanwhile, I had an astrologer friend by the name of Mead Roberts. I went to see him one day, and I noticed a poster on the wall that said "The Movement of Spiritual Inner Awareness," and it had a beautiful dancer on it. I thought it was a dance company that did spiritual dance. I said, "What is this poster here? I want so much to go see this dance company." He laughed and said, "Oh, that's the Movement of Spiritual Inner Awareness with John-Roger." I said, "John-Roger?" He said, "Yes, Muriel Engel and several of us are going to a seminar on Tuesday if you'd like to go." That was a few days in the future. And okay, I have to go, right? I mean, this is like, inevitable. This is my fate here. So, I went with them.

The seminar was at David and Heather Giorgio's home in Chatsworth, California, on August 7, 1972, which was exactly twenty years from the time I first "saw" J-R when I was twelve years old in junior high, just before I joined the circus. There was a little wooden platform in David's backyard with J-R's armchair on it. J-R was sitting in the chair, and about fifty to seventy-five people had spread blankets all around. They would pass the mike around, and we would put our names and whatever in the Light. Well, I immediately walked up to John-Roger and I said, "Are you that young blond man that's been in my dreams?" And he said,

"Yes, love, I've been working with you in this lifetime since about the time you were in junior high." Nailed it, right on the nose.

After the group had chanted the Hu, I watched the purple light bouncing off the trees. You know, it was just spectacular what was happening as J-R spoke. And the energy of the love...I was hooked—utterly, completely, and totally. I had never experienced anything as wonderful as this. I watched him like a hawk because I had never met a master before in the physical. In the tradition I was trained in, you worked strictly on the inner planes with the masters in the ashram. So having a real live master I could observe was really fun.

And let me tell you what a real live master looks like. John-Roger was completely attentive to people at every place we went. I particularly remember a time when we were traveling in Paris, France. We would go out to eat, and it didn't matter if it was the person running the elevator or the hotel sweeper—I don't care who it was—he would stop and evoke the divinity of that person. I watched him do it time and time again. How did he do that? Loving them...acknowledging them...and seeing them—really seeing who they are behind that façade. That impressed me so much because I had heard about Christ Consciousness, but this was the first time I ever saw it in action. I thought, "Oh, that's what a real Christed being looks like."

SHERWOOD DUANE
All of That Is Shifting Now

From my first seminar, I immediately became a seminar regular. At that time in Los Angeles, J-R was doing maybe five seminars a week. At some point, he went all the way up to seven. I came in with a lot to unlearn because my learned state was not very happy—low self-esteem, low self-worth. And all the while, I had this large ego, and I was just bumping around like a pinball machine guy. I did not feel comfortable with myself. I did not like myself—I really hated myself, truthfully. And I was covering up the majority of all that with the ego format. So, I was functioning primarily out of the ego.

At the seminars, we'd all line up and get to ask J-R a question. I did that at every seminar. And he was always very sweet and kind, and he'd look into my eyes. What would often happen is—I would have a question, I'd get in line, stand in the spot in front of him, and it would all get wiped right out of my consciousness. After having that experience a number of times, I would begin to try and hold onto the question, because I knew I was going to be blown out as soon as I stood in front of him. Eventually, I was able to actually ask him questions.

But in terms of comfort, some people were very, very comfortable with J-R. They were like, "My friend, my sweet man, I love you," and he loved them. And I was just outside of that loop. I didn't know how to get into that. And, truthfully, I don't know that I ever did. I'm closer to him now since he's transitioned than I ever was when he was on the planet. And I have a space for him inside of me that's far beyond anything I ever had when he was on the planet. But that was primarily a statement of my own discomfort with myself. My own discomfort with being loved and loving—and all of that is shifting now.

LYNN THAYER
No More Fear

When I met John-Roger in 1970, I wasn't really looking for anything or anyone "spiritual." I went to see him because my roommate had gone to one of his seminars, and of course, I didn't want to be left out of anything. So, I decided to attend the next one of J-R's twice-weekly seminars, which at that time were being held at a woman named Edna Garcia's home in El Monte, California.

I arrived about fifteen minutes before John-Roger was scheduled to start, and I found maybe ten people gathered in a room. They all said hello and introduced themselves, and then John-Roger came in and we all sat down.

My first reaction to J-R wasn't love or awe; it was… fear. As soon as I looked at J-R, I was very scared of him, despite his being clean-cut and having a great sense of humor. And I honestly don't remember anything he said that night. After the seminar, we all went out for pie and coffee with him, and after J-R left, people shared their "experiences" of seeing and feeling these fantastical, mystical things as he spoke during the seminar. Though I can't say I had the experiences they did, these stories didn't bother me, and I felt very welcomed by everyone, even by J-R. I didn't tell anyone that I was afraid of J-R; it was so deep and, in my opinion, irrational. Why would I feel that way?

But a part of me recognized there was something important for me at these seminars, so I set aside my fear and continued going to them. I noticed that at the end of each seminar, when J-R had finished speaking, people would go up and talk to him, which usually ended in a hug. By my third or fourth seminar, I knew I loved J-R, but the fear of him was still very present. How could I love and fear someone at the same time? I didn't know. I did know that I didn't want him to know anything about me, because if he knew more about me, I was sure he would kick me out of the group.

After the fourth seminar, I finally decided I had to go up to him, face to face, and ask him about my fear of him. So, when he finished speaking, people, as usual, lined up. The line wasn't long, and before I knew it, I was standing in front of him. I stood for a moment like a deer in the headlights, and he just looked at me with this little smile. I screwed up my courage and blurted out, "Why am I so afraid of you?"

He looked at me for a second, then said, "Because you can't hide anything from me, darlin'. I can look and see everything. Everything—especially the beauty which you have hidden so deeply."

"Beauty? Me?!"

"I will never hurt you," he continued, "because I love you unconditionally—no matter what."

I was stunned. He had seen into me, down to my very core. Then I got the biggest and best hug in my life from him, and I just surrendered and gave one back.

Since that moment, I have had no more fear, just a lot of trust and love. Though that didn't stop me from sometimes unintentionally testing that bond throughout the years.

What J-R said to me that night, and the absolute purity with which he said it, still lifts me and fills my heart with love.

KURT AND SANDY REINCKE
J-R Made It Real Easy to Quit

Sandy: When we wanted to give up cigarettes, J-R told us what to do. Put all the cigarettes in a bowl, the whole carton. And then you just start smoking until you get sick.

Kurt: Smoke until the bowl is empty. You smoke until they're gone—inhale-exhale, inhale-exhale, inhale-exhale. You never stop. You light the next one—inhale-exhale, inhale-exhale. After the first one and a half cigarettes, you sit there and your eyeballs are turning in your head.

Sandy: Then you got sort of sick and it was like, do you want to go and try it again? I think I said no. But the thing I thought of was, "Oh my God, I won't be able to have cigarettes and coffee in the morning!" I was up to two and a half packs or something a day. But I got up the next morning and had my coffee, and didn't crave a cigarette. I went for an aura balance shortly after that, and I never had another craving.

Kurt: I think I got to three cigarettes. I didn't finish the third one. I was done—I never smoked again. Didn't miss it.

Sandy: That's just how the Light works.

Kurt: It also helped that J-R said the Light doesn't really like cigarette smoke.

Sandy: He also said you couldn't go beyond the mental realm if you were addicted to cigarettes.

Kurt: Yeah, something like that. And that scared the shit out of me. How do I quit, you know?

Sandy: Do you want to get off the planet or not? It was like, you gotta give up smoking.

Kurt: But J-R made it real easy to quit. The way he told us to quit—man, it was foolproof.

Sandy: Well, it worked for us.

SUSAN GERKE
A Blossoming Flower

In 1972, I was visiting a friend in California who told me about John-Roger and his nightly talks in people's homes that she attended. She showed me his picture on the front page of "On the Light Side," MSIA's newsletter at that time. When I saw J-R's face, I swallowed hard and experienced something for which I have no words.

I began studying the teachings, having many inner experiences and dreams, and I wrote the following about J-R, my beloved spiritual teacher:

> *Presenting to us what we need to grow,*
> *Awakening heart centers of those who choose back,*
> *Showing us the keys so that we may unlock the doors,*
> *Always serving for the highest good,*
> *You are the one that I stand before like a blossoming flower.*

RACHAEL JAYNE
Being On Staff

In about 1972, I was sitting in J-R's office with him, and I was saying, "I just want to be on your staff, J-R." And I started to cry, wanting to be close to him. And he just sat there. He handed me the kleenex very neutrally, and his comment was, "Well, you will be. But you're in training now." And he said, "It's not like you'll be sitting at my feet, but you will be on my staff."

I think we talked a little bit about my ordination blessing at that time and what it meant to be in the female form because there was a line in my ordination, "Even though you're in the female form, your strength will be that of the Traveler." I asked him if it meant women are in some ways "less" than men, and he said, "Actually, women are more spiritually evolved than men, but they get caught in desire patterns more easily." It reminded me of what Sister Claire said in the movie Brother Sun, Sister Moon when she said, "I don't want to be understood, I want to understand. I don't want to be loved, I want to love…etc."

The biggest memory I have from that talk in his office is J-R telling me, "I will sit in my chair for as long as it takes until spirit directs me. And if I don't get direction, I may just sit for hours. And when I get direction, I follow it. Because if I stop listening to the direction, it will shut off."

I remember what a significant message that was to me. Ever since—and that was a long time ago—when I have those moments when the Traveler speaks, it's unequivocal, it's game over. I'm not going to question it, second-guess it, it's like a spiritual directive.

The way that J-R worked with me throughout the years and the positions I've been in, I was on his staff. Was I being paid to be on his staff? No. I mean, he had me working in the travel agency MSIA owned. He had me managing the hotel negotiations for conference for years. And after that, it was funny because the reason I became emcee at conference was because he kept egging me on. Even after I had breast surgery in April or May of one year—and it was June when we had conference—he had me go on stage and share about my PTS Masters class experience about God being my Partner.

Around that time, I had a very significant dream. I had just had a mastectomy, and I didn't yet know that I was going to have to have chemo. And I had a dream with J-R. I remember he said, "Well, it looks like it's going to be a longer haul." I said, "Is it going to take me out?" And he said, "No." He then asked me, "What do you want?" I said, "I want freedom." He said, "Then give yourself that. What else do you want?" I said, "I want my primary identity to be that of a Spiritual being." He said, "You're going to be learning services, right?" And I said, "No, I'm going to be facilitating the PTS Masters Class." He said, "Great."

That was all in a dream. As I was going through chemo, I began facilitating the MSS, and that was part of my identity as a spiritual being.

I went on to facilitate the DSS class, and I facilitated it for 16 years. With some overlap, I started doing more and more Insight. It was just time to move on from DSS. I love facilitating DSS. I love that class. And J-R gave me some really good coaching early on about facilitating. He said, "Make it fun. Because if you're not having fun, you're not going to be learning."

He also talked about some of the facilitators kind of being okay with reading the script, but not really coming from their experience. And he just talked about how important it was to share from your experience. I was very encouraged to be authentic and grounded in what I shared. When I was prepping for DSS, there were times when I read the script and found that I didn't comprehend the meaning of what was being shared in the lecturette. I would work on the content until I found my own experience with it. It was so important for me to come from authenticity in my own experience.

I think that's one of my strengths as a facilitator. Through my own demonstration, I give people permission to be human, because I am so aware of my own humanness and how it all fits into what we're doing.

ASHTAR-ATHENA
Template for the Golden Age

John-Roger said that in our particular format for MSIA seminars—sitting in a circle, everyone sitting equal, passing the microphone around so everyone has an equal say—we were setting the template for the Golden Age. No longer will you have the priest sitting separate and apart, officiating, and the congregation sitting down and being basically passive. We are proactive in being the Living Light in this time. What we're doing in MSIA is establishing the archetype for the new Aquarian Age education.

GLENN BARNETT
Sacred Contributions

In 1973, after attending several seminars, I was sitting near J-R at a seminar. At that time, he passed the microphone around the room and anyone who wanted to make a contribution could do so, which could be anything that was on the person's mind. It was a way of helping people to clear things within and become more attuned and open to the seminar that followed. There were perhaps fifty people in the room, and the microphone went around, and it seemed to take an eternity for everyone to have their say.

I was a little bored and, at one point, turned to a friend and made a snide remark about what someone had just shared. When I turned back to the front, J-R was looking at me with a very stern look on his face, such that I couldn't hold his gaze. I knew that he was upset with me.

During his seminar, he said, to no one in particular, but directly to me, "I have worked very hard to build the energy in this room, and I am not about to let you ruin it." I have always held contributions as sacred since that day.

ANNE SOELLER
Enthusiasm

I learned acceptance through J-R, which he always said is the first law of Spirit. Another step is understanding, and from that understanding came a great deal of enthusiasm. It seemed like the teachings came to me on levels, from acceptance to understanding to enthusiasm. So, I guess I really got kicked into this enthusiastic thing because I'd learned so much acceptance from J-R, so much understanding, and then my next level would be enthusiasm.

One year, we had a Conference of Enthusiasm. In those days, J-R said that Spirit would pick someone to be a key speaker. There might be several speakers, but sometimes there would only be one or two. This particular year, J-R approached me and asked if

I would speak at the Conference of Enthusiasm. I said, "Yes, I'd be delighted. I'd be honored to. How long will I have to speak?" He says, "Forty-five minutes." I had never spoken that long to anybody or any group in my life. I said, "How long are the other people going to be speaking?" He says, "Fifteen minutes." He had told me one time, "Anne, you're on stage twenty-four hours a day." So, here's my big moment.

I gave my talk, and it was so interesting. I was concerned about not having enough to say, and my talk ended right at that forty-five-minute mark. It was like, you know—Spirit just never lets you down. Once you make an intention with Spirit, once you make a commitment to do something for someone else through Spirit, Spirit will never let you down.

JACKIE PETERSON
MSIA Office Key

In 1973, I had one of the proudest moments in my young life. I was presented with my own key to the MSIA office, which I needed for the volunteer work I was doing. Five days a week, I left work and spent a couple of hours working in the MSIA office before picking up my daughter from daycare. It was the reason I had moved to Los Angeles the year before, to be close to MSIA and volunteer to assist in John-Roger's work. It was also lots of fun.

Pauli Sanderson and Candace Semigran, who had met J-R during his years teaching at Rosemead High School, would arrive around the same time I did, about 3:30 p.m. They both taught school—Pauli taught dance at Rosemead High and Candace, kindergarten. They spent their days teaching and their afternoons and evenings dedicated to getting J-R's teachings out and attending seminars. There was a lot to do in the office.

I tried transcribing J-R's seminar tapes, but I just couldn't stay awake—Pauli described me as "very entertaining." But she was amazing at it; she could just breeze along. Then she would take the transcriptions from a few seminars and write the Discourses and books. Of course, they went to J-R for editing. It was magical for me to watch. My job became printing those Discourses and books on our two Gestetner mimeograph machines. Back in 1973, copy machines had not been invented yet.

Then we would spread the pages all over our office (a converted two-car garage), collate them, and staple them with three staples down the left side. At my first conference, the Conference of Love in 1972, I purchased every book available by J-R. I got six of them for $10, all tied up with a purple ribbon. Now, I was printing those same books for others, plus new ones that seemed to be coming out all the time.

RUSSELL BISHOP
Awakening Is Internal Magic

Meeting and working with John-Roger has certainly been an adventure, one that began consciously in the summer of 1973 when I was married to a woman named Carol, who was an active seeker of all things mystical. One evening, she came home all excited about the next in the line of you've-got-to-meet-this-new-teacher-he's-the-best-one-yet. Thus began my introduction to John-Roger, the Mystical Traveler, and the Movement of Spiritual Inner Awareness.

Carol dragged me to a taped seminar, where I found the chanting and incense a bit odd, and she bought me a subscription to Discourses. However, Carol did not let me know these Discourses were on the way, so I was a bit surprised when the first one arrived in the mail. I read that first Discourse and literally threw it on the floor in front of her exclaiming, "Who is this nut case anyway? Seems like he must have read the Bible, taken the est training, and maybe even went through one of my programs. All he did was write it down and call it something special. Nuts!" Well, my language might have been a bit more colorful at the time, but you get the picture.

These Discourses kept coming one after the other, month after month. I paid no attention to them and Carol quietly put them on a bookshelf, out of the way, but in plain sight, in case I was ever curious. A couple of years went by, and in the spring of 1976, we were doing some spring cleaning when I came across this stack of 30-some Discourses.

So, I picked up the first Discourse, which I actually had read in 1973, muttering out loud, "What did that nut case (sanitized) have to say?" As I began to read it again, it all seemed new, fresh, and amazingly clear. I was being transformed and lifted in Spirit as I continued to read. When I finished, I exclaimed to Carol, "I never read this before!" When she reminded me that I had read it in 1973, I asked in a somewhat astonished voice, "Well, then, who changed the words?"

Changed the words, indeed! Something had changed, and that something was me. Or perhaps more accurately stated, my consciousness had shifted. As I came to learn, J-R was fond of reminding us that there was no way he could ever accurately reflect what the spiritual realms were; so, he spoke or wrote to occupy our minds while Spirit and the Traveler did its "magic" internally.

That internal magic is most simply described as awakening. Something awakens that was previously asleep. And something that is asleep was previously awake. Thus, the process of awakening is one of remembering something known but forgotten. This first Discourse, and the intervening years between my first reading and my real reading, had served to awaken me to that which is visible—but only to those who have eyes and are willing to see. Clearly, I had come more awake, rubbed the sleep out of my eyes, and begun to see that which was hiding in plain sight.

LEIGH-TAYLOR YOUNG
I Have Been Waiting for You

In 1972, I was drawn to study with a great Sidha guru, Baba Muktananda. I later realized this sacred involvement was a precursor to meeting John-Roger and embracing The Movement of Spiritual Inner Awareness.

During this time, a foremost university was doing consciousness experiments in Vancouver, Canada. I took part in one at the same time that I was following Muktananda. What transpired was an extraordinary visionary experience.

In one part of my vision, I was dressed in the beautiful red silk sari that Baba had given me, and he was walking me down a red carpet strewn with fresh flowers. With my six-year-old son by my side and a banner of purple light over our heads that spelled out Spiritual Aristocracy, Muktananda was giving me away in marriage. At the end of the carpet was my betrothed who placed a ring on my wedding finger with purple light shooting out of it. This man's face was so full of Light he had no discernible features. Just pure Light. The marriage took place. Within days of this experience, I met John-Roger.

I arrived home from Vancouver on a Friday, and on Sunday, my friend Sally Kirkland called saying she wanted to come over and play me the tape recording of her recent wedding. Sally is a remarkable actress and a truly outrageously genuine being of great spiritual depth. I met her through the actor Robert De Niro, a mutual friend. Shortly after Sally first arrived in Los Angeles to do films, she met John-Roger. She very often insisted that I needed to meet John-Roger. "You simply have to meet my amazing spiritual teacher John-Roger!" I would then patiently say, "Sally, I am a one guru woman and I am happy for you and I am happy and content with my teacher and thank you."

Sally showed up at my home that Sunday as I was resting from my time in Vancouver and because of my absolute love for Sally, I couldn't refuse to listen to the tape of her wedding, which had just taken place at an ashram in downtown Los Angeles called Prana. I learned from Sally that Prana was an acronym for Purple Rose Ashram of the New Age. She played the tape, and as I listened, I became aware of a very powerful loving energy. It moved me and I was silently very curious. She gave me three cassette tapes of John-Roger's seminars saying, "It is suggested to not listen to all at once, but I am going to leave them here for you to check out over time." "Honey," I said, "I am not making any promises."

After she left, I immediately put on a John-Roger cassette. I was riveted listening to all of them until one o'clock in the morning. At about two o'clock in the morning, I was hiking up Benedict

Canyon in Beverly Hills, exclaiming to myself, "Oh, my God, this man is telling me the truth!"

It was not that I had not heard or experienced profound truths elsewhere because indeed I had, but what kept running through me was a bliss of awareness that was so acute, I just kept repeating a mantra: "This is truth for me, this is God truth for me."

I was so excited I could hardly sleep. I called Sally at the rise of the sun and said, "Sally, when might I be able to meet John-Roger?" She was thrilled and said, "It is Monday now, and there is a seminar on Wednesday night, and I am going to call J-R and tell him about you and that you are coming!" I asked her not to, knowing that was useless.

On Wednesday night, I went to my first live seminar of John-Roger at Prana. It was the Fall of 1973.

I arrived at Prana feeling nervous and very excited but also very cautious, especially since I was extraordinarily shy in those days. I hid behind a pillar of sorts, as invisible as possible. I would peek around the pillar, ready to hear J-R the best I could, and still be unseen. Sally, of course, kept trying to bring me upfront, but with my urgent hushed whispers that I was fine and safe, she finally accepted my choice of place. I saw John-Roger enter from the side of the large seminar room with a few staff members, and Sally let out a loud shout while pointing, "J-R, there is the actress Leigh Taylor-Young I have been telling you about. She's behind that wall!" I was shocked, feeling "Oh God, may I just disappear" when I see J-R veer towards me through the room. As he approached me, I felt an instantaneous expanded state of excitement and alertness. A clarity such that scales seemed to be falling from my eyes. I was not blinking. He reached out and took my hand in both of his hands, looked into my eyes with Love beyond all Love, and sweetly and softly said, "Welcome." In my altered state, I managed a shy, "Thank you," as inwardly I heard him say, "I have been waiting for you." As he walked away and got into his blue chair to begin the seminar, I was in a state of Joy that I had never known. I was deeply One with him and being flooded in waves of bliss and recognition. At last, I was meeting my greatest love. All points of my existence converged in the deepest fulfillment. What I had always been looking for, and waiting for, was present and welcoming me home.

That night I had an exquisite dream in which a scene occurred that seemed to symbolize to me a great spiritual promise. John-Roger was standing at the top of the stairs of Great Light, and he was handing me a white rose. It was the spiritual promise. I said eagerly, "Are we engaged now? Can we get married now?" He responded with a tender smile, "We'll see."

I returned to Prana the very next day and bought every J-R tape and book available. Pauli McGary (now Sanderson) helped me load all of the boxes into my car with a wise admonition about spiritual indigestion. I was up all night devouring these materials, reading and listening well into the next day. That night, I attended the Thursday John-Roger seminar. On Friday, I asked to be a seminar leader, not even knowing what this was or what it involved, but by Sunday I was hosting my first taped J-R seminar. I was hiding behind the stairs, scared and shy, as four people who had arrived for the seminar were coaxing me to come out and lead the seminar. Sally Kirkland was a proud and encouraging supporter and walked me through the format. A year later, I often had one hundred-plus attendees squeezed into my home. I held these seminars every Sunday night for over five years. Craig Rand, earlier named Muktan, a former Satchidananda devotee, was my right hand, and we both became initiates and ministers and created very joyful and creative home MSIA events celebrating the teachings of John-Roger and Soul Transcendence.

Even though I was plunging wholeheartedly into MSIA, I was having moments of confusion as I had so much love and gratitude for Muktananda. By nature, I am very loyal, and I was having difficulty feeling torn between my devotion to Baba and the extraordinary feeling of coming home that I was experiencing with John-Roger.

Shortly afterward, I gave a reception for Baba in my home, which I had already requested to do before meeting John-Roger. It was a great honor for me to be able to hold this reception for him, and since I could invite anyone I wished to receive his blessing, with trepidation, I called and invited John-Roger. He said he would love to come. I awkwardly asked if he would like a chair as high as Baba's, and J-R laughed and said no—he wanted to be on the floor with everyone else.

In the Hindu tradition, when you come before the Guru, the men are on one side and the women on the other. I invited many people who were dear to me, including Olivia Hussey, a fellow actress whom I had introduced to Muktananda earlier. Baba had given us spiritual names together. He named her Muktabai, and I was given the name Mirabai, and he initiated us both at the same time. It was a bit disturbing to me that he gave me a different tone or mantra than he gave her and everyone else, which was Om Namah Shivaya. I thought quietly to myself that something must be wrong with me as perhaps I needed a "remedial" mantra! It later turned out that the tone Baba gave me was the mental tone that I later received from John-Roger. Baba already knew this was going to happen.

When I had the visionary experience in Vancouver, Baba was the one giving me away in marriage to a man with a purple ring. Now we were having a similar experience at this reception. I had placed a red carpet down in my home strewn with flowers. I was in the red sari that Baba had given me. John-Roger was in front of Baba on the floor at his feet, and I was in front of Baba on the floor at his feet. It was as though Baba was presiding over our ceremony. Later, J-R shared with me that this was when Baba transferred his spiritual authority with me and in a sense "gave me away" to John-Roger. This was the moment when my karma passed to J-R from Baba. My father gave me to the Beloved. They knew. I did not—yet.

A week later, I went on a retreat with Muktananda, and I felt him beginning to push me away energetically. I was in pain and confusion. I realized how important it was for me to get clear about who was now my spiritual teacher.

In order to resolve this, I decided I would go away on my own silent retreat to pray for God's guidance. I had left a message asking John-Roger to hold me in the Light. Just as I was leaving, he called. When I told him the issue and of my struggle, he said, "Remember, it is not loyalty to Baba or to me, it is loyalty to your own soul that is important. I would like you to take with you a tape called Loyalty to Your Soul." On my way out of town, I picked up the tape at Prana and spent a week by myself in Palm Springs listening to the tape, meditating and praying, and often sweating in communion with Spirit, pleading for clarity. It was intense for me as I deeply understood the need for a living master. And I loved them both.

Almost immediately after I returned, the phone rang, and it was John-Roger. I said, now clear in my consciousness, "Oh, J-R, I've come home. This is my family—this is my home—you are my Home." My true journey had now begun with John-Roger and Soul Transcendence.

Sometime later, I heard that Baba was critically ill. I was about to leave the house to go and see him when the phone rang. It was J-R. He said, "When you see Baba, please give him my great love and tell him I honor him and I am with him." When I got to San Francisco, Baba was in a hospital room with his devoted Swami valet, and a long line of his beloveds were patiently waiting to see him one at a time. When it was my turn to enter, I lost all decorum and threw myself onto Baba's chest, weeping. He was bare from the waist up, with just a sheet wrapped around him, and he was beating me gently on my back, whispering to me in Hindi while I was crying and sweating from love. My heart was directly over his heart, and I saw a huge beam of purple light come right through me into Baba. This Light was pouring over us both in profound love for him from the Heavens. He just kept holding me close. Finally, it was time to go, and that was the last time I saw Baba. Just as I returned to my home, the phone rang, and I told J-R what had happened. He said, "Good"— nothing but a loving, deep, and rich "Good." I knew that J-R's love had touched deeply into Baba. Muktananda passed away some years later. He has always remained my Baba.

I have had many adventures during my life on earth; many highs and lows in career, personal life, finances, and physical health, but always ascending in my Spirit with the Traveler and the Christ. J-R was there intimately to steady me as I walked through it all. He supported me with loving beyond any measure.

He was, and he is, my Friend in this world and in what is already in Spirit and what is to come. If I close my eyes, I can see his eyes and they are the eyes of God, the eyes of eternal love. He is with me always. I know this as he continues to awaken me in my Soul and into the Heart of God.

KEITH MOORE
Travels with the Traveler

Two spiritual luminaries first met on the physical level in October 1972. It was an occasion of tremendous importance for many on the planet who follow the flow of spirit. John-Roger has described his meeting with Satya Sai Baba as a form of total communication, one of pure love with no blocks or resistances. Sai Baba said that the Movement of Spiritual Inner Awareness would sweep the planet. It was indeed a true blending of east and west.

Traveling Light

In September of 1972, A trip to India seemed remote, unlikely, undesirable, and entirely out of the question for me. As a matter of fact, on my list of places I would most like to go, India ranked 97th just in front of the North Pole and just behind Folsom Prison. But when the Light hits and moves you, you don't think about what you want or need. You just hold your breath and hang on.

My rational processes were saying, "No, you can't go. You can't leave your chiropractic practice for three weeks—you can't afford it—you never wanted to go to India." On and on with 17 different reasons why it couldn't be done. I knew that the trip was impossible, and that is why I agreed to put the entire matter in the Light "for the highest good." I felt very safe—after all, it was now down to just days before the plane was to leave and we had friends who had been planning the trip for months and still weren't sure if they were ready.

Thursday at noon four days before lift-off, we decided to go (that was if God, J. R., the kids, my patients, the president of the bank, my landlord, and grandma were willing).

Now keep in mind that we didn't have passports, tickets, shots, anything. The first step was to dash to L. A. from Ojai and get the passports. The lady at the desk said, "No way you can get a passport in less than 10 days." We hit her, everybody in the building, and the entire U.S. Foreign Service with a shot of Light. The passports were ready in 22 hours. So, with this approach, miracle followed miracle, and the following Monday at 9:00, we boarded the plane. A doctor had been found to take my practice, a close relative in the hospital was cured of a serious illness, the money for the tickets showed up, we made six freeway trips to the city without an accident, and last but not least, we got a sitter for our young boys. All the ends had been tied up, last-minute miracles for the last-minute crises, and a real buy on a big bright green trunk for $8.88 at Thrifty Drug.

Little did I know as I settled into my seat that in less than thirteen hours, I would be dashing through the subways of Paris carrying that damned green trunk with J-R, his staff, and six other people. Also, little did I anticipate that this episode would be followed closely by a plane search for bombs by the Israeli authorities, a camel ride by the Arabian Ocean, nursing nine very sick Vietnamese war orphans in the back of a 747; being a passenger in a death-defying taxi race through the streets of Bombay at 2 o'clock in the morning; mind-blowing interviews with Sri Sathya Sai Baba; eating off palm leaves at a stone-age village; witnessing a battle between a cobra and a mongoose; sitting in the midst of 4,000 chanting Hindus who were in varying states of religious ecstasy; and having a midnight supper in a small Bohemian cafe in the heart of Paris with J-R, the staff and other members of the Light family. I was expecting little but received much.

The flight over the pole to Paris was uneventful and as I sat there at 40,000 feet sipping Bordeaux, earphones tuned to the channel with the choir singing. In fact, I had indeed made a final departure.

There is an aura of excitement in and around every international jetport, and Orly is no exception. People are rushing here and there conversing in different tongues. I must admit I was a little bewildered by it all, but I took courage as I saw the Hilton Hotel sign lighting up the Paris night. I was sure that Conrad Hilton would protect me until our flight to Bombay left sixteen hours later, but alas, that was not what the Light had in store.

We stopped at customs to be processed when an Air France official walked up to Jeri Silver and said, "Dr. Hinkins awaits you on the other side." Jeri replied, "Yes, yes, I know all about that, but is he here at the airport?" J-R, Phillip, Wesley, and Michael had been in Paris for ten days taking side trips through Europe, and we had hoped they would meet us and I am pleased to say we were not disappointed.

Before I continue, it is important to make a few brief statements about our small band, which was making the trek from L.A. to India. We were composed of three groups, actually. There were the folks who set the trip up from the Baba Center in Hollywood, another contingent from the Baba Center in San Diego, and a few of us who were going because J-R was going. J-R's reputation had preceded him, and many of the people were looking forward to meeting him for one reason or another. The devotees of Sai Baba were delightful, courageous, kind, and to a person wonderfully spiritual. Each of us was expressing through our own individuality, each playing a role in this traveling dream. If at any time in this ongoing narrative I poke fun at any or all of us, I do so with the greatest love and respect, keeping in mind that what I report is not necessarily how it was, but merely how I saw it.

Now by this time, we were through customs and had made our way into the great lobby of Orly Airport. And what to my wondering eyes should appear but the Mystical Traveler and three Light grenadiers.

Throughout the entire journey, it was remarkable to me how well-dressed and groomed these four were. Even in the wilds of India, they looked as though they had just stepped out of the proverbial bandbox. On this particular occasion, however, J-R was cloaked in a black overcoat that was about four sizes too big for him, and his hair was a bit unruly. As he talked and greeted the various arrivals, one of the doctors from the Baba group came up to me and said, "Who is the character in the black overcoat? Is he trying to sell us some postcards?" "Postcards, indeed, sir," says I, "that happens to be Dr. John-Roger Hinkins, Light of the new age, founder and director of the Movement of Spiritual Inner Awareness, my teacher and master." I could tell from his quizzical expression that he was not impressed, but then again, I had seen a picture of his guru, a 4 ft., 10 in., Indian with a giant Afro hairdo that gave him an electrified look, wearing an orange dress. I didn't really understand how he could be so picky about the way my leader looked. But as we stood watching J-R move through the group sharing his warmth and friendship, taking charge of the situation, getting people placed in the proper taxis and busses to their respective destinations, my friend's attitude began to take on a new Light. J-R's adeptness and aplomb at handling and moving us all through every crisis and emergency was indeed miraculous and was in a large part responsible for his new title Mystical Tour Director (MTD).

Karma in the Subway

It seemed that some of us had karma to work out from a previous existence in regard to underground tunnels, so we soon found ourselves being led by the MTD through the subways of Paris, an intricate people mover built through the extensive catacombs under this romantic city. It was "follow the leader" and you had better be quick or you'd be standing inside the car looking out at the rest of the party on the platform—which happened to me several times. I narrowly escaped being a subway door sandwich, green trunk and all.

From the Orly substation to the Louvre Museum sortie (exit) we rattled and clacked, changing trains intermittently, and finally arriving at our destination, a small, quaint, family-run hotel, the Hotel Saint-Marie. J-R and the staff had been staying here for a week and the management had fallen in love with them as did everyone they came in contact with during this Light Journey around the world.

Next, we went for a midnight supper in the upper room of the Cafe Beaujolais, a petite Bohemian restaurant in the heart of Paris, where again Love had preceded us and we were greeted with warmth and graciousness by all. Of the many adventures and experiences the trip afforded, somehow this meal in the upper room was, to me, the most rewarding. Perhaps it was the magic of Paris, the intimacy of the Light company—whatever it was, it is difficult to place a word-level on. The food and wine were delicious and the conversation and camaraderie placed us, to say the least, in a high state.

We reluctantly returned to our respective hotel rooms which were side by side. My wife Muriel and I had just snuggled into a cloud-like feather mattress when from the room next door housing J-R and the staff came choruses of uproarious laughter. We were later to hear the precious tale I'd call…

Wesley Accepts a Gift

Unbeknownst to the rest of us, Wesley (one of J-R's personal staff guys) had gone downstairs to the restaurant to pay the bill. And as Americans do, they had left the tip on the table. However, it is the custom in France to pay the tip as you pay the check. Because Wesley didn't do that, the cashier became very irate and began to berate poor Wesley in the most vociferous Parisienne manner. Wesley, who really didn't know what was going on, gestured apologetically to no avail. Fortunately, he was rescued by the waitress who assured the cashier that we were quite generous and had left the tip on the table.

Now it was the cashier's turn to be red-faced and apologetic. In his desperation to get back into Wesley's good graces, he insisted that Wesley accept a gift, as a token of his repentance. The gift was a fine French cigarette. Wesley thanked him and tried to explain he did not smoke, but so as not to re-offend, he accepted the cigarette and started to put it in his pocket. The apologetic Frenchman would not have this, however, and insisted that Wesley enjoy his gift to the fullest and proceeded to light the cigarette. So, seeing little choice, Wesley accepted and puffed and coughed up the stairs.

Now, Wesley did not want us in the upper chamber to think he had taken up the vice of tobacco, so he pinched out the butt and placed it neatly in his coat pocket. Taking his place at the end of the table and rejoining the conversation, he soon noticed wisps of smoke emitting from his pocket. Keeping his composure, he discreetly attempted to put out the fire by exerting inconspicuous pressures on the smoldering cigarette in his jacket—which was accomplished without drawing attention to himself.

It wasn't until they returned to their hotel room and J-R asked Wesley how he got the big hole burnt in his coat that the truth was told with the resulting early morning hilarity which startled us as we dozed.

A Minor Detail

In our hurried four-day preparation, we had a man fly to San Francisco in an attempt to get a quickie visa for India. However, that day had been a Hindu religious holiday and the embassy was closed, so, no joy.

I had learned from spending several years abroad, that the career of an embassy worker consisted primarily of skill in taking holidays. Not only are the holidays of the host nation observed but, also, those of one's native land, both real and imagined. This practice diminishes the number of workdays in a year considerably. In any event, we now found ourselves halfway around the world with no visa—and our plane was to depart at 1:00 p.m. the day we arrived. When J-R was not on the spot, my dear friend, Robert Silver, looked after me. Robert had made the trip several times before and his knowledge and assistance were invaluable. So, off to the Indian embassy in Paris we went.

If the amount of constructive work being done at an embassy is any gauge, it is difficult to tell if an embassy is open or closed. You must go by whether or not the front door is unlocked and if there are people standing around. Standing around is what one does most at an embassy. Our papers were all in order, requiring only the signature of a minor official. Fortunately, the signature was obtained—at the eleventh hour—and we made it to our plane with no time to spare.

The plane made two stops en route to Bombay. The first was at Tel Aviv where the craft was boarded by the Israeli authorities searching for bombs, suspicious-looking Arab-type persons, and other mysterious and questionable items. Passports were checked and faces scrutinized by young Jews in mod dress (no Gestapo type uniforms for these boys). All this attention was due to the horror at the Olympic games that summer.

Muriel and I had seats which proved a constant source of entertainment for us during the flight. As credentials were being surveyed and storage areas checked with bomb-detecting devices, a young Israeli man came up and stood in the aisle by our seats. I thought he was waiting for a vacant restroom. I have this nervous habit of popping my chewing gum and I noticed that this young man had an interesting reaction; every time I would pop my gum he would nearly jump out of his skin. It wasn't until Muriel elbowed me in the ribs that I realized he was a member of the bomb squad and any suspicious noise sort of...alerted him.

Welcome to India

As we emerged from the plane at Bombay airport, I knew we were in India. The stifling heat and the acrid smell were all somehow familiar to me. I stepped reluctantly toward Indian soil. After an arduous customs inspection, a few of us decided to take refuge at the Sun and Sand Hotel by the Arabian Ocean.

On this trek around the globe, we were conveyed by every possible means of transportation, jet plane, ox cart, motorcycle, camelback, and shoe leather. But the most ubiquitous method of transport in any country is the taxicab. Cab drivers are indeed a breed apart and general contributors to the world's charm.

In India, taxis were secured by the airport attendant who told the driver where we wished to go. The driver spoke only Tolegook. Our taxi was occupied by myself and three ladies; I assumed the role of male protector and off we went in search of the seaside hotel.

After a few minutes in the cab, I had a sinking feeling in the pit of my stomach that was soon to be replaced by stark terror. We went for a ride on thoroughfares to roads of ever-decreasing size until we were at last creeping along a narrow dirt street teeming with poverty-stricken Indians and lined with grubby lean-tos which served as commercial stalls.

In the midst of this huddle of fragrant humanity, our cab's motor stalled and refused to start. Now, panic time. I knew that these people were so poor that they would slit my throat for my damp sweat socks. My emotions and imagination ran amuck. The fears, of course, were entirely unfounded because if it were possible to lay a word label on the Indian people it would include gentle, kind, peaceful, and loving. In about fifteen minutes we secured another cab (through the office of the Mystical Traveler) and were on our way.

Some people have had unpleasant times with the beggars in the large cities, but in our experience, all the Indian people were, as I said, gentle and kind, the beggars included—persistent, but kind.

The Beauty of Mysore State

Next, a short plane trip to Bangalore, a city of several million in the beautiful southern state of Mysore. Several days were spent in preparation for our visit to Sai Baba's ashram, Prasanthi Nilayam (the Abode of Peace), near the village of Putta Parthi. Mosquito netting, blankets, sheets, etc., were secured and we had brought inflatable mattresses from home, a foresight which was fortunate to be sure.

A ride through the streets of Bangalore would make anything at Disneyland seem tame. All conveyances, whether ox cart or truck, drove in the center of the road, only moving to the side as oncoming traffic approached. The cab drivers created a cacophony with their auto horns constantly beeping and tooting. Even driving unaccompanied in the remote countryside our driver would honk and beep relentlessly.

In exchanging our money, we decided to get the most rupees possible for our dollars. The going bank rate was 7.5 rupees to the dollar, but the notorious black market offered nine and possibly ten. So, an entire morning was spent in wheeling and dealing in shadowy back rooms down dark alleys with clever little Indians looking furtively over their shoulder and into the dark corners. All for good reason: I learned later that the penalty if they were caught, was twelve years imprisonment. They say that Indian jails would make a Mexican jail look like a Holiday Inn. At any rate, it was all very exciting and melodramatic.

In the first two days in India, I became sure my diet would consist exclusively of tea and toast because I found nothing else during that time that was in any way edible. I resigned myself to a very limited food regimen, though menus did expand for me later. On the third day, taxis were secured for the 100-mile excursion into the hinterlands of Mysore where we were assured Sai Baba awaited us.

The countryside was remarkably incongruous. The semitropical vegetation was lush and beautiful and yet the animals and people appeared lean, hungry, and almost emaciated. Thousands of years of primitive agriculture had depleted the land of its vital nutrients. Suddenly we entered a village where our cars were surrounded by scores of children staring sweetly at the strange-looking foreigners. This was our first experience with the Indian people outside the large cities and proved most delightful. Despite the depleted soil, somehow the streets and shops were full of vegetables and produce from the nearby farms. The citizens were proud of their harvest. The mayor conducted a short, enthusiastic tour of the main shopping area. Politicians are politicians the world over. You would have thought we were registered voters and the election was tomorrow.

A strange thing happened to me in this village. As we approached the village my eyes began to tear uncontrollably (as they did again when we left). During the short stay, I was walking up the street and noticed my dear friend, Dr. Herb Daly of Ventura, walking toward me. We met and embraced as though we were meeting after a long separation, when in fact we had seen each other that very morning. I had the feeling that long ago we two were small children, playing here in this same dirt street.

Sri Sathya Sai Baba

One hour later we made our way through a phalanx of beggars and entered the gates of the ashram, Prasanthi Nilayam. No begging is allowed inside the walls, so these unfortunates gathered just outside the gates. I was to pass through these gates several times during the next few days and the filth and squalor of the beggar's life are indelibly etched in my memory.

As we entered the grounds, an Indian in the customary attire (that resembled a bed sheet) beckoned us with excited hand gestures toward the huge open-air temple saying, "Bhajans, come quick, bhajans!" Anxious to get our first glimpse of Baba we moved forward quickly. It was then that I committed the first in a long sequence of transgressions against the local customs and traditions. As I ran, I stepped inside the sacred circle which runs around the temple--which could have been okay except I had my shoes on. My guide noticed and commanded me to please remove them, motioning to a gigantic pile of sandals where they should be left. I flashed back to my childhood family reunions and a game where everyone would take their shoes off, pile them in the center, and the first one to find his shoes and put them on, won the contest. My mind did a quick number with me in the midst of several thousand Hindus playing find the shoes. I decided that I would probably win because mine were the only fifty-dollar Flor- sheim boots in the pile.

The temple consisted of a roof over 100 feet high supported by brick pillars some twenty feet apart. Save for these pillars, it is open on three sides, the fourth being a large stage with the small ceremonial shrine, a large chair, and above it all a giant picture of Baba looking down benevolently on his chelas. The structure would hold around 10,000 people sitting cross-legged on its sandy floor.

I made my way to the front and lotused in a vacant spot. The bhajans were in full swing, rhythmic two-liners that gained in tempo led by a single voice that sang the chant once, then the group sang the same line following his pace from slow to very rapid and back again. I knew this was very heavy stuff because the fellow on my right was really freaked out, eyes closed, head bobbing, knees flop- ping and hands clapping...this must be samadhi (religious ecstasy) I surmised. My gaze darted around to catch the entire scene. Some were doing this guy's trip and some were just sitting silently. Others were talking among themselves. Kinda like back home... some were doin it and some weren't. Bob Silver and Herb Daly had taught me a couple of bhajans; a familiar one came along and I really got with it, running the guy on my right a very close second.

On coming down, I had another look around, and there he was...the Baba. What a sight. The afro hair cut had been short- ened, cut closer to the head, well-shaped...it looked good. His face was strong, forceful; his eyes told that he was in command and still that gentleness, that kindness, that lovingness came through. He was leading the chants with a unique and enchanting, rotating hand motion punctuated by an occasional finger flourish as though he were writing something in the air. (I learned later that was exactly what he was doing.) He wore an immaculate orange fitted gown, floor-length with three-quarter sleeves. He was short, not quite five feet, his shoulders and body were excellently proportioned and powerfully built. His movements were pure grace without being at all effeminate. His early training had been in the arts, especially music and dance. He moved deftly from the stage down among the people, cat-like, accepting letters, giving silent blessings with gestures of the hand, writing the name of God in Sanskrit on children's slates. His followers were indeed in awe and full of reverence.

It was contagious. I remembered twenty years before going with Australian friends to watch the Queen of England pass by. I assured myself it was just for the beer drinking and camaraderie, but as she and the prince consort passed, I cheered as loud as anyone. Greatness has a transcendent quality. The music stopped; Baba took the flowered chain from his neck, placing it on the elephant shrine. Baba garlands Gita. He disappeared off stage and it was over.

A Day at the Ashram

A day at the Nilayam began just before dawn. We were awakened by the chanters, who run the walls of the ashram in two groups. We laid on the porch where we had made our sleeping quarters and listened to the distinctive and beautiful choruses, one rapidly approaching, the other fading into the distance, counterpoint to counterpoint. A peaceful start to a peaceful day in the Abode.

We gathered for another appearance of Baba and he walked again through the crowd, talking here and there to the people gathered. Then at one point, Baba stopped talking, closed his fist, made a circular motion in the air about three feet from my head, and a japala (a crystal beaded necklace) appeared as if by magic. I could hear its jangling noise a split second before my eyes saw it dangling from his hand. He presented it to a lady from Los Angeles who wept with tears of joy.

I had heard of Baba's so-called manifestations and frankly had my reservations. Evidently, I was not the only one, for after Baba had manifested a second piece of jewelry, a university math professor asked him to take his wedding ring and put Baba's picture on it in place of its present surface. Baba explained that the professor's ring was conventionally made and, therefore, imperfect, and it was impossible to put a perfect image on an imperfect object. The professor smiled slyly as though he had won the first round. On a subsequent smaller group interview Baba took the mathematics professor's ring, closed his hand around it, blew twice on the closed fist, and when the fingers opened there in place of his ring was one made of silver with a beautiful moonstone. Baba looked deep into the professor's eyes and said, "how is that for mathematics?"

The private meetings between J-R, the staff, and Sal Baba must have been fascinating. I suppose it will be some time before they are related in detail, if at all. So, I would like to share some observations and conversations which came my way.

An American girl named Vajia had lived at the ashram for two years, as did several other western devotees. They had no specific job but worked at being of service in whatever way they could. They visited with our party helping us as they did other guests. Vajia was the local expert on Bababilia, in particular his materialized objects. Her eyes widened in amazement when she saw the ring and medallion Baba had manifested for J-R. She said that she had never seen any to compare with them in all the time she had been there. She was truly impressed. And rightly so, for the diamond ring, which J-R still wears, is very large and impressively brilliant; when the light is right, Baba's reflection can be seen in it.

I asked J-R if he might have it appraised. To which he replied something like, "It might not be in the best of taste to have such a generous gift appraised."

An interesting side-note is that all the rings Baba materializes are the exact size for the person for whom they are made. The only near exception we witnessed was one he pulled from the ethers for a lady with arthritic hands. Baba struggled to slip the ring past her swollen knuckle, explaining that it was the correct size for the space just beyond the calcific joint. He promptly sent it back from whence it came and immediately manufactured a more fitting item. I believe it was a small medal.

The large medallion Baba presented to J-R consisted of four metal letters fused together. L.O.V.E. It is my understanding that on giving this piece to J-R, he said, "You are the love of the western world."

Through several group interviews, many personal confrontations, witnessing at least a half dozen of the manifestations, the personal opinions varied from complete disbelief in Baba's supernatural qualities, to neutral...just observing, to acceptance, and devotion. So, the adage that each person has in his heart the answer to his quest took on added meaning. I would like to describe the other manifestations I witnessed, not in an attempt to prove or disprove, but merely to tell what I saw.

On beginning the second interview, Baba asked if we were hungry.

We said yes, and he made the now-familiar circling gesture, opened the hand, and there in his palm was a pile of what looked to be loosely packed brown sugar. As he distributed portions of the prasad (food blessed by the master) we found that it was a delicious confection. When it was gone, he inquired if we would like some more. We again replied in the affirmative and he did It again. During that same interview, he manifested a small statue of Krishna for his interpreter, who was always present during interviews, although Baba's English was quite sufficient. As the statue was being passed around, Mark Holmes drew my attention to the casting marks on the statue's base. When asked if these apparent miracles were to prove his divinity, Baba answered, "No, they are acts of love." Gifts from the guru to his friends, as it were.

On another occasion, I was sitting cross-legged in front of the residence when Baba came out to select his next interview. As he turned to re-enter the house, a mother pushed her blind son toward him. Baba spun on his heels, pointed his finger at the child and black ash shot out of his fingertips, gently striking the boy first in one eye and then the other. All this happened not five feet in front of me. I was again dumbfounded.

There are many things in the art of legerdemain that I do not know, and being involved in the physical sciences, I tend to look on this type of phenomenon with a rather critical eye, however, when it was all over, my attitude concerning Baba's materializations had gone from complete disbelief to a hesitant admission that it possibly could be a legitimate manifestation.

Finally, in a brief private interview with Muriel and me, Baba displayed his abilities of clairvoyance and impressed us with a personal description of our lives and characters, which ended with the manifestation of a small medal.

Actually, the first hour of our stay when J-R saw Baba eye to eye, he surprised us all by saying "OK, I'm ready to leave." Evidently, all the business which he had come thousands of miles to transact took place on another level and in the twinkling of an eye. Some of the group prevailed on his good graces and he consented to stay a few more days so that the rest of us could do our thing with Baba.

J-R had vouched for the safety and well-being of some of us who had requested that assistance and so on the third day when he told us that he was leaving, some of us wished to go with him. Those who remained became very ill. J-R had foreseen this happening, hence, the reason for our departure.

From Rags to Riches

The Ashoka in Bangalore was one of the most luxurious hotels in which we had stayed. After the austerity of the ashram, it was sheer delight. We spent two days resting and relaxing, talking about the recent adventure. Muriel and I had been introduced to Princess Emilia Karfota Sanganhi, a member of the royal family in Bangalore when she had been in the States, and through our mutual friends, the Dalys, we renewed this pleasant friendship. A late dinner one evening found J-R sitting next to the Maharaja's daughter. Both displayed a royal bearing, not a haughtiness but an elegant grace. I have watched John-Roger relate to princesses and peasants, taxi drivers and tycoons, drug addicts and dowagers. I never cease to be amazed at this ability to relate to everyone but never change himself.

My eight-year-old son, Charles, was playing paper airplanes with a small friend in our living room one day and between roaring airplane noises, I heard his friend ask, "Who's that in the picture?" Reply: "That's J-R." Question: "Is he your friend?" Reply: "He is everybody's friend."...more airplane noises.

The Bombay 500

The 747 which was to take us from Bombay to Paris cracked a windshield in a monsoon coming from Saigon, and consequently, our departure time was postponed 24 hours. This allowed us to spend a lovely afternoon on the Arabian Ocean playing soccer with Indian children, taking hilarious camel rides, watching a traveling beggar family of acrobats perform tricks and tumbling, plus precious spontaneous seminars with J-R.

That night the delay was discovered so we were loaded into taxis bound for a hotel on the other side of the city. The drivers decided to race to the hotel. We spent a death-defying thirty minutes racing pell-mell through the streets of Bombay. I was aware of the danger but was having too much fun to ask the drivers to stop. Muriel glanced out the window and asked what were those objects lying by the curb. She was surprised to find that the endless rows of forms lying by the curbside were people sleeping. If one of the taxis had gone out of control many of the sleepers would have made their transitions.

Suffer the Little Children to Come Unto Me

Upon boarding the 747, something drew me to the back of the plane, and there I encountered a strange sight accompanied by a stranger smell. Seat-belted into the last row of seats were nine Vietnamese war orphans, all suffering from diarrhea and vomiting. All were sick, several were near death, too feeble to cry or make a sound. We learned from the distressed lady who was taking them to foster parents in Paris that because of the delay and visa problems, they were forced to sleep for the last 24 hours on the airport's concrete floor. They had taken no nourishment, and already being in a fragile state were indeed in trouble. She was asked an obvious but necessary question, "Do you want assistance?"

What followed was twelve hours of the greatest Light service imaginable. The entire Light company with J-R leading the action nursed, changed diapers, bathed, dressed, loved, healed, cuddled, and generally ministered to those infants for the rest of the trip. The result was an unforgettable miracle. The metamorphosis that took place at 40,000 feet between Bombay and Paris saw these babies snatched from the jaws of death and despair and delivered to new parents in bright and shining style.

I thought as I witnessed the parents accepting their new charges that if they could have seen these babies twelve hours before, they would not have believed the change. My eyes filled with tears as I saw J-R carry the baby who had been the sickest off the plane. He stopped for a moment, touching the little fellow under the chin, and said, "Bertrand, you are going to be OK now." Poor Bertrand, who had been expressionless and glassy-eyed through the entire trip, managed a feeble smile.

The Light was so bright. I will never forget it.

Onward and Upward, Etc.

Muriel and I were off to do Paris, London, and Edinburgh. The Light staff and J-R were bound for Miami and everyone else to New York and Los Angeles. The excitement and thrills of a lifetime had been packed into a few weeks, traversing the physical realm with the Mystical Traveler. What new joys and experiences await us with his guidance on the other levels, always lifting higher, traveling free, traveling Light?

EAST COAST (PENNSYLVANIA, NEW YORK, FLORIDA)

VICTORIA MONTGOMERY
Deep Tears Started Coming

The first time I heard J R's voice and saw his photograph was in 1971. I had been invited to a friend's karate studio to hear a cassette tape that he had brought back from California. I was living in Pennsylvania at the time. I had traveled to India and was wearing Indian clothes and was very involved in learning how to meditate. I was hoping for a meditative experience.

I remember lying on the floor, and there was a photograph of John-Roger. He looked rather conservative—he wasn't an Indian guru with a turban. The tape started and I heard his voice. It was so familiar, and I remember my eyes were closed and these deep tears started coming out of my eyes. I just knew in the sound of his voice that I had connected in some way to an energy, to a loving, that was going to show me how to get back home.

Even now, so many years later, I'm feeling my heart open just thinking of that moment. I was in college at the time and going through what we all go through in college—trying to balance studying and partying. Once a week I would go to a taped seminar and the hectic part of the week would come into balance. A group of us started going regularly to these seminars, and then we invited J-R to come to Pennsylvania. We had gotten a house together in the country, and we were all so excited.

The first time I saw him physically, I was so happy to meet somebody like that. At that time, there was still an Indian influence with a lot of the people who found him. So, we would decorate the house. We would sing songs like "Sri John-Roger Light and Sound," and we put flowers around the stage. He was so natural and relaxed and so right on with some of the things he told us. We were always laughing. I remember a lot of wonderful moments when he would come to visit. He told us that our beat-up old cars were never going to make it across the country! So it took a while to get out to California for the first Conference, but we did. I remember wanting to be close, so I moved out to California and became a part of Prana, the MSIA ashram.

JOHN JURKOFSKY
I Felt a Truth in It

I heard J-R for the first time in 1972 at a meeting of people listening to a tape-recorded lecture by him. A friend had seen a notice on a bulletin board at the University of Pennsylvania for a seminar called Soul Transcendence. It sounded intriguing so I decided to go. When we got there, there were a couple of MSIA "old-timers" who played a J-R cassette tape. I was convicted by my Soul, my Spirit, of the truth of what I was hearing. So, I started going to different seminars on different nights.

I felt a truth in it. When I heard J-R's words—and heard his voice and saw his demeanor—he didn't seem to have any urgency. He just delivered the information. I needed something that would transcend my previous teachings. Something that offered a different way of doing it than having an intermediary work for me, having a priest at the altar do it. He presented this idea that it's already present and I just have to take the time to go inside and work with it. I have to bring my awareness into a place where I can avail myself of the energies of the inner world. It was all on me. I could spend four hours when I had time or I could spend only a half-hour if I didn't have time.

When J-R came to Pennsylvania to visit, he would sit on a winding staircase. We all sat way out into the next room and he would just talk to us. My experience of J-R was that he was extraordinarily ordinary—and yet he was ordinary with such profundity. It seemed like absolute truth was often expressed in the way he brought the energy forward in his communications.

SHEILA STECKEL
I Can Still Feel the Joy

Early in my association with MSIA, I went to Joan Beisel's loft on Canal Street in New York City. J-R was there talking to several people who were asking him questions, mostly about how he gets his information. He shared generously.

This was the first time I saw J-R in such an up-close and personal way. When I saw him, I wanted desperately to thank him for the Discourses I was receiving—they were so meaningful to me. I struggled to go over to him, but my shyness paralyzed me and I couldn't move. However, I knew from the conversation that he was about to leave.

What to do? I had to thank him, and I didn't want to lose this opportunity. Finally, when I got up enough courage to walk the few steps over and thank him, he whispered in my ear, "I am always with you." I couldn't possibly describe how I felt when he said that. I only know that somehow, I left the loft, got to the train station, and flew home on the subway in complete bliss. I can still feel the joy that it brought me.

CRAIG REID
He Knew What Was in My Mind
and My Heart

I was raised in the Presbyterian Church, but I had so many questions that were not answered by the church that I set out on my own spiritual quest. As J-R would say, I became a "spiritual tramp." I went to the spiritualist church, to mediums and psychics, to meetings of the A.R.E (Edgar Cayce's group), the Spiritual Frontiers Fellowship, and the Yogashakti Yoga Ashram. I looked into the teachings of Baba Sawan Singh and Kirpal Singh, Guru Maharaj Ji, Baba Ram Dass, Eckankar, and many others.

I met Dolores Bell (now Angela Bell)—who became one of my dearest lifelong friends—at a Mark-Age meditation meeting in Miami in 1969. I eventually left the Mark-Age group after discovering that the two individuals that headed the group were doing some pretty negative stuff. Angela and I then began attending meetings of a small group of Hispanic women who were doing healing meditations. They were beautiful, loving souls and we had many wonderful sessions with them.

In 1975, Angela introduced me to MSIA and John-Roger through Rama Fox. I was a single father with two kids in diapers at that time, having just emerged from a traumatic marriage. That year, Angela and I went to my first live John-Roger seminar at the Festival of the Light Centers. John-Roger was a keynote speaker for the event. I was very aware of the powerfully loving vibes in the room. J-R seemed to be a down-to-earth guy with a twinkle in his eye who spoke very plainly, yet profoundly, and pulled no punches, even telling a few jokes.

In the weeks and months that followed, Angela took me to some taped seminars in North Miami at the home of Dick and Rose Haussling. The loving at those seminars was palpable, and I felt like I belonged there—that I had "come home." Something I really liked about the seminars was J-R's humor. He wasn't taking himself or us too seriously. There were lots of jokes, and there was a buoyancy and joyfulness about what he was doing that lifted me and opened my heart.

Of course, given my experience with some of the other spiritual teachers I had encountered, I was a bit cautious and maybe even suspicious of J-R at first. But I kept coming back to those wonderful seminars at Dick and Rose's, where I continued to feel like I had come home, that I was among people who truly seemed to care about me and each other.

It wasn't long before I followed Angela's suggestion to sign up for Discourses and write a letter of intent to study for initiation with John-Roger. As soon as I started reading the monthly Discourses, I felt that things were being accelerated in my life. Things were moving fast, and I felt this invisible hand holding me up and urging me along, ever so gently putting me back on the path each time I started to veer away from it, and constantly emanating a wonderful warmth and loving. Each month's Discourse seemed to deal with something I was going through right at that moment or had just gone through or would be going through shortly. I became aware of J-R's spirit working with me on the inner realms. I felt safe and protected despite the fact that some of the lessons that were coming to me—now fast and furious—were hard and perplexing. But the inner support, love, and guidance I was receiving was becoming more and more evident and kept me from getting stuck in anything too long.

Some years later, I remarried, having met a wonderful woman, Christine, who joined me in MSIA. We had a child together, and not long after Noah's birth, J-R gave him a baby blessing. J-R told us that Noah had come down through the school of the Holy of Holies and had lived at the time when there were giants on the Earth—literally giants—and that he had actually been a giant.

That was a mind-blowing week, which took place in April of 1978. Our son had his baby blessing, I received my Causal initiation from J-R himself, I was ordained by Michael Sun as a minister in MSIA*, and I took my first Insight I seminar. I was floating on air for weeks after that and felt like I was the most blessed person on the planet.

I later had the opportunity to share with J-R at an MSIA retreat we attended. I had been considering having a vasectomy and I wanted to know if that would be a clear action, spiritually. When I nervously started to introduce my question, "I've been considering having a vasectomy...," before I could get the rest of it out, he responded, "That action would be clear for you." Startled that he had answered my question before I had a chance to complete asking it, I suddenly realized that he knew what was in my mind and my heart, practically before I did. Wow! That strengthened my connection with J-R even more.

Sometime after taking Insight I, Christine and I signed up for what they were calling a Ministerial Training. At one point, they had us set our chairs up in rows and sit down in them. Then we were asked to take off our shoes and socks and close our eyes. At that point, the assistants, some of them being J-R's staff members, each came to one row with a bowl of water. The assistant would go down the line and, with one bowl of water for each of us, proceed to wash our feet. When Phillip Anthony came to me and began washing my feet, I was transported into a glorious realm of Spirit. I was in a state of bliss and felt such love and light surrounding me as never before. I felt as though Lord Jesus himself was washing my feet. Even now when I recount that experience, I can feel an incredible feeling of love and Light flowing through me.

In 1983, we moved up to Charlottesville, Virginia, where we have remained ever since—longer than I've lived in any town in my whole life. In 1988, thanks to Angela Bell's encouragement and assistance, we were able to come out to L.A. for the J-R tribute dinner and to see him pass the remaining keys of the Traveler Consciousness over to John Morton. It was a fabulous event, and we got to meet many of our spiritual brothers and sisters from all over the world and renew some old and dear acquaintances. This was a magical event, which included a great video tribute to J-R—a precursor to the movie about J-R's life that came out in 2014.

That would be the last time I would see J-R in the physical. But I was not worried—I knew that he would be leaving the body someday and I also felt a very strong connection with him on the inner where the lion's share of the work was being done. As time went by, my connection with John Morton would grow deeper as well.

Before I came into the Movement, I did not have dreams about J-R, letting me know he was working with me. I didn't have any of those mystical experiences that many people who come into MSIA have. The first time I saw J-R physically he was not familiar to me at all. It took me time to accept him and to come to the place where I knew that I wanted to work with him. I was pretty much flying blind—feeling my way along. What I did experience that really resonated with me was the strong feeling of loving that emanated from him and those who followed him. As I opened myself more and more to Spirit and to J-R, I could see the love in his eyes and in his smile, I could hear it in his voice and the words he spoke, and I began to feel it growing inside of me. That was what drew me to him and brought me to the place where I absolutely knew I wanted to work with him.

When J-R left his physical body in October of 2014, I felt such a rush of love for him and a great sadness to know he would no longer be around physically. But I also had a real sense of relief that he didn't have to deal with pain and the physical discomforts that can come as we age. No more pain, no more suffering, no more lugging around the dense physical body. I think that in Spirit there must be a great relief when the body drops and you get to fly away free. And ever since J-R's passing I have felt him much more strongly within my heart—I am just flooded with his love and Light, to the point where I sometimes think I might float up into the air.

ANGELA BELL
The Gift of Life for the Second Time

In 1973–74 while living in Florida, I was diagnosed with the last stages of uterine cancer with a 25 percent chance of survival. I was a single mother with two children under ten years of age. My quest at that time was to find a teacher who could take me home to God. I was preparing myself to die.

At the time, I had access to the community room of an association I belonged to. Dick Haussling, who was an MSIA seminar leader, asked me if he could use the community room for one of his seminars, and I agreed to let him use it. Soon after, he sent me a ticket to attend a live event with John-Roger. My first meeting with J-R, in his white suit and full beard, was a loving meeting. I commented to him that I received his loving heart, and he said, "You got it."

Shortly after that, Dick invited me to his home seminar. He said, "I know you are quite ill, but our meetings are very loving and

I think you might benefit." When I entered his home, I saw a large framed picture of J R on the entrance wall, and as I looked at it, it turned into a fountain of Light. That certainly caught my attention!

When the seminar started, I lay down on the floor and went out somewhere. During the seminar, J-R told a joke and I came to, sat up, and laughed. At that moment I knew he could be my wayshower home to God—I could ride on his humor. Dick told me about Discourses—I said, "Sign me up." He told me about aura balances*—I said, "Sign me up." He told me about Light Studies—I said, "Sign me up." The next time J-R was in town, I was ready to go.

During my Light Study with J-R, I felt like I suddenly came out of a deep sleep. He told me that I had a disease that needed to be addressed. I then had an aura balance, and during the aura balance, my disease left and went into remission. I never had chemo, radiation, or surgery. I was given the gift of life for the second time—once when I was born, and once again when I woke up and committed to myself and my journey home to God. This Traveler was my guy!

I have been studying in MSIA ever since that time in 1973 when I was very ill with uterine cancer. As of this writing, I am eighty-five and have had a blessed life. At one point, I needed J-R on the outer and needed to be near him physically. However, as I moved more into the Traveler's teachings, I found him on the inner and he has always been with me as my beloved inner master.

* Aura Balance is a service offered by MSIA for clearing the aura that surrounds the physical body.

EXPANDING INWARDLY AND OUTWARDLY (1974-1978)

Stories in this chapter reference some of the organizations and services that grew around MSIA as it began to experience exponential growth. During this period, MSIA purchased Prana (an ashram and home of the MSIA offices—now called Peace Awareness Labyrinth and Gardens) and was given property near Lake Arrowhead in the San Bernardino Mountains where they created a retreat center. John-Roger also founded a number of organizations, including Baraka (a holistic healthcare center), Prana Theological Seminary—now Peace Theological Seminary and College of Philosophy—and Insight Seminars (educational organizations). The organization was also providing spiritual services such as aura balances and initiations. In this section are also stories of MSIA reaching new cities in the U.S. and Australia, and some recollections of inspiring and life-changing moments.

PRANA

In 1974, MSIA purchased the old Guasti mansion—also once owned by the famous movie director Busby Berkeley—near mid-city Los Angeles that had been modified to become a retirement home for physicians. It was subsequently renovated for use as MSIA's administrative offices and residences for those studying in MSIA. It was named Prana, which means "breath of life" in Sanskrit, and it was decided that the acronym PRANA would stand for "Purple Rose Ashram of the New Age.

ASHTAR-ATHENA
A Dream and a Blessing

In 1974 when my husband and I were living in Santa Barbara, John-Roger called us one day and said, "I want you to come down and check out this property we're considering buying—tell me what you think about it." It was the old Busby Berkeley estate in Los Angeles. As we drove up to it, I said, "Oh my heavens, John-Roger, I had a dream of this place!" And he said, "Tell me the dream, tell me everything about the dream."

Well, I had this dream where I saw Sai Baba standing on a balcony with his hand upraised, which means, "Have no fear, I am here." It's a blessing mudra and also a warding off of anything that you could be concerned about. It's called the abhaya mudra, which means the "fear-dispelling gesture." He was standing like that on the balcony right over the entrance. J-R said, "That's our sign. We will purchase this property."

God wanted us in this area of Los Angeles. Why? Because we all needed to earn a living and had jobs or professions that required being in an area where there was work. What are we going to do living up in the forest somewhere? So, 120 of us ended up living at the ashram, which was called Prana. When we moved in, the area was like a war zone. Even though there were lots of churches, there were also the hoods, the gangs—you know, fighting. We began to have open-house garden parties on the lawn as fundraisers where anyone could come and eat. Years later we planted a peace pole with the words, "May peace prevail on earth" in the languages of the people who were living in the area.

YVONNE MOCHEL
We Were on a Journey Together

I was one of the first to move into Prana. My husband and I had just separated, and I was a generation older than just about everyone there. I'd had my own home, and here I was with these "kids," some of whom had never picked up their clothes or made their own bed. To deal with all of this I would say to myself, "I love this—I'm just holding for this whole process." J-R acknowledged it, like "Yes, you are doing that."

I felt like I was basically holding because there was such a difference in age. What was going on around me in so many ways was like these kids playing. Everybody was growing at their own rate. For example, we'd have a wonderful chocolate cake with frosting on top that somebody made. Then somebody else would run their finger all the way through the cake, lick their finger, and keep on walking. It was like that kind of "basic self" world going on.* When I saw this, I was like, "Gasp!" I couldn't quite figure out how that was okay...

But slowly, things began to change. At some point, we were cleaning our rooms with some kind of responsibility. Nothing was forced. Nothing was like, "You gotta follow the rules." It wasn't about the rules. It was about the beingness and the consciousness as a group. I loved being there, I loved being part of all of that. In my ordination blessing** it says, "Your ministry is not necessarily a verbal ministry. It's one of holding in the peace of God's consciousness in the silence." For me that meant if you see something that needs to be done, you just go do that. It's pretty effortless and natural. When I got a "Minister of the Year" award, it was obviously a shock to me. As I was walking up, J-R said, "You didn't think they saw all the things you were doing, did you?" And it was like, "No, I didn't."

That was a time when there were a lot of opportunities to be of service in a natural way because there was a level of growing that people were catching up with. How do we handle this world on the physical? J-R was building a foundation for us in such a beautiful way on every level. On Prana's 25th anniversary, the physical grounds and space, and the energy were how I had dreamed they would be. J-R knew that—he knew what was available. For him, it was not that it had to be right now. It was about "It is what it is, and we're just lifting all the time." I was so grateful that I had the reference of being there at the beginning and seeing it just keep lift, lift, lift.

We would do fundraisers to support the work we were doing at Prana, and these fundraisers involved being outdoors. One time it was going to rain, so we got in a circle on the front porch of Prana and called in the Light, asking for good weather for this event. When we got through, we looked up and there's this blue circle right above us with the gray clouds all around it. It was so perfect. It was one of those moments of knowing that we were on a journey together, and there was something about the group that was so important.

* *According to MSIA, the basic self is that part of our consciousness that is like a four or five-year-old child that tries to assert its desires and wishes upon the conscious self.*

** *Students in MSIA can be ordained as ministers of Light, consciously dedicating themselves to being of service, and during the ordination ceremony they receive a "blessing."*

RACHAEL JAYNE
Move Into Prana

One of the significant moments I had with J-R in a dream was after I had heard that there was going to be an ashram, the Purple Rose Ashram of the New Age. And I thought there was no way I would ever move into a community with a bunch of people. I was dead set against it.

So, I had a dream. J-R looked right into my eyes. He said, "You want Christ Consciousness? Move into Prana."

At that point, there was no more discussion or inner debate. I moved into PRANA! It wasn't like every night I would get those kinds of directive dreams, but when I needed that kind of direction, J-R was always there.

Fast forward to 1974 or 1975 when J-R would come to Prana and do amazing sharings with all of us; we'd have individual sharing.

At one particular sharing, I remember I started crying. I said to him, "I feel like I miss you." Because he had definitely pulled back. And he said, "Well, you agreed to it in another consciousness. Why do you think I pulled back?"

I answered, "To train me?" He said, "Exactly right." Basically, it was more about finding him inside of me and not depending on him outside of me. I am so, so grateful that I got that training because one of the things I have to say is my inner connection to the Traveler is the most precious thing in my life, hands down, the thing I trust the most.

PENELOPE BRIGHT
Prana Was Our Home

Prana was the home for a small group of us, right from the opening in August 1974. When we first moved in, the house had pretty much gone to seed after its heyday as the Busby Berkeley mansion (Busby Berkeley was the Hollywood film director whose films featured lots of female dancers shot from above and making kaleidoscope-like patterns with their arms and legs). It had been sold and turned into a retirement home for physicians. By the time MSIA bought it, it was in need of a serious cleaning, oceans of paint, and lots of tender loving care. The last we had in abundance.

Most of us were in our mid-to-late twenties, with the energy of youth, and had dedicated ourselves to living a life of Service. Almost all of us held full-time jobs to pay for our room and board; a few held jobs with the organization, as bookkeepers or secretaries; some of us went to school, came home, and worked. Lord, did we work!

Unlike today, when there is a household staff to keep things up, back then we all had weekly household chores like washing floors, vacuuming, dusting, etc., all the things needed to generally keep the house clean and maintained. Each of us also had two days of kitchen duty which included ordering food, cooking dinner, washing dishes, or baking bread. There were those who, when it was their turn to cook, would instead bring home twenty or so large pizzas. There were others who, when it was their cooking day, made the same dishes, again and again. We were definitely not listed in the Michelin Guide. Food complaints abounded.

We had Dharma Day every Saturday, which is when we tackled the bigger jobs or special projects, like putting in a huge organic garden, landscape maintenance, window washing, deep cleaning, painting, and replacing a century of old wiring and plumbing. There were certain individuals who came with excellent skills, much like building contractors. They would take the lead on projects in their area of expertise. Everyone worked at something, like cleaning out one of the basement "grottos," re-roofing the house, or installing industrial shelving in the lower half of the Carriage House, a separate building toward the back of the property.

Sometimes J-R would show up on a Dharma Day just to see how things were going. He would quietly wander through the public rooms, into the kitchen, and out through the dining room to the gardens. He would often say a few words to someone about a personal problem or about the work in which they were engaged. And sometimes it would change that person's perspective—or their entire life.

We had a large laundry room in the basement and, being the hippies that we were, we installed a Free Box. The idea was that if someone was finished with a garment, they would place it in the Free Box for others to potentially use. (Waste Not, Want Not, as the saying goes.) Shopping the Free Box was an adventure. But the Box (eventually a small alcove) got out of hand many times, over-flowing with ratty undergarments and soiled bedding. One of the house jobs was to cull it every couple of weeks; some things were immediately trashed; whatever could be salvaged by laundering was then folded and placed on the rack or the shelves; the rest went to charity shops. All in the flow.

J-R had already started to travel a fair amount, but when J-R was in town, Prana hosted two seminars a week. So, we set up teams to manage folding chairs, help people park (and after the Seminars, some of the guys would walk people to their cars), and clean up and put everything away again. After some Seminars, we rolled up the rugs in the foyer and danced like the joyful hippies we were. Some of us were musicians and formed singing groups and bands. After the first few weeks living there, late one night, J-R quietly went about the house, dropping off cans of Lysol cleaner by each of the rooms, encouraging us to "keep it clean."

Since we had a goal of paying Prana off in five years instead of thirty, which is the usual course of a mortgage (and we owed a HUGE sum in the minds of some residents), we did many things to achieve our objective. Most bedrooms housed two or sometimes three people to maximize the amount of income that could be put toward the mortgage. We held fund-raisers. And we held a huge garage sale with everything we had brought to Prana that we no longer needed. J-R's staff guys cleaned out J-R's house, and other non-residents brought their items to be sold. It was great! We also started charging money for huge dinners and afternoon teas. And, yes, we did pay the mortgage off in five years. That's J-R for you. It was great fun and hard work, and we loved it.

J-R called Prana "The Home of the Traveler," and in the early days, he came to visit often. One evening, someone told one of the residents her car had been broken into. She went out and checked. Sure enough, a crowbar had been taken to the trunk and it was all bent up. She called the police and was told it would be an hour or two. Her room was at the far end of the lower West Wing. It was getting late, and there was no one around to let anyone in, so she needed to wait where she could hear the doorbell. When she got to the foyer, she noticed there was some kind of meeting in the small formal dining room (called the Small Seminar Room), and she checked it out. J-R was leading a Light Circle, so she joined in. There were about fifteen people, and each of them would share whatever was present and then get feedback from the group. When it was her turn, she shared about waiting for the police. She recalls J-R saying that she had made good use of her time, that she did what had to be done, and then, rather than doing nothing or sitting in her upset, she did the next thing in front of her to do, which was join the Circle. These were the kinds of learnings that came from being at Prana.

For a few people, kitchen duty was baking bread, and they were experts. They would get home from work and head to the back of the kitchen to start the wheat grinder working. (The theory was that homemade bread was healthier for us.) As soon as the cooks served dinner and as the dishwashers were cleaning up, the baker would start making the dough in the commercial mixer.

They made multiple loaves each week. By the time of the second rise, it would be getting late. Those loaves would come out of the oven sometime after 11:00 pm. The house would be quiet, lights out, not a soul around…but one by one, people would start showing up, drawn by the smell of fresh-baked bread. They would stand around the kitchen (with a pound or so of butter) eating and laughing. Sometimes the baker would take some of the dough, roll it out flat on the huge stainless-steel tables, fill them with honey, raisins, cinnamon, and nuts, roll them up, and cut them into rolls for breakfast. Those rolls rarely made it past dawn.

While we had plenty of fun, that isn't to say all was Love and Light. We had our share of disagreements and, along with announcements and such, sometimes they got addressed in our weekly Thursday night House Meetings. At one meeting, various residents participated in a "skit" performed in several languages about how to do better at scrubbing the dishes, pots, and pans after dinner. Another meeting included a review of recent movies, acted out with imaginary Samurai swords and shouting in *faux* Japanese.

One of our early participants was a woman who had lived at Synanon, a large residential building right on the sand at Santa Monica Beach, where ex-drug users could live, work and come together in "clearing sessions," a form of (some would say, rather brutal) group counseling. Some of those techniques and processes from that group became a part of our "getting along" with each other in House Meetings, in the form of "Light Circles." And the woman who shared those techniques became a true teacher to many of us. J-R would attend House Meetings occasionally, but generally, he gave us a lot of freedom to sort ourselves out. And mostly, we did.

During Saturday Dharma Day, one of the tasks was to take care of the kids, usually taking them out for the day. The families with children all lived in the lower west wing and, in the beginning, we had anywhere from five to eight kids ranging in age from about fourteen months to eleven years. The kids loved going on these weekly day trips and often movies were involved. Much to the disappointment of the boys in the group, including the male group leader, they had strict instructions that there were to be no horror movies. Nonetheless, on one such Saturday, the group leader took them to a horror flick, and one of the kids ended up having terrible nightmares. Her mother railed and complained bitterly at the next House Meeting, but no one, not even the kids, was willing to disclose who chose the horror film. The mom only found out twenty years later when someone admitted they had been the culprit but had been unwilling to admit it and face her fury.

Living in close quarters as we did, there were many opportunities for (ahem) Love to blossom between the (young and healthy) residents. But the Prana Rules were very clear: no alcohol, no drugs, no smoking, no warm-blooded pets, and above all, no sex at Prana between unmarried persons, gay or straight. This led to any number of quietly resourceful practices (which shall be left to the imagination), and we often didn't even find out that two people had been dating outside of Prana until they announced they were getting married.

Weddings at Prana were and are super-special. The house itself was built in 1911-1912 by an Italian winemaker named Secondo Guasti of Guasti Vineyards. The marble-floored foyer is large and open, with tall windows facing the front and the rear of the property. It is covered in dark wood paneling carved with flowers and vines. There are ceiling murals and an extravagant, carpeted, curved staircase that connects the upstairs rooms (now offices) with the ground floor. Many brides have made their way down those stairs to a room full of guests and their groom awaiting them.

Christmas at Prana was always a magical event. Our tree each year was huge—over ten feet tall and loaded with as many ornaments as we could find. It would be set up in the foyer or in the curve of the winding staircase. Each person would draw the name of another resident and set about finding the best present for that person, whether or not they knew them well. There was a limit to the cost of the gift so that no one would feel compelled to spend more than they could afford. Of course, some people would also buy or make gifts for their friends and family as well, and most of us doted on the kids, making for an enormous pile of wrapped goodies under the tree.

Christmas morning was a huge frenzy, led chiefly by the older kids. Everyone was encouraged to show up early in their pajamas, bathrobe, and slippers. Hot chocolate and sugary baked goods were *de rigueur*, while the children enthusiastically ripped off wrapping paper and played with their toys, squealing and shouting with joy.

Living in close quarters at Prana, especially in the early days, brought opportunities to learn about communicable diseases and the hygiene practices that would halt them. As fortune would have it, there were a few medical personnel who lived there at the time and educated us regarding cure and containment. With more than a hundred people soon living there, we often had outbreaks of common colds and flu, as well as rashes of indeterminate origin (eventually traced to a harsh detergent in the laundry), head lice, and even pinworms. Nevertheless, we sailed on.

More than anything, Prana was a place where we learned to live from our hearts and souls, to get along with others who were different from ourselves, and to have the good of the group foremost in our actions and decisions. We learned to pay closer attention to what we were doing, where we were looking, and what we were thinking and saying. No one who lived there for any length of time went away unchanged. At times, it was admittedly challenging. At others, it was bliss–all the loving, joy, and creativity came bubbling up out of the most unexpected places.

Prana (which means life-force in Sanskrit) was our home for however long we stayed there. We became a spiritual family, connected in heart and soul, if not genetically. Many still remain family and friends to this day. It wasn't so much what we did there, although that was a large part of it; it was more how we learned and grew inwardly from all the loving and the caring and joy while we did what was needed. And, in the midst of it all was J-R, so often at the home of the Traveler.

GLENN BARNETT
Fellowship and Endless Rounds of Work

It seemed that most of us at Prana were strangers, gathered from across the country into a fellowship of we knew not what. Many of us were ex-hippies and druggies, and Prana was a place and existed at a time to let that all go. While we were getting to know each other—and the expected rounds of he'n and she'n—we settled into an endless round of work, which we did willingly.

Consider that we each had our own personal chores to do—cooking, cleaning, food management—and volunteering for even more work. Then every Saturday was group work, like cleaning, painting, or construction. We put up shelving in the products area, and we bored through solid cement to create a darkroom for Betty Bennett, the official MSIA photographer. All of her pictures were processed there. The Movement Newspaper was produced and mailed from Prana. We collated, stapled, and mailed out booklets and other materials. For some, Saturday work included working at the church property that was J-R's home in Mandeville Canyon—digging trails, planting trees, landscaping, and a thousand other chores.

When J-R started doing retreats at Lake Arrowhead, we were the group that installed showers, laid carpet, and dug trenches for toilet facilities. We also formed the bulk of the participants at the early retreats. When J-R and Russell Bishop introduced the idea of Insight, it was done at a Prana house meeting. I remember J-R saying that if we did not participate in Insight, then he did not know why we were living there. So, we became the pioneers of Insight. Later, Prana Theological Seminary (PTS) was born at Prana and administered through Prana.

BOB STRIMPEL
A Special Energy

I remember all the work parties at Prana. On Saturdays, we would work all day doing things like tearing down tree stumps and taking out concrete walls. I remember painting the hallways in the east wing. Everybody worked really hard, but the energy was there. It wasn't like it was drudgery because we had a lot of fun working together. J-R would show up and see how we were doing.

There were personalities, friction, and stuff that had to be worked out. I remember an incident with Kathy Jeffares, who was just a powerhouse of energy. We were building the trails up at J-R's house in Mandeville Canyon, and she started rolling these rocks down the hill. I saw people down there at the bottom, and I started freaking out—she's going to kill somebody! So, we "got into it," and Kathy didn't hold anything back. Later, at a Prana house meeting, the incident was mentioned, and J-R said, "Well, just give each other a hug." So, we did. The tension between us released, and that was it. That's the way it was—he just had this ability to cut to the chase.

I remember J-R saying that the house worshipped us. And I thought, "That's really true. It's a special energy. You're being blessed, because the Light focus at Prana is something else." It still is.

MARIE GERHART
What Is True Love?

While living at Prana, I—like most people of a youthful age—was always looking for a life partner. I went through various ones, and after a while, I thought, "Isn't there somebody that I'd like to stay with longer?"

J-R took me aside one seminar night. We went into a small conference room and he said, "Look, you've been asking for a relationship, but that's all you get is a relationship. You can have a relationship with a cactus but you just get stuck. What you need to ask for is true love, and then you have to decide what true love looks like—what is true love on all the levels. And then you begin to live it, live it in your life on all those levels. People who recognize it the same way you do will be attracted to you. So then, you just choose." That was very revealing and a really good experience for me.

Another time, he talked with me about what love looks like. He said, "When you see your special person, what do you think? Do you think, 'I wonder if they're comfortable? Do they need a pillow? Are they hungry? Maybe I could make a sandwich'—little things like that to be concerned about, and caring." After some years of working with his advice, I did meet my husband, and we've had a long and happy marriage.

LOUISE WYATT
Love, or Something to Shake Us Awake

Shortly after my daddy passed away, I was feeling a lot of emotional pain as well as guilt. I was attending a seminar at Prana, and J-R was walking around and talking to people, as he did back then, before the seminar started. I closed my eyes and "stuck" a smile on my face so he wouldn't know how I was really feeling. We all know how well that works! Suddenly I felt a presence standing in front of me. I opened my eyes and saw J-R looking at me sternly, saying that the smile I had plastered on my face was not fooling him and that I needed to snap out of it. It really shocked me. Then he abruptly turned around and walked away.

I was starting to feel hurt and angry when suddenly I realized that the pain, the hurt, and the guilt I had been feeling were gone. He had taken away my pain. I realized at that moment how deeply J-R loves me, and loves all of us, and how he gives us exactly what we need at that specific time—be it love, or something to shake us awake.

JACKIE PETERSON
Grace Had Been Extended

My husband and I were newlyweds and money was tight, so we had to budget. We didn't want to spend more than we had, so we would cash our paychecks and put a budgeted amount in envelopes for the month. One Friday night, we had a weekend of fun planned, so we cashed our paychecks and put all the money in a drawer, planning to put it in the envelopes on Sunday night. We had a great weekend.

On Sunday, we opened the drawer to divvy up the money into our envelopes, and we found nothing. The drawer was empty—the money was gone. How could this be? This was Prana. It was an ashram. Everyone living there was family. We rushed around and told everyone. We thought of suspects. We blamed the teenagers living next door, but we had no proof. We were broke, and we were heartbroken at the violation of our living space, our home.

At a seminar a few months later, Jim and I were sitting in the front row to the right of the stage. J-R was doing the seminar, and right in the middle of it he turns to us and says, "That money stolen was karma balanced. And you got off cheap." Turning back to the group he went on with the seminar. I sat there stunned, rooted to my chair. The Light went through me, and I knew that grace had been extended.

What no one knew was that I had gone on a stealing spree when I was a teenager. I had met a girl who loved to steal stuff from stores, and she taught me how to do it. For about three months I became a thief. I stole things I wanted, and I even stole things I didn't want. I finally stopped when I stopped hanging out with this girl. I stopped for two reasons: One was that the fear of getting caught became more than the desire for the things. The other was that it was simply wrong to steal and it didn't match up inside of me, to my own personal self-image. It wasn't who I wanted to be inside. I had just turned seventeen, and my inner guidance was surfacing more and more in my life and directing me. I didn't like me as a thief.

Years went by—and I mean years—when a letter came in the mail. The letter writer reminded me about the lost cash, and then went on to say that they had stolen it. So, it wasn't the teenagers we were so sure had done it. This person had been staying at Prana, had been using drugs, and had stolen the money to pay for drugs. The person was now in Alcoholics Anonymous and wanted to make amends. A schedule of payments was set up, and every payment was made, on time and in full. The amends were complete.

ALEXANDRA ROBERTS
Born Again

In 1977 I was a young girl modeling in New York, engaged to be married, very into the world, and deeply miserable inside—not on a spiritual path at all. Knowing there was so much more but not knowing where the "more" was, I just left everything, packed up, and moved to Los Angeles—knowing hardly anyone there. Two weeks after my move to L.A., I was invited to a large party at a home owned by a woman who ran *The Hollywood Reporter* magazine.

At the party, I gravitated to a beautiful man named Carl Parsons, a publicist at the time who was in MSIA. He was wearing a small, deep blue button on his jacket lapel with a swirling symbol that read *MSIA*. I asked him about his button and symbol, and he told me about this man, J-R. I did not want to leave Carl's side. I was entranced, in love, mesmerized by his stories. Sensing this in me, Carl said that I could meet J-R, but first I had to go to three taped seminars—meetings where recordings of a J-R talk were played—before I could attend a live seminar at Prana.

So, for the next three weeks, I drove to Carl's place and he would play taped J-R seminars for me, just him and me. I remember being so enthralled, so alive, so... everything! At last, I was able to attend the live seminar at Prana. The place was packed. I went by myself and just inwardly listened—not understanding much of what J-R was saying—but I was in rapture with this man. After the seminar was over, I extended my hand and said to him, "Hi, I'm Alexandra Roberts and I am new to MSIA." He looked at me, and in a millisecond with a twinkle in his eye, he said, "You're not new to MSIA," and walked away.

My life, my world, my beingness were never the same again! I never looked back. Whoever that girl was who had lived in New York was now born again. J-R's love took this lost girl—who was not sure what real love, real beauty, real beingness were—and the miracles began. This inner immense love affair began back then, and it has not ended.

ERIC DELGADILLO
Love All Ways (Always)—Regardless

Once I was sharing with J-R about a family member and he told me to stop, so I did. He then said, "We do not love any ways, we love all ways (always)—regardless." In my mind, I got the message, and then when I started to wander off, J-R took me to a room in Prana that is now the reception area, and said, "Eric, everyone you will ever meet, see, touch, smell, or hear—on any and all levels—I have been a personal member of their family." My mind began to wonder, "What? How?" He then said, "I have been their brother, sister, father, or mother. So, treat everyone and love everyone as if they were me."

Then it was time for him to give the seminar. So, I got up and went to the front where I always sat, right below his feet, and once more just closed my eyes. He took me to places that I can't even begin to describe.

TANNIS BENEDICT
I Couldn't Wait to Start Over, Whatever It Took

I discovered John-Roger in the spring of 1974. I was young and going through a very challenging time. I had so many questions about why my life was such a mess and how I was going to get out of it, and J-R had the answers. In fact, he had all the answers to every question I ever had. Finding him was like being struck by a bolt of lightning. His teachings immediately spoke to me and I came into alignment with them right away. This path was for me! J-R was going to make all the difference in my world, and he did. I soaked up J-R's weekly seminars at Prana and got on Discourses.

However, if my life wasn't bad enough when I came into the Movement, after about four months of being on Discourses, my fragile life fell completely apart. I lost my job, was evicted from my home, had no money in the bank, no friends who could help, and—just to make sure Spirit had my attention—I was in the middle of a name change and I suddenly had no current photo ID. It was as if someone came along and erased my life off the planet. I was living out of my car with two small children and nowhere to go and no one to help.

I never prayed harder asking God for help. I had been seeing flashes of purple light, so I knew the Mystical Traveler was with me. But did the Traveler know I needed help right now! This misery went on for three weeks, and then something happened at one of J-R's seminars at Prana.

It was the end of summer. I didn't know many people in MSIA yet, and I didn't see anyone I knew at the seminar. I was standing there alone, lost in the crowd when J-R walked in. I could see him in the distance talking to a couple of people—then it seemed that he purposefully weaved in and around people straight to me. I had never been introduced to J-R and had never spoken with him until this time. He looked me straight in the eyes, and with a powerful energy I felt coming at me, he asked, "How are you?" I replied, "I don't know." Then, he asked, "What do you mean you don't know?" I replied, "I don't know if I'm coming or going." With that same piercing energy, he said, "It's not out there, you know." And then he walked around me and up to his chair in the front of the room. I had been hit energetically by his words, but I didn't get it. My head was spinning. I felt disoriented and needed to ground myself.

I went to get a glass of water in the back, but on my way, a guy I knew stopped me by the reception room to chat. He grabbed my arm and started talking, but I couldn't hear a word he was saying. I was so distressed—and lost. Suddenly time slowed down, and the voice of the man gripping my arm faded out. I was standing in front of the doorway to the reception room and noticed how light it still was outside on this long hot summer day. Still in slow motion, I pulled my arm from the young man's grip, looked at my watch, and said, "Isn't it interesting that it's so late, and yet I can still see outside?"

At that moment J-R suddenly appeared in the reception doorway only a few feet from me. He locked onto my eyes with that intense energy, then quickly shut the door in my face. I was stunned. I stood there paralyzed for a moment trying to make sense of why he did that. Then I slowly turned to look upfront where J-R always sat in his blue chair. There he was, about forty feet away! He was settled into his blue chair reading through a stack of 3 X 5 cards of questions that we always gave him. But wait. I just saw him in the reception room! How could he be in two places at once? I later realized that I had seen his radiant body—it was J-R's spirit body that closed the door in my face. Okay, I got the message! "Stop looking outside for answers." J-R had given me the experience I needed to turn me around from seeking outwardly for answers to seeking within. That was when I finally surrendered and went inside, which was the beginning of my movement of spiritual "inner" awareness. It's funny, I don't remember how I got out of crisis during that time, but I felt a peaceful connection to the Traveler and Holy Spirit that somehow guided me through and out of it in an easy way.

I loved being in the Movement. I stayed on Discourses and finished all twelve years, but it was hard raising two children by myself and trying to work and have a career. I didn't have the time to develop lasting friendships with others in MSIA, although I would have loved to. My life was happening outside of the Movement, and I eventually married a wonderful man in 1985, Brian Frankish. My life took a slow turn away from MSIA, and by 1988 my Initiation had become inactive.

Nevertheless, the late 1980s were a wonderful time for me. My husband's career was taking off. He produced a film titled Field of Dreams during that time and I was blessed to be a part of it. The film had a spiritual message and amazing things happened during the filming. I saw fireflies appear in the cornfield and fog roll in when the director called for action. People were touched by the film's spiritual message, and hearts opened. The experience was joyful and magical. I sent Light to the project every day—before, during, and after filming. Even though I no longer had MSIA in my life on the outside, I had it on the inside. Life was good.

Life has its challenges, however, and over the next twenty-five years, I experienced many of them. I went through much grief and sorrow, but I never stopped praying to God and invoking the Holy Spirit. And yet, I always felt something was missing during that time. I had never harbored any negative feelings or against-ness toward J-R or MSIA, so I didn't really understand how or why I had drifted away. I just did.

Many years went by without thinking about J-R. There were two occasions, however, when I saw J-R—both in Century City in the early 2000s. Each time he was by himself, walking around and people watching. He appeared to be really enjoying himself. He passed by closely—seeming to almost float by—but never looked at me, although I was gaping at him. He seemed to be in another world, and I noticed that no one else was looking at him. I tried to follow him, but he disappeared. I later realized that I had seen his radiant body… again. I wondered if it had been a call for me to come home—but I didn't act on it at the time.

Through the grace of God, I got a third chance. One day in the summer of 2013, a dear friend visited me from Hawaii. I was planning her visit and wanted to take her to a meditation garden somewhere in the city. I thought of several places, but then Prana popped into my mind and I immediately was set on taking her there. I hadn't been to Prana for almost thirty years, and I was looking forward to seeing what it looked like after all that time.

As soon as I walked in, I knew I was home—just like that. It hit me like a ton of bricks. My love for J-R resurfaced and was instantaneous. I felt him deep in my soul, and I couldn't wait to start over, whatever it took. I yearned again for J-R's teachings. I yearned to see who was still in MSIA, to meet them and develop those friendships I had always wanted.

I wrote J-R right away, and I thank God he was still with us on the planet. I was told I would have to start over with Discourses and most likely with my initiations. I had left as a mental initiate, but I honestly didn't care if I had to start over. I felt joyful about everything. I heard back from J-R within a few weeks that he had reactivated my initiation tone where I left off on the mental level. I was thrilled and burst into tears of joy! It was so unexpected, and I knew J-R was extending me grace.

For years during my absence, I had felt lonely on my spiritual path. I kept missing a group of people I could connect with spiritually, and they were here all along—in MSIA, my spiritual family. I am thrilled to be back home—back in the heart of MSIA, the heart of the Traveler.

The contrast I experience after being gone for almost thirty years is like walking into a dark room and turning on the light. A part of me was asleep, and now I'm awakening. The Light for me is brighter now. My life is brighter. My love is deeper and I'm filled with gratitude. I'm seeing everything as if it were new. I feel supported and loved in a way I hadn't for years. Yes, I am still blessed to have a beautiful marriage, but I now experience the love in my marriage more profoundly than ever before. And I am able to extend that love to others as I see everyone with new eyes and a bigger and more open heart.

I am so grateful for the journey the Traveler has taken me on. I look back on the years I was gone and I can now see how perfect it was. I had karma to complete and balance, and I see how that might not have been possible had I stayed physically in the Movement. I had people to meet and experiences to have that I might never have had the opportunity to do.

I will be forever grateful to our beloved John-Roger for carrying the mantle of the Mystical Traveler Consciousness, and for my good fortune of having met him. For me, he was the embodiment of the highest Divine Consciousness, yet still just a regular normal guy. He would look at me and I knew he knew what I was thinking and how I was feeling. I knew he knew everything about me. I could share his thoughts sometimes at seminars when I was in perfect alignment with the Traveler Consciousness. Several times at Prana before a seminar, he passed by me and I saw his eyes as pure radiant light! I felt the powerful energy field around him. Indeed, he did close the door to my continual search on the outside looking for answers, and opened the door to my spiritual path of inner awareness where I began connecting to the Oneness! I loved him—I love him now in spirit where I was always intended to meet him. Thank you, J-R for being the Wayshower and for bringing me home. I am so blessed!

LAKE ARROWHEAD

A retreat property in Lake Arrowhead, California,
which was donated to MSIA in 1974.

SHERWOOD DUANE
A Divine and Sacred Time

Up at Lake Arrowhead, we used to have these horrendous work parties that were fabulous—but we worked like slaves. We called them retreats, and we paid for them. Breakfast was early, like at 6:30 a.m., and then we'd start work usually at 8:00, clearing the ground, digging plumbing trenches and trails—grunt work. I was one of the crew members who dug trails. Bob Strimpel was like Paul Bunyan—he was tearing the trails up, and we were doing our best to keep up with him. J-R would direct us, saying, "The trail goes here… The trail goes there." We were cutting the trail in. And during the summer it was hot as a bitch sometimes, so there was a lot of sweating that went on. And dirt—a lot of dirt. Sweat and dirt, which kind of describes the grunt work up there.

People who were in the kitchen were not getting dirty like we were, but they were sweating. The kitchen was super-hot and crowded and jammed up, with usually 15–20 people in there. It was like a madhouse. We would all work until 5:00 or 6:00 p.m., which was a pretty full day. And in the evening, we would go down into the sanctuary—which was really a garage with a fireplace—and J-R would be with us. Sometimes we would all share, but many times only he would share. Sometimes there were events that involved music. Mostly, it was a very divine and sacred time.

I remember being in the sanctuary one time when Jesus came into the room—and that is beyond words. Another time, J-R was in a very deep place—deep, deep, deep—and talking to us, and he closed his eyes. The room was dimly lit at the time. It was so sacred you could cut it with a knife. I think he said, "My teacher just came into the room." We all fell apart. Everybody was crying. It was the Spirit walking through the room. We couldn't hold ourselves together. It just washed over us and took our breath away. Tears flooded out. And we knew we were in the presence of God, the Divine, of Jesus the Lord. Those were some mighty high times.

GLENN BARNETT
Getting in the Game

Around 1976, we had set up an impromptu volleyball court at Lake Arrowhead in the cul-de-sac of the entry road. After lunch, many people went over there to play volleyball, and I found myself walking in that direction with J-R beside me. We made small talk as we walked until we reached the edge of the court, and then we stood and watched the game for a few seconds.

I was content just watching. After all, I was no kind of athlete. I had had polio as a child and one of my arms was disabled. When I got out of the iron lung and back into school, I was always the last one chosen for the team—so I had stopped trying. Then suddenly, J R said to me, "Well, I don't know about you, but I'm going to play." He took two steps and turned around, looked at me, smiled, and said, "And I'm not that good." Well, I was busted—I had to get in the game.

So, he went on one side and I took the other and we played volleyball. I discovered I could actually hit the ball, and I had fun! It was a moment of emotional healing for me. And I found out that J-R actually was pretty good at volleyball.

KURT REINCKE, SANDY REINCKE, & JACKIE PETERSON
Which Way the Tree Would Fall

Kurt: One experience at Lake Arrowhead that had an impact on me was when David Giorgio and I cut down a tree. We were both debating which way the tree would fall. I looked at the tree and figured which would be the heaviest side; "It's gotta go that way, it's leaning that way. Why would it go any other way?" And J R kept saying, "I don't know if it's going to go that way."

I made a comment like, "You be a nice Traveler and let me worry about the tree." And J-R said, "Okay." So, I started cutting that sucker, and when I started cutting—instead of the tree going back the way I expected—it started turning. I said, "What the hell is going on!" It turned and fell right across the road. I nearly crapped my pants! I should have listened to J-R… I should have listened. The tree took down electrical wires and blacked out the whole neighborhood. J-R never said anything about it. He just went on to the next thing— "Let's get this tree out of here." I ran like crazy and started cutting up that tree.

Sandy: That was J-R—good loving. There was a lesson in it for all of us: pulling together, everybody pulls together. And then we all got the opportunity to be good neighbors.

Jackie: Yeah, we took all the food we had brought for the entire retreat and made dinners for the whole neighborhood that had been blacked out. The whole group got together, and we carried food from door to door to feed everybody.

BARAKA HOLISTIC CENTER

*A healthcare center founded by MSIA members
in Santa Monica, California, in 1976.*

MURIEL MOORE
Baraka: Challenges and Joy

My husband, Keith, was a chiropractor, and we were involved with opening the Baraka Holistic Center in Santa Monica in 1976 with about thirty-five practitioners and staff. Coming to the Baraka Center every day was a challenge—or a joy—to each person, in their own way. For many of us, it was being stretched to the limit: learning cooperation and group dynamics, learning to deal with other points of view and strong egos, and learning how to make business decisions from a spiritual viewpoint for the highest good of all concerned.

In his book, Baraka, J-R states, "It is very well known that we all must partake of life according to where we come from and where we are going, according to our life destinies. So, you can't ask for the truth for a group; you can only ask for truth for yourself. You have a right to ask for the truth for yourself; you do not have the right to inflict your truth or preferences on others." That was a balancing act for some.

For the administrative staff, the challenge was to keep the wheels turning as seamlessly as possible for the practitioners— so the environment would be supportive, and healing could take place for ourselves and for our patients. Our goal was to make sure Baraka was a place for healing, for the highest good of all concerned. It was gratifying when we learned that a Baraka patient had been heard on Christian television saying, "As soon as I walked into Baraka, I felt the Holy Spirit!"

KEITH MOORE
Baraka: Exchange of Blessings

"Baraka, a Holistic Center for Therapy and Research" was the official name of the nonprofit corporation, which became the Baraka Healthcare Center (1976–1990). Baraka is a word that appears in several African languages and has many different meanings, most having to do with the "exchange of blessings."

I was one of Baraka's founders, and I continued as a practitioner and administrative officer until 1983. The founding committee was made up of MSIA members, most of whom were healthcare practitioners. J-R's teachings had attracted a number of healthcare professionals into MSIA from various disciplines, such as chiropractic, acupuncture, allopathic medicine, psychotherapy, and nutrition. This group met to discuss the possibility that an MSIA healing center could become a reality. Much grand speculation abounded. From this enthusiastic group, a small healing center was opened with donated furniture and equipment, a small staff, and several volunteers.

This humble start-up grew during the next seven years to be the finest and largest multi-disciplinary healthcare center in the world—according to an evaluation team from the World Health Organization—with a staff of seventeen practitioners and eighteen administrative personnel.

Despite the founders' grand intentions, when asked what the purpose of Baraka was, J-R replied very matter-of-factly, "So you all could work out your karma with each other." His involvement in the day-to-day activities was through his personal/spiritual relationship with most of the practitioners and staff who, because of his influence, worked together to embody the principles of acceptance, cooperation, understanding, and enthusiasm. J-R's counsel was always available.

Many MSIAers came to the clinic for their healthcare. In addition, the practitioners often brought patients from their private practices who were not in MSIA. The general public loved the Baraka experience. Initially, most practitioners were in MSIA. However, even in the beginning, there was a "buzz" about what we were doing, so interest and participation developed with non-MSIA practitioners.

"For the highest good of all concerned" was the core J-R teaching that we integrated into the clinic philosophy. The most popular weekly event was a meditation workshop using J R's Sacred Tones book. The Baraka logo was an open hand extended in loving service. In the palm was the dove of peace, a purple rose in its mouth, representing the Mystical Traveler Consciousness.* The staff would gather before each shift started, call in the Light, and chant Ani-Hu—*Hu* being an ancient name for God and *Ani* bringing in the quality of empathy. Many patients would come early just to be in the reception room where they could hear the chant and experience the energy.

* *The Mystical Traveler Consciousness was an extremely loving spiritual consciousness that John-Roger received in 1963, which was often experienced by students of MSIA as a purple light.*

INSIGHT TRAINING SEMINARS

A series of personal growth seminars created in 1978.

RUSSELL BISHOP
Talking About the Teachings vs. Living the Teachings

When I first began my relationship with J-R and MSIA, the Movement (MSIA) seemed like a mismatched collection of characters with heavy overtones of my days as a hippie. John-Roger often said that the Movement was made up of a bunch of non-joiners, people who wouldn't want to join anything. That's certainly what we looked like back then.

It became increasingly clear to me that many people suffered from a disconnect between their spiritual values and making daily life work. For many, it seemed like a choice—you could be poor or you could be pure, you could be successful in the physical world or you could be successful in the spiritual world. The more I learned, the more I saw that there was no disconnect between the inner and the outer worlds. In fact, it seemed to me that if you could truly live the spiritual teachings, you could integrate them quite well into the world of everyday life.

So, one autumn afternoon in 1977—while on a break during a training I was running in Seattle—I wrote J-R a letter. The gist of the letter was that, while I had no way of knowing how people were doing spiritually, it seemed to me that many were missing the point—that a person could do well spiritually as well as doing well in the physical world. That it wasn't a choice of either/or. It was both.

In that letter, I suggested to J-R that if this made sense, then I could design a training program that would help people integrate their spiritual values with their daily lives in a way that would support success in both worlds. The basic principles of the training would be couched in non-religious terms; rather, we would focus on response-ability (the ability to respond), accountability (willingness to own the outcome), intention (what is it you really want and why), and how to integrate all three into an ever-more successful life. I further suggested that just as anyone studying with MSIA would find harmony with what was being taught, so also would anyone from nearly any religious point of view or walk of life.

J-R completely surprised me when, a few days after I mailed the letter, my phone rang in Eugene, Oregon, where I was living and working at the time. J-R said, "Hello," and asked if I had a few minutes to talk. Well, J-R and I had never spoken, so this was beyond a complete surprise. Of course, I had a few minutes! Lots of them in fact. All he wanted.

At the end of the call, we arranged to speak in November when I was planning to attend an MSIA retreat in the Valley of the Moon in Sonoma, California. We also agreed to have me run a little workshop during the retreat that would follow the basics of what I had in mind for the seminar. We called that workshop, *Actualizing Spirit.* It was during that same retreat that I was ordained.

J-R and I did speak a little at the retreat; mostly, however, I spoke with Edgar Veytia and Michael Sun, members of J-R's personal staff at the time, who recorded our lengthy question and answer session. Evidently, J-R listened to the tape on the drive back to Los Angeles. He then called me a few days later, and we began mapping out the possibilities that led to the creation of Insight Training Seminars.

That first seminar had 150 participants who gathered in the downstairs ballroom of the Miramar Hotel in Santa Monica, California, January 4–8, 1978. J R was one of those participants. He actually took part in the seminar, usually preferring to sit in the very last row on the end.

I remember one sharing in particular that caught a lot of attention. One gentleman was sharing how challenging his life was—that he just didn't understand how it could be that challenging. When I asked him what it was that he didn't understand, he replied, "Well, I do six to eight hours of spiritual exercises—chanting the sacred names of God—every day and still things don't seem to be working out." Somewhat astonished, I asked him if he really meant that he did six to eight hours of spiritual exercises every day—as in every day. When he assured me that it was indeed so, I replied, "What a great way to avoid your life!"

Well, the air went out of the room in a hurry—after all, everyone there was a minister and an initiate. All heads turned in unison toward J-R, who just sat there, nodding his head up and down in affirmation of that apparently heretical statement of mine.

Things took a big turn from there, as people began confronting the difference between the word level and the experience level—between talking about the teachings and actually living the teachings. When the seminar came to an end, J-R stood up and hugged every single person there. The line was long and it took quite some time for this to take place. Apparently, he was not prone to doing anything like this with such a large group.

A few days later, J-R called to let me know that 126 people who were not in that first training had signed up with MSIA for another one—which we had not prepared for at the time. And 123 of the first group of 150 had signed up for an advanced course—which we also did not have ready at that time.

I eventually agreed to move down to Los Angeles from Oregon and head up Insight Training Seminars. J-R shared with me that he had received some rather critical letters from people who thought we were polluting, if not perverting, the teachings of the Traveler. I had also received a few similar letters. As I was feeling a bit sick to my stomach—my basic self didn't like the feelings of rejection—J-R said two very powerful things to me. The first was, "They crucified Jesus, so don't expect any better." He amplified that a bit in terms of what kinds of negativity came at him. That helped quite a bit.

What really got me was when he said, and I'm paraphrasing here, "It doesn't really matter if we do another one of these or not. We have now trained all the ministers and initiates I need to do this work."

Clearly, our beloved J-R did keep things going, to say the least. Whether it's through Insight Seminars, University of Santa Monica, Peace Theological Seminary and College of Philosophy, or any of the myriad tapes, books, and seminars that he created through MSIA, he's still training ministers and initiates to do this work. I am eternally grateful that these teachings keep on teaching—and I see my job as to keep on learning.

JACKIE PETERSON
It Doesn't Have to Be Hard

J-R was always open to new things, new ideas, and new ways to expand, especially if it had to do with personal growth. The 1970s brought lots of that.

Living at Prana was a 24-hour-a-day lesson in personal growth. We were packed together, with varying levels of social skills, yet all committed to making this work—physically, financially, and spiritually. It was hard work and hard on us. Then along comes Russell Bishop with his stories of a better way to clean up our acts. He was a Lifespring facilitator, and as he experienced working with J-R, he saw a better way, a way to bring more loving into the work he was doing. He discussed this with J-R, and Insight was born. The first training was scheduled in 1978, and I wanted to be in it. Although it was expensive, and I didn't have the money, I put down a deposit anyway—not just for me, but for me and my husband, Jim. Somehow, we came up with the rest, rented a room in a hotel, and off we went.

Because the concepts Insight was based on seem like an accepted way of thinking today, it is hard to explain how new, how revolutionary, how extraordinary it was at the time. It took me and twisted me all around so I could see myself from a completely different angle. It gave me a safe space to go inside and look—long and hard—at myself. It gave me mirrors so I could see my own reflection as I had never seen it before.

We loved it so much that an Insight II was quickly scheduled. There was a moment in Insight II that has stayed with me. It was a process where many people were going very deep inside. For some, it was difficult and even painful. A space was created to make this inner journey safe, so I decided to take my own inner journey. As I was in the process, one of the assistants came up to me, looked right at me, and said, "It doesn't have to be hard." A light went through me right then and there. I stood up—both physically and inside myself—and walked away. That has become one of my cornerstone statements to myself.

INITIATION

Through initiation, students in MSIA are connected to the Sound Current, the audible energy that flows from God through all realms.

DARRELL CLAUSEN
A Delightful Treat

When I first started subscribing to Discourses, the monthly study booklets from MSIA, I didn't know anything about the process of initiation into the Sound Current, or even that there was such a thing. It wasn't until a few years later that I learned initiations were ways to conceptualize one's understanding of a process that was beyond understanding. To me, initiations were steps to be counted in MSIA, and I felt that aiming for something was better than not aiming for anything. Naturally, I was pleased whenever I was notified of an initiation to the Sound Current—one more step taken, I thought.

Later, I heard or read that you were not supposed to ask J-R if you were ready for your next initiation. Supposedly, he said it was because it was an individual process, and for some people, it could be a short time between initiations, and for others, it could be years. He didn't like to say no and tell you that you weren't ready yet. Still, after some time had passed since my last initiation, I wondered if it was really only a kind of test to see if I was really ready for my next initiation. Like, "If I didn't ask, I wouldn't get it, right?" But I figured that the worst thing he could say would be "No," so as long as I could accept that answer and was okay with it, I would shoot for the moon and go ahead and ask him. Shortly afterward, while I was assisting at an Insight training, I noticed that J-R and I were all alone in the room together. It was my chance to ask.

As I watched him straighten up some papers, I gathered up my courage and approached him. When I asked him if I was ready for my next initiation, his eyes flickered up above my head—like he was often known to do—and then he looked me straight in the eye and said, "No." Fair enough, I thought—asked and answered. Even though I secretly hoped he would say "Yes," I willingly accepted his answer.

As I turned to walk away, something pulled at me. I felt like I was spun in a circle, as if I had stepped into a revolving door. One moment I was turning to walk away from J-R, and the next I was spinning completely around and past him in a 360-degree circle back to face the direction I had been heading. Except there was a difference now—the profound sadness I had just begun to feel was gone, dissipated into nothingness. I was free from whatever longing, whatever wistfulness I had created for myself as a result of J-R's answer. I turned and looked over my shoulder at J-R, but he was looking down at something else and had already moved on. Well done, J-R! What a delightful treat to receive.

LINDA BOSTON
Chanting All the Time

I've had a lot of wonderful moments with J-R. When I first got my initiation, I asked him, "Do you just chant all the time?" He said, "Yes." And I said, "Really?" And he responded, "Well, right now I'm talking… so, not chanting, I'm talking. But I'm going to stop and let you talk, and then I'll be chanting." And I remember thinking, "Wow, that's amazing! This is just going to be my whole life—I'm going to be chanting."

I remember going to Prana right after that, and J-R was doing a seminar. I was sitting right in the front row, and somebody sang a song. J-R said, "Now that's what I call chanting your tone to rock and roll." And I just went, "Oh my God, he's talking right to me! And he knows I was chanting because I was trying to do my tone."

VALERIE RAMBO
A Feeling of Everything Being in the Proper Place and Time

I was very drawn in by the whole idea of Soul Transcendence, becoming aware of oneself as a Soul and as one with God, even though I had little knowledge of what that was or what it meant. I did understand the phrase, "Not one soul will be lost." And I loved the sound of the phrase, "Going home into the heart of God."

My very first initiation was the only time I ever met one-on-one with John-Roger. I arrived at his home in the hills, and when it was my turn, he asked me to follow him up some stairs. I don't recall much of what took place, because I was overwhelmed with a feeling of everything being in the proper place and time. I do remember that he gave me my tone to chant and asked me if I had any questions. Sitting in a place like that—the heart of God as I now call it—it was rather difficult to ask my mundane, prepared questions. I felt rather stupid, but I went ahead and asked my questions.

My husband and I were having difficulty getting along, and I was hoping that John-Roger would see my side and tell me I was right and my husband was wrong. Well, John-Roger—with all his wisdom and loving—made a comment that we both were fine and just had different views on things. I was so happy to have my tone to chant in my daily spiritual exercises and a new goal of getting to the next level of initiation. My husband and I did not stay together, but we did part in a loving way and have stayed in touch over the many years.

MSIA COMMUNITIES OUTSIDE OF CALIFORNIA: LIFE IMPACT

VIRGINIA RIDGEWAY
We Had Many Long Conversations

When I was twenty-one—after a period of sex, drugs, and rock 'n' roll—I had this epiphany that the only thing that really made sense was knowing God. First, I came across Yogananda in 1971 and studied his meditation and spiritual teachings through the Self Realization Fellowship. Then, in late 1973 or early 1974, I got a reading with a young man named Michael Bookbinder, which introduced me to MSIA. J-R came into town with his staff a few months later to give a live seminar. During the seminar, I had a vision of being present with the karmic board and all of the Light beings, and J-R was there too. And I remember that I had agreed to come in and work with J-R this lifetime—and I wept with the loving of that recognition! It was really an amazing experience for me even, though it was not uncommon for me to see angels and ghosts and things like that. But to have that kind of vision that told me what I was here to do and showed me how those decisions are made in Spirit—that was pretty amazing.

At that time, I was living in Glassboro, New Jersey, just twenty minutes outside Philly, in a communal house with five other adults and my two young daughters. All the people in my house had started Discourses and loved MSIA. We turned our home into a Light Center, with a very large picture (2' x 3') of J-R on the living room wall, and we held weekly seminars featuring recorded lectures by John-Roger.

I was searching for my next steps in life at that time. In the fall of 1976, Michael Bookbinder mentioned that there was no Light Center nor formal MSIA community on the Front Range in Colorado and suggested I trek to Colorado to anchor an MSIA Light community there. Since I had never been self-supporting, Michael trained me to teach people how to use Bach flower remedies, which were just coming to the States, and to teach about angels, auras, etc.—topics I was already innately knowledgeable about. He also suggested I go to the massage school in Boulder and noted that massage was something I would be good at.

So, I arranged for my older daughter to stay with a girlfriend of mine until I could find a house for us, then packed up my car with the youngest of my two daughters and a trunk full of belongings. I was terrified! I had never been outside Pennsylvania and New Jersey and had never been completely on my own. Having been divorced for only a year, I had no experience of supporting myself and my daughters. I had only $1,000 in my pocket, and I knew only one person in Colorado, a Philadelphia MSIAer who had moved there with her boyfriend a month earlier. My daughter and I slept on her living room floor for a month.

I was able to find some part-time jobs, including waitressing at a macrobiotic restaurant and clerking in a health food store. I was also soon teaching the esoteric classes I had been trained to facilitate, doing readings on an irregular basis, and had enrolled in the Boulder School of Massage Therapy. People would come in and take my classes, and they would end up getting involved with MSIA. And then Michael Bookbinder and Michael Hayes, who was his apprentice, would come out and teach classes, which would bring in more people.

But the move to Colorado continued to be very, very challenging. My friend had brought my older daughter to Colorado, and the girls and I moved ten times that first year—living in teepees, tents, basement furnace rooms, and new friends' living rooms. Also, my car broke down, and we had to hitchhike everywhere. Needless to say, it was often scary.

One of the possessions I had brought to Colorado in the trunk of my car and kept with me always was the big picture of J-R that had been on the living room wall of the Glassboro Light Center. I kept it at the foot of my bed—which was usually just a mattress on the floor since I moved so often. I talked to that picture every night about my fears, trepidations, doubts—and about my aspirations, my hopes, and my love of J-R and Spirit.

In 1978, I did the first Insight I open to the public, and then a few months later, I took the first Insight II in Philadelphia, which was co-facilitated by J-R and Russ Bishop. During the Insight II, Russell confronted me about something during a mingling exercise. All my fears and feelings of unworthiness came up, and I kind of freaked out on Russell. At that point, J-R walked up to me and said, "Virginia, you and I have had many long conversations, so I know who you are. But these people don't know you—and they won't unless you talk to them."

That was great advice—but the most significant piece of what he said was the part about me having had many long conversations with him. The only long conversations we had were the ones I had in my bedroom with his picture! In the moment J-R spoke to me about our "many long conversations," I understood that he truly is always with me—as he has said many times to all of us. I "got it" in some way that was deep, eternal, and well beyond words. From that moment onward, I trusted J-R completely and have loved him always in a way I cannot begin to describe.

I still do. I know that his transition to being more fully in Spirit does not change anything about the loving that he was, that I am, and that we shared. I know he is still always with me, as is the Traveler Consciousness, the Christ, my own Soul, and Spirit.

DAWN WHITE
Purple Rose

My story begins when I was one year old in Sydney, Australia, in 1963. My mum had been searching for the meaning of life, and she suddenly became consumed with the idea of growing a purple rose. She had seen the majestic vision on the inner and did all she could to manifest it in the rose garden we had at home. She did not realize the significance of this vision until we discovered MSIA when I was around thirteen.

At that time, we had embarked on a glorious spiritual quest, investigating several varieties of yoga, Swami Venkatesananda's beautiful teachings, Sun Bear (Native American teacher), Mind Dynamics, the Dalai Lama, the Aboriginal Evangelical Church (they were so warmly welcoming), and the Church of the Mystic Christ which worked through the great Lord Melchizedek.

Finally, around 1975, we found MSIA outwardly by reading The Movement Newspaper in a new age bookstore in Perth, Australia. The resonance was immediate, pure, and true, and we started on Discourses. And to discover that the purple rose was a significant symbol in MSIA clinched the deal. I see now—more clearly than ever—the connection was always there with our most gloriously loving J-R, and that igniting the connection outwardly took it to a whole new level.

My experiences both inner and outer with J-R continue to be many. I always experience the most divine, loving, fun, practical, and joyful energies with him. I am so proud of all that MSIA is, and all of us who have made it so. For me, the J-R experience has only become richer through his passing, even more profound and joyfully loving, which I did not know was possible. And the blessings of MSIA run deep and true, with many veins of gold and Light still to be mined.

ANDREW BAILLIE
With J-R You Have Complete Freedom

I was working in a hotel in Buenos Aires in 1978, and I didn't like the manager. As you may remember, it was quite a mess in Argentina at that time. My co-workers at the hotel didn't like the manager either, so we all signed a letter of complaint to the hotel's management. As a result, we were all fired—which wasn't very good for me, since I was recently married and had to support

a daughter who was just a few months old. Because I knew Buenos Aires very well, I was able to get a temporary job as a tourist
guide. My first assignment was to pick up a couple of Americans
at the airport and drive them around Buenos Aires for a few days.
I went to the airport, and I found the two guys. One was Edgar
Veytia, who was the president of MSIA at the time, and the other
man, who was a little bit plumper, was J-R. I didn't know anything
about him, but during the three days I drove them around Buenos Aires, the first thing I noticed was that he was watching me,
which was interesting. And I also noticed that he was very adroit
at jaywalking when we walked across an avenue through the cars.

When I got home, I told my wife that I had met somebody very
interesting, somebody I was able to converse with in a way that
was totally new to me. It was the first time I hadn't felt attacked in
a conversation, where I would usually have to defend myself and I
could never express what I wanted to say. It was the first time I felt
really respected, that my ideas were respected. What especially
connected me to him was that in our conversations he would
never reply by saying, "Yes, but..." Instead, he'd say, "Ah, yes...
Have you considered this?" That was like magic to me, because
then the conversation would open up. I discovered that you can
talk about anything with J-R—you have complete freedom.

I felt so connected to J-R by the end of his visit that when I
drove him to the airport, I almost got into the plane with him!
I told him, "I'm going to go and see what you do in the States."
However, it took me nearly two years to get there because it was
very difficult at that time to even leave Argentina. You could forget
about getting a visa unless you had connections, and we were just
nobody. But then everything aligned perfectly to get me there. I
was able to sell my apartment and travel to England, where I was
helped by various people, including J-R, and I arrived in L.A. two
years later and went to Prana.

Being interested in architecture, I was given an opportunity
to work on building geodesic domes, which MSIA had an interest
in back then, and seemed really sensational to me. While I was
working on the domes, I began to do some reading, and I started
having interesting experiences—some very interesting experi-

EXPANDING INWARDLY AND OUTWARDLY (1974-1978) ☼ 139

ences. I then decided to return to Prana to see if I could be of service, so I asked the MSIA staff what was needed. In response, they placed a pile of Discourses in front of me and told me they had to be translated. Translating the Discourses into Spanish then became my work, the function I had in MSIA. Although I was the one who had had a personal experience with J-R, my wife, whose name is Adrienna, came with me on this journey and helped me very much as we worked on the Discourses. I spent countless hours translating them, then Adrienna would type up my translations, and finally, they were published. So that is the story of how I arrived in L.A. and became part of the Movement.

When I spent those three days with J-R in Buenos Aires in late 1978, the sense I had was that he came there to place columns of Light. I think it was during those three days when he placed the first Light column in Buenos Aires, and this has resulted in the thriving community of MSIA ministers that exists today.

The year 1978 was apparently a very significant year for other MSIAers as well. I recently learned from John Morton that he was ordained on November 26 of that year during his Insight II, which was co-facilitated by J-R. John said that he made a dynamic life decision at that time, and two weeks later moved to Los Angeles. Vincent Dupont, currently one of the MSIA presidents, arrived at around the same time as well, so there was a lot going on in 1978.

CECILE PICKENS
A Warm, Strong, Golden Breeze

Back in the mid-1970s, psychics were big news, and some fairly well-known ones were coming to New Orleans, Louisiana, where I lived at the time. A friend and I had been making plans to go see a famous psychic when my friend phoned to say a man from California was in town and was going to speak at the apartment of her friend Martin. And Martin said that we absolutely had to hear him! "Did I want to go? Sure, why not? Sounds like fun."

This was J-R's first trip to New Orleans—I think it was in 1976, or maybe 1975. It was already dark when we arrived, parked, and headed to Martin's door. As the door opened, I saw and felt a warm, strong, golden breeze enfold me. It was a beautiful golden color with pure, bright alabaster-white flecks in it. As I recall, I took a step back, either physically or mentally—it was so beautiful and unexpected. "Wow," I thought, "this guy is really something!" Little did I know…

We went in and took a seat. Michael Sun and crew were singing those great old MSIA songs they had written, and then J-R started talking. As I listened, I still remember thinking, "This is how I always imagined Jesus talked and taught." It was all about love, and kindness and forgiveness, and peace and oneness, and all good things.

I also remember one of his closing remarks. It was the one about, "If you knew the secret sorrow of your own worst enemy, you would not add one thing—they have enough." What a concept! This is something I'd been wanting and waiting to hear. Needless to say, this led to an aura balance (one of the MSIA services), a Light Study (a counseling session with J-R), Discourses, home seminars, Insight in L.A., and moving to California in the summer of 1979. And no, we never did check out the "famous psychic" in New Orleans!

NORMA JEAN FARLAND
Purple Light

I was born into a large family in the Midwest, and I brought in lots of karma to work out—I have been told that my Soul took on more than most people do in one lifetime. I had many painful and challenging experiences growing up, and as a result, I created lots of hurt, anger, and resentment—I felt like a victim. I had to transcend issues such as alcoholism, drug addiction, incest, violence, religious training, self-hate, and a broken heart due to unfulfilling relationships that were brought to me for learning.

In 1977, a friend introduced me to Donna Wright, a minister in MSIA who did a healing on me and invited me to a home seminar. At the seminar, I experienced the essence of my Soul as ever so pure. I did not believe anything I heard J-R say, but I recognized the energy as greater and purer than anything I had ever experienced, and I knew this energy was my home. I got the Ani-Hu and Hu and other tones to use, and I heard about the purple light that some people believed indicated the presence of the Mystical Traveler, the spiritual consciousness J-R was said to work with.

Seeing colors was not unfamiliar to me, but I laughed at the concept of the Mystical Traveler. It sounded so funny and not at all in alignment with my belief structure. I said jokingly, "Okay, Mystical Traveler, if you are real, I want to see the purple this week, and then I will believe you are there and you are real." Well, guess what? That week, I saw the purple in a way I could not deny, and I followed the energy. So, I signed up for Discourses and continued attending seminars.

Since then, it has been a long journey of clearing, forgiving, and transcending lots of karma and judgments, for which I am so grateful to J-R and Spirit. I now realize that the purple light and the Traveler had been working with me for probably about five years before I met J-R physically. J-R's teachings saved my life, and I'm so grateful for J-R's life on this plane as a demonstration of his teachings for me to learn from.

In the early years, J-R was in my dreams, which I really needed to validate my relationship with the Traveler. I rarely remember anything now, but I know the inner connection. I never had the pleasure of being close to J-R in the physical, but now that he has passed, I am grateful that I have relied on the inner connection. I used to write to him about my troubles, and it helped to clear things. His love carried me through so many things.

ANNIE PETERS
Spiritual Wholeness

In September of 1972, the third week of my freshman year in college, I was in a seriously bad motorcycle accident. While riding on the back of a motorcycle with a guy I had just met, a car drove into my shin and nearly severed my left leg below the knee. Over the next four years, I had surgeries every four to six months and spent my whole college career on crutches. By 1976, the doctors were finally beginning to say, "Anne, nothing we are trying is working—with bone grafts, skin grafts, and even more bone grafts," and they said, "You should have your lower leg amputated." Terrified, I began searching for healing in a very serious way my senior year, including finding alternative healing, which was just coming onto the scene at that time.

It was then that I hooked up, as we'd say nowadays, with a fellow student named Michael Slom—who had this twinkle and this light about him—and one of the first things I learned about him was that he had a spiritual teacher named John-Roger. Michael took me to some taped seminars in Philadelphia, and I was fascinated, although I didn't know quite what to make of it all. You would go to someone's home and meet people, and then everyone would lie down on the floor and fall asleep while the tape was playing. There was nothing like it in my experience up to that point. But I was open and desperate for healing—just desperate for some kind of healing.

In the spring of 1976, Michael took me to hear J-R speak in Baltimore, and after the seminar, J-R saw me on crutches and asked me what had happened to my leg. As I told him, he put his hand on my sacrum, rubbed my lower back a little, and said, "You'll feel some energy in a few days." And of course, the dreams and the inner awakening began to happen. After that, I said, "Okay, I'm getting Discourses—I'm going to do this whole thing." Nothing changed in a few days with my leg, but I began doing spiritual exercises and going to more seminars. By 1978, I got very involved with Insight when it started on the East Coast.

There's a very powerful process in Insight that I participated in, and afterward, I was crying and releasing, and people were surrounding me with love and holding me. J-R was at that training too. As I sobbed, it was as if a gate or barrier at my left knee opened and lifted, and energy poured in. Energy poured into my leg so vibrantly that I could hear it; a brilliant light turned on in my leg; it was nothing short of the Holy Spirit arriving in my physical body.

At that moment, in the deepest part of me, I understood I was completely whole on every level, in every way. I knew I was going to be fine. And I knew I could lose my left leg, I could lose my arms, I could lose my sight, I could lose whatever—and I would still be whole and fine. I was going to have a wonderful life no matter what happened. Just then, J-R came over to me, put his hand on my leg, and said some things. I literally fell to my knees in gratitude. In the months after that, when I sat down to do spiritual exercises, that same energy and sound poured into my left leg and knit the broken bones. So, one day at work three months later, as I walked down the hall, I suddenly realized I wasn't using my crutch or cane—without noticing the shift, I could now bear weight on that leg again. It was a moment of tremendous celebration!

I am having a wonderful life, and I would be having a wonderful life even without that lower left leg that was attached to my body when I was born. I owe it all to J-R. From that first time he put his hands on my back, it took three years, not three days, but in the course of a lifetime, that's not much.

And so I feel unbounded gratitude that it was not just a physical healing, but that I came to know my spiritual wholeness through this path of physical injury in a way that's now unshakeable in me. Here it is, forty-plus years later. And that spiritual knowledge of me as a divine being to whom a miracle could happen—to whom the Holy Spirit can come and dwell herein—I haven't needed to have that happen again.

It's been my prayer that I learn my lessons not through physical pain and angst because that was hard on the people around me. For the most part, Spirit has granted me that wish. I walk freely now, hiking and exploring this beautiful world, and though I walk with a cane, I try to make every step, every time my cane strikes the ground, a prayer, a blessing, a thank-you. So, I've been very loyal to J-R, not just because of that healing, but because it's the path for me. It's my work in this life—it's at the core of who I am.

ANGEL HARPER
Flesh and Blood

When I was a senior in college taking a mysticism class, our daily homework was to do fifteen minutes of meditation and write in a journal about it. We could choose the form of meditation we wanted, and after researching and trying different chants and modes of meditation, I chose to chant the name "God." Day after day, I'd chant "God" in our college chapel or under a big willow tree outside. One afternoon while I was chanting in the chapel with my eyes closed, a beautiful presence appeared. In surprise I shot my eyes open, only to see nothing there but the chapel. I closed my eyes again, and pop!—there was the presence again. I didn't move, hardly wanting to breathe, so that I could stay with this amazing, all-encompassing, loving, and knowing being. I finally opened my eyes, as that was all I could take then. I knew this was what I had been looking for.

I asked my professor if she had ever had this experience, and she just told me to continue on with what I was doing. I read lots of books but couldn't find exactly what I'd experienced in them. Eventually, I put the experience on my inner shelf, while I moved into my outer life of getting married, having children, and exploring my Catholic teachings, especially the Catholic mystics. It wasn't until nine years later that I felt the impulse to connect with my earlier experience of that wondrous presence. I was pulled to check out many different paths to find that one—that beautiful presence who accepted me just as I am.

One day, I attended a Rolfing demonstration given by a young man. Rolfing is a type of deep tissue massage developed by Ida Rolf. During the presentation, I heard a voice whisper in my right ear, "Ask him if he does meditation." I looked at the people on either side of me, "Did you hear that voice say something about meditation?" They hadn't heard anything and thought I was a little crazy. On the break, I went up to the Rolfer and asked him if he did meditation and if he was part of a group. He said, "Yes." So, I said, "Okay, I'll sign up for one of these Rolfing sessions, and when I come, please tell me about the group and the meditation." When I went for my session, the Rolfer asked me if I'd mind listening to some music. I was happy to have background music, so he put on a tape that started with a man's voice introducing the album "Songs of a Loving Heart." At the first sound of the voice of the man doing the introduction, I suddenly sat upright on the Rolfing table in instant recognition! "Who is that man?" I asked excitedly. "John-Roger," the Rolfer replied. "At last," I told him, "That is the one, the presence I have been looking for." The feel or vibration of the voice was the same as the presence I had met nine years ago in my college meditation.

A while later, I saw John-Roger in person at an Insight training. I went up to him and touched his arm in different places as if trying to understand his physicality. He smiled at me and said, "Yes—flesh and blood." I said, "But you don't look like that on the other side." And he responded, "That's right because this is flesh and blood." J-R gave me the precious blessing of meeting him inwardly first—and that one is still with me, and even more.

INSPIRING MOMENTS

MARY BEARD
The Voice Was Calling Me Home

When I was a young woman of thirty in 1975, I was yearning for something I'd felt my whole life but didn't know what it was. I'd begun studying astrology with Barbara Shere in Berkeley, and I felt a strong connection to her and to her spiritual nature. She invited me to something called a seminar and assuming it had to do with astrology, I said, "Sure." When I arrived at her home, I felt awkward since everyone else seemed to know each other and were very warm and affectionate with one another. After a bit of food, we went into a room and Barbara called in the Light—something I didn't quite understand, but I liked it. Then everyone began to chant "Hu." I sat quietly, not really knowing what was going on but feeling swept up in the energy. She then put on a tape, "The Dilemma of Man and the White Light Meditation."

As a man's voice started to speak, I began to leave my body. I scrunched down on the floor in a corner of the room, not so much to get away but to feel protected and safe. My body felt like it was melting. I realized the voice I was hearing was the one I had heard inside me my whole life and I felt it was calling me home. I saw many lifetimes where I had followed teachers and gurus and always ended up feeling betrayed. I saw myself coming into this lifetime with my jaw set, ready to defy any teacher and to follow no one. I would do it myself! And now I was being asked to surrender—but not to someone, not to something outside myself—rather to surrender to myself, to my soul's journey.

It felt so very different from what I'd experienced before. And I could only say "Yes" with all my heart.

When the tape was over and the lights turned on, I got up but couldn't speak. Barbara approached me and looked concerned, but I motioned that I was okay. I left quickly and walked down the hill to my car. Driving home, I had to pull over to the side of the road several times because I was crying so hard I couldn't see.

Several weeks later, John-Roger came to Northern California for a seminar. While he spoke, it looked like he was looking at me almost the whole time, referencing events I'd just experienced, like a recent vacation I had been on. But the weird thing was that his face kept changing, and at the end of the evening, I still didn't know what he looked like! The next day, I visited Barbara to talk about my experience at the seminar. She showed me a photo of J-R, and his face stood still long enough for me to see what he looked like. I'd never had strange experiences like this before, but it all seemed so perfect.

My relationship with J-R was always an inner one, with occasional meetings in the physical. I am profoundly grateful that I am living at this time, that the voice I heard inside manifested in an outer form as well as in increased awareness of the inner form. My soul has yearned so long—it feels like eons—for the time when I would be called home again and once more know the oneness of Spirit from which I came.

PATTI RAYNER
A Spiritual Father

My first and most impactful memory of J-R was the day of my first aura balance in early 1975. I had only been to a few taped seminars, and yet here I was going to J-R's house in Mandeville Canyon for something that sounded very weird, but very alluring.

As I prepared to go, I wasn't sure whether I should take my three rambunctious sons—twelve, thirteen, and fourteen years old—with me. But I surrendered to the possibility of their spiritual advancement and heaved them into the car. After putting the fear of God into them if they even dared to get out of line, I headed to the house and parked near J-R's long brown limousine.

Before I could even turn off the ignition, my boys had jumped out of the car and were all over that limo, oohing and aahing and looking into the windows. I was horrified, and as I was reading the riot act to them, who did I see quickly walking toward us but J-R himself! Oh God, we had done the unforgivable and touched his car. But no, that was not it at all. J-R, with keys in hand, opened the limo and before I could catch my breath to apologize, we all found ourselves sitting inside the limo with J-R explaining every bell and whistle to the boys!

I realized I had an aura balance appointment that I would be late for in a minute, so I was in a dilemma—sit with the living Mystical Traveler or go to a weird-sounding session with someone else. Hmm—I was frozen. J-R finally said, "It's okay, Patti, I'll take care of the boys while you have your aura balance." During the one-hour session, J-R must have popped in four or five times to update me on what was going on: they were driving the 4-wheelers, they were with the staff on the mopeds, they were in the game room, etc.

That was the day I gave my sons over to their spiritual father. He taught them all the things that their physical father was unable to—how to be men in this world, how to make a positive difference in the world, how to know God, how to know themselves, how to avoid the many pitfalls of teenager-hood, how to facilitate personal growth trainings, how to keep their hearts open, and how to be great men. And most of all, how it feels to have a real father. My precious John-Roger taught me that I was not alone in the raising of my sons, and he was there for us every step of the way into their adulthood, as he guided us into the realms of Spirit.

ASHTAR-ATHENA
Loyalty to Soul

I remember a seminar that J-R said he gave specifically for me because sometimes I would wrestle in my mind about loyalties: "Should I be loyal to Jesus? Should I be loyal to Sai Baba? Should I be loyal to John-Roger?" Sometimes I'd go through that angst. And the name of the seminar is "Loyalty to the Soul."

J-R said, "It's important to be loyal to who you are as a Spirit." And he told me personally, "Never be loyal to a little organization like MSIA, or to this body," speaking of his body. "Be loyal to who you are inside, and then you will be loyal to everything." That was the biggest key for me because that was my spiritual path—loyalty to Soul.

ERIC DELGADILLO
Following Jesus

I recall one time when I was alone with J-R I felt this urgent need to share with him my love for the Christ, as expressed through Jesus.

I stood up, looked at him, and said, "J-R, you know how much I love you... But if Jesus were to walk into this room and call my name, I would follow him out that door."

To which J-R responded, "And I would be right behind you!"

CHAPTER FOUR

LEARNING LESSONS, FINDING JOY, AND FACING CHALLENGES (1979-1987)

The stories in this chapter reflect the patterns of ups and downs that seem to be part of the human experience. Moments of great joy and loving, moments of tears and learning lessons, moments of going within to navigate challenging situations—all these experiences make up the fabric of life. Even MSIA itself and J-R faced challenges from those who would discredit them. It's all a reminder that we are on a planet that is designed to shake things up every once in a while.

During these years, MSIA continued to disseminate the Traveler's teachings through technologies available at the time—including videotapes, audiotapes, and the use of cable television stations. Affiliated organizations—such as Insight and Peace Theological Seminary—continued to expand, and MSIA acquired Windermere Ranch in Santa Barbara, California. The first of the PAT IV trips to the Middle East took place in 1984 when J-R and over a hundred students embarked on a spiritual journey together.

At the end of this chapter, students share how they were inspired by John Morton, who would soon take on the mantle of the Mystical Traveler.

LEARNING LESSONS THROUGH DIRECT EXPERIENCES WITH THE TRAVELER

WIN HAMPTON
A Hug Is a Simple Thing, Right?

When I was fifteen, I had an awakening where I had direct experience and memories of having been embodied before, and that I was back in a body again. I experienced transcendental states of awareness, states of God consciousness, the difference between my ego and my Self as a spiritual being, and experiences of other realms of existence. From that point on, my questing intensified. I read all the religious and spiritual texts I could find. I began practicing yoga, became a vegetarian, and tried to figure out what worked in hopes of getting into further transcendental experience. I was not interested in mental knowledge, but instead I was seeking experiential methods to explore transcendence.

When I turned twenty-three in 1979, I reached an impasse. Up to that time, I had been studying books and practicing yogic teachings as best as I could, but the books just weren't doing it. I decided that I needed a guide, someone who could show me the way. I wanted a guide who would know and understand, by experience, the deeper knowledge within the various spiritual and religious texts I was reading; who would have detailed first-hand knowledge about practices that led to transcendence; who would be impeccable in the world, honest, forthright, and caring; who would demonstrate integrity and spiritual knowing and not just talk about it. This guide would know all about those other realms of existence I had experienced, and would know what they were, and would know how to get there and travel in those realms. Pretty tall order!

In August of 1979, I reached the end of my rope, so to speak, and decided to go on a pilgrimage to find such a teacher. I was planning to go to India, but just before I left, a close friend of mine, Linn, said she thought I should go with her down to the little town of Alamogordo in southern New Mexico. She was going there to begin a program to teach counseling. I said, "No, I'm about to leave on my pilgrimage." She repeated that I needed to go with her, so I asked, "Why are you being so adamant about this?" She then shared about a dream she had where I went to Alamogordo and stayed there and enrolled in the program. I knew she was a prophetic dreamer because I had seen that verified before, so I asked, "What's going on in Alamogordo?"

It turned out there was an organization there called the Quimby Center that involved a group of folks who were way into spiritual studies and practices. Linn's perception was that they were a pretty high group, practicing something called "aura balancing" and working with the Light and the Christ energy. It did sound interesting, so I agreed to go. I thought, "Why not? This can be the beginning of my pilgrimage." When we arrived in Alamogordo, we went to a house in the neighborhood where I could see white light all over the house. I hadn't ever seen that before. We went in and Linn introduced me to a fellow named Robert Waterman, and within twenty minutes, it came clear to me that I wanted to enroll in their counseling training program.

Some of my teachers were Ellavivian Power, Robert Waterman, Ron and Mary Hulnick, Marya Foley, and Berti Klein. In Robert's classes, we used a wide variety of study materials, including some books by John-Roger. At that time, these books were just one part of the reading list. During one of Robert's classes, he played a J-R seminar tape, and I vividly remember that, as soon as he turned the cassette on, I went unconscious and only came back to awareness to hear the final words, "Baruch Bashan."

Around this time, I had a dream in which I was walking through a garden, an olive grove like you would find in the Middle

East. The trees were very old and knurled. I noticed four men walking along a central walkway through the olive grove, and I saw that the man in the middle of the group seemed to be the leader. As I looked over at them, he looked at me and our eyes met. I saw that he was fully aware of me. The olive grove was quiet and peaceful as the four men walked and talked together. I could see a great deal of camaraderie and caring between them. There was something about this man in the middle that was attracting me. I began to follow along, and from time to time, our eyes would meet. As I looked into his eyes, I saw purposefulness, peacefulness, and a simple acceptance. There was no rush, no expectancy, and there was a sense that all was well. I felt that I wanted to know and relate with this man the way his companions were. I wanted to be with him. That was the dream.

In October, we heard there was a training called Insight, which our teachers highly recommended, coming to a town nearby, so all of us students signed up. As I walked into the training room, I saw in the back of the room a man who had a bit of a potbelly and was wearing a T-shirt and blue jeans. As my eyes landed on him, a bell began tolling inside my chest—a deep tolling sound reverberating throughout my body. Within the sound, there was a presence and recognition of some sort. Holy shit! I looked at this guy and did a double-take. This was the guy who had been in my dream!

I asked the people next to me, "Who is that guy back there in the blue jeans?" Someone said, "That's John-Roger." I asked, "Who is John-Roger?" They said something like, "Oh, he's the head honcho in charge of the training—he's a spiritual teacher." Then I started piecing things together, "Oh right, we've been reading some of his books for class." And, "Oh yeah, he's the guy who does those seminars we listen to on cassettes in Robert's class." I was having a deep resonating experience moving through me. I then knew that this was the teacher I had been looking for. This guy knows Spirit, he knows the inner realms, and he teaches others how to do it. My knowing this was not a rational, logical thing. It was a knowing that seemed to come out of the resonating tolling taking place inside.

Needless to say, that training was a huge life-changing experience for me. At one point in the training, we all had the opportunity to walk on stage to a microphone that was set up there, and J-R would "read our beads," so to speak. When I finally worked up the courage to do it, I mostly went blank and checked out as J-R talked to me. But I do remember a couple of things. He said I was a maverick who lived out on the edges of things and didn't really commit. And he said I might consider how well that was working for me.

I also got a hug from J-R at the end of the training. You might think that a hug is a simple thing, right? But it is challenging to describe what happened when I hugged John-Roger. At this time in my life, I had the perception and awareness of energy fields, auras, and other things going on. I was aware that John-Roger's aura was quite large—it filled the room. When I hugged him, there was a tremendous amount of activity taking place in the auras. I perceived his aura as a field of energy that naturally began to straighten and balance any other field it touched. Just the way water flows downhill in a very natural way, finding the lowest level and flowing into it, his energy was like that. As I hugged him, his energy flowed into all the places in my energy field, very subtly and naturally, and began straightening, purifying, and balancing. I experienced this so powerfully that it made me dizzy, and I reeled a bit as I walked away.

During and after the training, I grilled everyone about John-Roger. What does he do? How does one get involved? I learned there was an organization called MSIA. I began to learn about Soul Transcendence, the audible life stream, and Shabd Yoga. This was right up my alley—a kind of mystery school as I conceived it. I wanted initiation and ordination immediately! "Nope," I was told, "you have to go on Discourses for two years first." So, I ordered Discourses the next day, and I was initiated and ordained two years later.

My relationship with J-R has been almost entirely an inner relationship. After the initial dream where I first met him—and by the way, he looked in the dream exactly how he looked when I saw him physically—I began to work with him in my dreams regularly. For a number of years, our inner meetings were usually about a particular teaching. In the dream, we would meet up, sometimes just the two of us, but more often there would be a group present, and sometimes I would recognize other members of the group. J-R would show me a door, take out a key, and open the door. Then he would give the key to me and have me open the door. Sometimes, the key would be more like a set of feelings or a thought process.

Typically, when I woke up and remembered the dream, I could see and feel the key but would be unable to translate it into my conscious mind. Usually, the dreams had a strong feeling of comfort and wellbeing that stayed with me when I awoke. This went on for about fifteen years during which I was experiencing intense challenges in my outer life. Often, when I woke up, I really didn't want to resume my outer life, which was so difficult. Then began a period when I would just hang out with J-R in my dreams—which were not so much training sessions at this point. During this time, we became very close friends in my dreams. It may sound strange, but my relationship with J-R in the inner was as grounded and solid as any relationship I have ever had in my waking life.

Throughout this time, my life gradually improved as the challenges and issues I was dealing with began to resolve. My awareness shifted and expanded. I started to recognize the inner realms we traveled through in the nightdream state or when I sat down to do spiritual exercises. I developed reference points.

I never felt the need to be with John-Roger physically, because our inner relationship was so rich and full. He would answer specific questions for me on the inner. I once sent him a physical letter asking about another spiritual teacher. Shortly afterward, he came in a dream and showed me where this teacher was on the inner and where I was in relationship to this teacher. This provided the clarification I was looking for. In this way, I learned to get verification for things inside myself.

Around the time I received my Soul initiation, J-R came to me and told me that he would no longer be doing as much for me. He said that I now had the keys and I needed to start using them. After that, he showed up less often, and when he did, it was more in the context of just being together. Around this time, he stopped appearing to me as he looks in the physical body. Sometimes he would look like he did in his twenties. One time I saw him looking very old, and then he changed to looking very young. He reminded me that he was neither young nor old, and he told me not to get caught up in the illusion of age or death.

John-Roger totally fulfilled the criteria I had been looking for in a spiritual teacher. Over the thirty-five years that I knew him physically, his guidance helped me awaken spiritually. He is the most clear and loving person I have ever met. When he died from the physical body, I was so grateful for my inner relationship with him. I knew him best in his radiant form, which has not changed. I miss his physical presence deeply at times, but in my inner life, I still get to spend some time with him now and then.

J-R is the dearest of friends, a true friend who has transformed my life in amazing ways. My life has changed dramatically since I first met J-R, such that I now live a balanced life of peace, abundance, and loving inside myself that I once only dreamed of.

ANNIE PETERS
Learning to Listen

J-R had that knack for going to a person's level. Once in an Insight Training, I asked him a question. As he answered me, in my mind, I started grooving on the energy—"This is so amazing, my heart is so open, I love this so much!" Then I realized J-R was saying something to me, and I asked, "Would you repeat that?" And he said, "No." I said, "What?" He said, "No, you don't listen—I'm not going to repeat it."

And that was such a great teaching because listening is not my first, strongest sense. To this day, my whole life, I always have to keep working on listening—on all the levels, but even just basically not tuning out because I'm following some sweet daydream in my mind.

RUSSELL BISHOP
Awakening to the Loving:
What is Your Carrier Wave?

A few days after the first Insight Seminar in January 1978, J-R called and told me that it looked like there would be lots more people who would follow in the footsteps of that original group of 150. Would I be interested in leading a not-for-profit company we could call Insight and make these trainings available to those who might be seeking greater loving in their lives?

Let me think about it. OK, I thought about it.

The next month, I moved from Northern California and we launched Insight from a spare bedroom in the house I had rented in Santa Monica. Most days began with me driving up to J-R's Mandeville Canyon home where he would sit with me for hours going over each element of the seminar. What's the purpose of this exercise? How could we make it even better? What would happen if we tweaked this piece just a little bit?

J-R was working with me to refine the seminar so it could hold the spiritual frequencies that would help people awaken more fully to who they truly are, to their natural loving. As I would come to learn later, he was also working with me to help me awaken more fully to the loving frequency we were intending to convey to others.

As part of the refining process, J-R began co-facilitating seminars with me all over the world. What a blessing! And a strengthener.

We would often tune in to the same issue or awareness as we worked with individual participants. It was as though we could finish each other's sentences and we would seamlessly integrate our observations, questions, and suggestions. Occasionally, some-one would seem to resist what I had to share, and yet when J-R would intercede with the same observation, the resistance would melt away.

On a break during one of those seminars, J-R and I discussed the sharing we had just finished. These kinds of in-the-moment debriefs were normal, often adding additional bits of insight or awareness to our process. I later came to understand that J-R did those debriefs more for my own awakening than anything else. This particular conversation was one of those. It went something like this:

J-R: *"Russell, did you notice that Steve seemed to resist what you had to share with him and that when I shared the same thing, there was no resistance at all?"*

RB: *"Yeah, well what's your point? Of course, he got it from you – after all, you're J-R, aren't you?"*

J-R (*ignoring my cutesy comment*): *"The information was the same from both of us, but his reaction was not."*

RB: *"OK . . . and?"*

J-R: *"While the information was the same, the carrier wave was different."*

RB: *"Say some more – what's a carrier wave?"*

J-R: *"A carrier wave is the frequency on which the information flows. It's like a radio or TV station – each station broadcasts on a frequency (carrier wave). While the content or information is different from hour to hour, the carrier wave, the broadcast frequency, is the same.*

"Russell, you have the gift to perceive areas that can be improved and how to get there. So do I. However, when you offer the information, it often comes on a carrier wave of criticism.

"When I share the information, it comes on a carrier wave of loving. I don't share anything until that carrier wave of loving is present, and then I share the information.

"Not all your sharing comes on the criticism wave, but when it does, the first thing the person notices or feels is the criticism, then the information. If the person is sufficiently aware, they can rise above the criticism frequency and receive the information anyway. If not, then they move into resistance.

"They're not resisting the information, although that's just how it may seem to you. They're resisting the frequency of criticism.

"When I share with them, the first thing they notice or feel is the carrier wave of loving, followed by the information.

*Most people readily accept the loving frequency which makes
receiving the information much easier."*

As you might imagine, this sharing with J-R was illuminating
in many ways. The aspect of me that carries criticism is the aspect
that cares deeply. Somehow, the criticism carrier wave doesn't
seem to communicate caring!

Of course, I am most critical of my own self. Equally obvious,
the carrier wave of criticism doesn't work any better from me to
me than it does for anyone else.

Over these many years, J-R continues to work with me to
refine my energetic carrier waves, to access the profound loving
within. The more loving I am with my own self, the more my carrier wave of loving is available to everyone else.

JULIANA ROSE
Not Attached to Outcomes

Once I send the Light to someone, I let it go, because I'm not
attached to outcomes—it's always for the highest good.

I especially got clear on this when I asked J-R many years ago
at a PAT training if he was working with my children, and he took
a really long time to come up with an answer. I was thinking, "Oh,
my God, he's going to say, 'Those little brats—I don't think so!'" But
he looked at me and said, "Inasmuch as they allow." My children—
my daughter and my son—are not in the Movement, and that's
perfectly fine. They have, thank God, never been against the Movement or had any issue with me being in the Movement. And I've
given them books over the years. But they're not really involved.

So, when J-R said that to me, it got really clear in me not to be
attached to what happens to other people, even the ones you love
a lot and who are close to you in your inner circle—where you
really want them to have the benefit of what you think would be
good for them. So, I just let it go. I send the Light, I hold the Light,
and let it go. I'm not invested in the outcome.

NATHALIE FRANKS
Listen for the Inner Feedback

One time, MSIA President Paul Kaye's mother was hosting a dinner for J R at her home in England. I usually went there by car, but for some unknown reason, I decided to take the bus this time. Sitting opposite me on the bus was a rather disheveled character. All of a sudden, he slumped forward. Thinking he must be ill, I called in the Light, and the bus conductor was asked to call an ambulance.

Inwardly, I heard to hold his shoulders and to lay him down. I saw purple everywhere, and I sensed that he was transitioning—which he was. I kept holding the Light. Soon the ambulance arrived, and the man was taken away. Feeling rather shaken—I had never seen anyone die before—I continued my journey.

When I arrived at the house, I went straight over to J-R. He pulled me to him and gave me one of his amazing hugs, in which I sensed all of the karma of what I had witnessed being dissolved. I told him what had happened, and he said, "We needed you there to assist with his transition." What I learned from this experience is to listen for inner feedback before I move on anything, to check things out, and to lean into an action to see if it's clear.

JACKIE PETERSON
You Were All Supposed to Die

January 1, 1982, just after dark, we were on our way to Prana to drop off a wedding gift I had made for Pauli McGary (now Pauli Sanderson). Jim, my husband, was driving while wearing a seatbelt. I was in the front passenger seat, unbelted. We were in a discussion about wearing seatbelts which were not required at the time. In the back sat my 12-year-old daughter, El, also unbelted, and our one-and-a-half-year-old baby, Melissa, in a car seat that had been bolted to the frame of the car because my husband was nuts about her safety.

We were traveling in the far right "slow" lane as we were preparing to exit the freeway when I felt a jolt. The car went dark inside as it tipped onto my side, the headlights from other cars that lit up the interior vanished. My eyes went wide and my mouth hung open in shock as I heard glass breaking. The next thing I heard just in my right ear was a kind of huff and sigh as J-R's voice came through saying, "Close your mouth and close your eyes." His voice had that kind of exaggerated patience that implied, "I have to tell you everything." Being very familiar with J-R's voice and doing as he suggested, I clamped my eyes and mouth shut. I heard Jim say, "Light" and that was all I knew as inside I said to myself, "Yes, light."

My awareness was completely enveloped and totally subsumed by loving. Had I had a body to be aware of, it would have felt like being enveloped in cotton balls and down made of pure loving. My beingness was comforting, embracing, and existing in this essence of love. There was nothing else, no body, no memory, nothing but loving. This loving was tangible. It was completely fulfilling.

I felt a shock as I was pushed into my body and was instantly aware that the car had stopped upright. There were people all around the car trying to get the doors opened but they were all stuck. I knew Jim was trying to get out. I turned and hit both feet against my door as the strangers pulled and the door gave way. They reached for me but my only concern was for my children as I raced to get to them. I pulled Melissa from the car seat as Jim had freed himself and gotten El out. He was bleeding profusely from where the car roof had crashed into his head during one of the rolls the car had taken as it had rolled up onto the embankment then back out onto the freeway. Jim remained conscious the whole time and steered the car to the edge of the freeway so we would not be hit by other cars.

People wrapped me in blankets as I sat on the ground with my arms around my children. Jim took care of whatever business there was to be taken care of after he assured himself we were all OK. Paramedics arrived and one asked me if I had been knocked unconscious. "I have never been more conscious in all my life," I replied. I was still in this space where I was aware of the physical world but part of me was still in the loving and the awareness of the loving made the world seem somehow less urgent.

The paramedics wrapped Jim's head. He looked like the walking wounded with his clothing covered in blood and head wrapped in white blood-soaked gauze. He talked with witnesses.

One car drove up and the man who got out went right to Jim. Jim later shared that the man saw the whole thing. The other car was going about 90 miles an hour weaving through traffic. It was an old car, the kind with steel bumpers, and had hit us in the left rear taillight tipping the car onto the embankment. The man chased the car as long as he could trying to get the license number but the car outran him.

Jim refused the ambulance for the entire family as he knew the local hospital had a very poor reputation and instead, we went with the tow truck. We called Prana from the tow yard and a lovely minister picked us up and brought us to St. John's Hospital in Santa Monica.

At St. John's, everyone was given a room and I wandered between the rooms checking on my family. I watched for a while as they picked glass from Jim's head and examined the children. I assured everyone I was fine. I was very fine. I was still partially in this loving awareness. One nurse stopped me in the hallway and said, "I have never seen a mother so calm." I smiled.

The next day we all went to the tow yard to retrieve things from our car, including Pauli's gift. The entire staff came out to look at us. One said, "This car came in last night and we were sure no one lived. None of us can believe you are here and walking."

There was nothing salvageable. All of the glass was broken. The car had skidded upside down for so long on the freeway that there were holes in the tops of the fenders. Ivy and dirt from the embankment were embedded in the back window. There was blood everywhere.

We all went home and life seemed to move in slow motion as we recovered. About two weeks later, Jim and I were talking about the accident. I said to him, "I am so glad you said, 'Light' as the car started rolling." He responded, "I said 'light' three times." Boom!

The veil dropped and I was again fully in my body. The awareness of the loving embrace of Spirit became a memory rather than a constant presence.

The insurance agent came to visit us at home. He took a look at us and listened to our story. Right there and then he wrote us a check for the full amount of our uninsured coverage, wished us luck, and left.

Another couple of weeks and we were all going to a seminar at 2101. As we approached the building, we saw J-R just arriving. He saw us and broke from his group. When he was close, he shared, "The negative forces took a swipe at you. That's why they couldn't find the car that hit you. It was like a ghost. You were all supposed to die except the baby." He hugged each of us and was again swept up into the crowd as we stood on the sidewalk staring after him.

It took us about six months to start feeling more normal again. Jim lost his sense of humor for about a year but it did come back. The insurance money became the down payment for our first house. Blessings can come in strange packages.

NANCY CARTER
Jewels of Communication

I was new to J-R when, after many years of television and film work, I found myself editing videos for NOW Productions, which was located in the basement of J-R's Mandeville Canyon house. One evening I needed some labels, so I walked from the video room into the long corridor that connected to the audio room where the labels were stored. I was surprised to find J-R in the corridor, speaking to one of the staff members. My experience was that J-R, with sword of truth in hand, was communicating something firmly and clearly to the staff member!

At first, I hesitated, but J-R waved me through—so I picked up my labels from the audio room and passed back through the corridor a second time. As I walked down the corridor, I realized that while J-R was delivering what would ordinarily be described as a scolding, the picture that formed in my mind was of jewels dropping from his lips. Jewels!

I am forever grateful for that experience. I learned that it is okay to be direct and pointed with another person if it is warranted, but being pointed does not need to be accompanied by judgment.

ANDREA BARKLEY
I Found Hope and Faith

I was living in Phoenix, Arizona, in 1982 when I had a nervous breakdown. I was dealing with all kinds of things coming out of my unconscious and subconscious. I was hospitalized, and while there I had a spiritual awakening. I was feeling God all around. I felt that when the trees were blowing, God was waving to me. Things were cropping up that were unusual—like coincidences—and I was getting some answers to my questions. One of my questions was, "Where are my people?" And the answer was, "You shall know them by their vibes."

A year and a half later—after my recovery—I was visiting my mother in California when she turned on the cable television station, and there was a man named John-Roger speaking on a show called That Which Is. I thought, "This guy is really interesting!"—and the people in the audience were listening to him so intently—so I became interested. My parents wanted to help me, so they bought me some of the J-R tapes from the television show. Watching these J-R tapes helped me to feel better.

I decided to look into this further, and one of my first experiences was a live J-R seminar in San Diego. I found hope and faith listening to J-R, and I got educated about a lot of things—it was like a crash course in what's going on. Later I got initiated, and I faithfully attended home seminars every week in Chandler, Arizona. During the seminars, I would feel a pressure on my forehead, and there were times when I would semi-fall asleep in the middle of a seminar; these were signs to me.

Then I started taking PAT trainings, and I had interesting experiences—shifts in consciousness. J-R answered some of my questions, and I felt the memory come through. I thought, "Oh, this is real. He's pulling up some stuff I need to release, some karma." I was attracted to MSIA and J-R's teachings because I really needed a foundation. I needed a group that was going to be nurturing and supportive. I needed teachings that were reasonable and where there was freedom. In MSIA, I found a situation where a person could be themselves and learn who they are through a gentle process—or at least a process where you can learn to trust and go, "Oh, I can handle that."

MICHAEL FRANKEL
Falling in Love with the Teachings

I was in my early twenties and living in Santa Monica when I was introduced to MSIA. The first time I heard John-Roger speak was in a large auditorium—I think it was the L.A. Convention Center. I didn't go up front to meet him, because at that time I wasn't especially impressed—but I was curious.

I started going to Insight graduations for a while, and then I ended up going to a "home seminar" at Prana. When the Ani-Hu chant began and I joined the chanting with my eyes closed, I felt like somebody had hooked me up to a thousand volts of electricity. I heard this very loud buzzing sound and felt it all through my body. I thought everybody would be standing around looking at me when I opened my eyes, but instead, they all still had their eyes closed. I didn't know what it was, but I was hooked—I wanted more of it.

Even though my initial response to John-Roger had been kind of so-so, now when I went to seminars, everything he said went inside of me as, "Yes, that's true." It all made sense to me in a way that I couldn't deny. And I began to have a lot of experiences where I was definitely out of my body—I would go to sleep in the middle of a seminar, and afterward, I'd start talking about what was in the seminar. I would have no conscious memory of hearing it, but somehow it got in there.

Knowing how I was back in 1983 in my twenties—I had a tendency to idolize people and things that I liked—I think it was Spirit's way of protecting me that I never fell in love with John-Roger the personality. What I fell in love with were the teachings and the wisdom and the absolute truth of what I got inside that was being taught. And it was the kind of thing I couldn't deny— no matter how I tried, I couldn't deny the truth of what he said.

At the time I got into MSIA, I had heard a lot about how it was a cult. But what I very quickly realized was that—despite what I had been warned about—I was never told I couldn't do anything, I was never forced to give anything up, and I never signed away anything. I was encouraged to love God, to love my fellow man, to be kind to other people, and to take care of myself. It's kind of hard to go wrong with those things.

RICHARD STAMEGNA
I Was Home

One time in 1984 when I was seeing a new patient in my chiropractic practice in South Carolina, we were having a conversation about spiritual matters. He asked if I would like some information about a person he was involved with in California. At that time, something was happening in my meditations and I was tracking it to see what it was—so I said, "No, since something is going on with me right now and I am trying to see what it is and where it's going." He said, "Fine, maybe later." So, a while later, he asked again, and this time I said, "Yes, I would." He handed me an MSIA booklet. I opened it, and without really reading or seeing anything, I immediately said, "This is what has been going on with me. How strange…" Not a conscious mind event at all! And I knew, without doubt, this was it.

I found out about an upcoming event with J-R in Miami and set my sights on it. Miami is a long day's drive from my home in

South Carolina, so I planned my timing carefully. I made it to South Florida in good time and stopped at a gas station to get final directions to the Miami Convention Center. The woman there did not speak English. Time was passing. I stopped at another place, and the next person I asked for directions also did not speak English. More time was passing, which made me increasingly uncomfortable.

I finally found the convention center and rushed out of the car. I entered the enormous building, but nothing was going on anywhere. The impossibility of this is starting to paralyze me. I wandered down a hallway and saw an older man sitting on a stool. I asked him where the MSIA event was and he said, "There is nothing going on today." "No John-Roger?" He said, "No."

I was stunned into silence. I just stood there with this loud buzzing in my ears. The gentleman then asked if I wanted the Miami Beach Convention Center or the Miami Convention Center. I say, "There are two?" "Yes, indeed," he says. He gives me directions and the only thing I really hear is to go over a bridge. I am out of control, late, my brain is buzzing, and I am very upset! Somehow, I drive directly to the Miami Beach Convention Center—just as if I knew where I was going.

Inside, there was a big reception desk with people milling around. Since I was late, I walked around the desk to get to the room for the event. I opened the door and ran right into J-R, who was standing there, facing me! Now I was in shock. J-R looked at me and said, "You don't have a name tag." I said, "I am Richard," and he stepped toward me and hugged me, and everything dropped away. I have never been the same since.

The Light was called in shortly after, and then the Ani-Hu was chanted, which I had never heard before. When I opened my eyes from the chanting, I was someplace else. Home.

THERESA HOCKING
He Is Always with Me

When I was on a PAT IV trip with John-Roger in 1985 in Italy, my karma was very much with me. I was feeling emotional and discouraged. The issue I was dealing with was somewhat embarrassing, so I told no one about it or how I was feeling. Not being able to express the pain or talk about my feelings was part of my challenge.

I thought it was strange that J-R kept appearing in my path, walking in front of me, sometimes "accidentally" bumping into me in a crowd. When I was in a hotel one afternoon, I saw J-R looking into a huge mirror in the hallway, sort of fixing his hair. I kept walking down the hall, but I was laughing inside because the idea of J-R checking his hair in a hallway mirror was so out of character. I knew that his appearance was not a primary concern for him, whereas his initiates, including me, were a primary concern.

As I kept walking, inside myself I suddenly understood: John-Roger was making it clear to me that he is always with me—I am not alone. After that realization, I essentially never saw him again on that month-long trip, unless he was at the front of a room giving a seminar. This was a large group, perhaps 135 MSIA people, so he had many people's needs to attend to.

That was many years ago, and life has only gotten better since then. (And I finally did get the issue resolved!) I know John-Roger is with me, probably all the time, but I am most aware of this when I consciously connect with him. Even though his body left the planet, there is no change. He is always with me, just as he said he would be. I am blessed.

KATHLEEN FLEMING
The Light and the Energy Filled the Room

I got very involved in the Insight community around 1985 to 1986. I assisted at seminars and I took all the offshoots of the Insight Seminars, such as the Business Seminar. One time, John-Roger and Russell Bishop were coming to town to do a weekend seminar, and they were looking for assistants—volunteers to help with logistics in the seminar room.

Those who had taken the Business Seminar were given first choice of assisting, so that's how I got to be in the room. Having previously studied neurolinguistic programming, I was totally blown away during the seminar by what John-Roger could do with people in reprogramming childhood traumas and that kind of thing. The man just blew me away! At the end of the seminar, some of the assisting team who were in MSIA gifted those of us who were not in MSIA with our first year of Discourses.

The next time I remember seeing John-Roger was at a Spiritual Warrior Retreat in Orlando, Florida. When he and John Morton came in, the Light and the energy filled the room as they walked upfront. It's amazing that anybody has that kind of really loving, open energy that they can do that. I don't know how to explain it. I've experienced it many times, especially when the two of them are together. It's like the energy is not just doubled, it's increased geometrically when the two of them come into the room together.

SANDI BROWNE
Laughter Is a Powerful Healer

When I was at an Insight Super II (an Insight II seminar in which all participants are previous Insight II graduates) in 1986 in Los Angeles facilitated by John-Roger and Michael Feder, we were asked to look at what limited our happiness and our freedom. What beliefs did we hold that kept us from loving ourselves and others? Several people raised their hands, and one was called on to begin sharing. During the sharing, an old sadness engulfed me—one that had been there for as long as I could remember. Tears pushed against my eyelids, and despair seemed to ooze from my pores.

During a pause in the sharing, my hand went up, but they called on another participant—and then another, and then another. Finally, my hand shot up as high as I could reach, but Michael Feder was looking at someone on the other side of the circle. Then J-R playfully punched him in the arm and said, "Let's call on Sandi—over there." I stood up, extremely grateful to be called on, and my words faltered as I tried to communicate what was happening inside me.

"Take your time. You have all the time you need," J-R encouraged me. Half-crying, I blurted out, "I'm not lovable." Years of tears pressed on me, demanding to be expressed. Through my tears, I saw J-R stand up and begin to walk across the circle toward me, so I rushed forward to meet him halfway. He put one arm around me, and in a voice you would use to comfort children, he said, "And so…you're not lovable?"

His words nailed something in me. My mind scurried to figure out why I wasn't lovable. What came out was, "Men don't love me." J-R looked at me in disbelief and began to chuckle, "Men don't love you?" His chuckles turned into warm loving laughter— "That's the most ridiculous thing I've ever heard!" In my mind I thought, "He's right, it is ridiculous!" and I joined in his laughter. I laughed, J-R laughed, and everyone joined in as if we had just heard the funniest joke in the world. And in that laughter, I felt this giant illusion of being unlovable shatter around me, like a glass bubble that exploded, and the shards were magically whisked away. I felt free, enlarged somehow. That particular limiting belief had lost its power over me.

I flew out of Los Angeles walking freer and arrived back in Austin, Texas, where I was to facilitate an evening workshop for graduates of Insight I. I stood at the front of the room with twenty eager Insight graduates wanting to hear about the Super II and having J-R as a facilitator. "How did the Super II go? What did you learn?" they asked. I chuckled, and said, "You won't believe it. After I spent all that money for the training, the airfare, the hotel, the meals—all that money, and what I learned was to laugh!"

As I tried to explain that I had shared a limiting belief of not being lovable, I couldn't stop laughing long enough to finish the thought. My spirit-filled laughter was so contagious that the group caught it and began to join me in laughing uproariously. Struggling to get my words out, I said, "It is ridiculous. We are lovable because that's who we are."

I took a breath, curbed my emotions, and when the group calmed down a bit, I said, "So my learning from Insight Super II is that you don't need to take any more Insight trainings—just laugh." The room broke up again—heartfelt laughter that moved inner mountains. In front of me, I saw bubbles of illusion bursting like soap suds all over the room. In Super II, and in that Insight room in Austin, I learned that laughter is a powerful healer.

JOYFUL MEMORIES

PAULA BELDENGREEN
The Twaji

When I took my first Insight training, I heard people mentioning MSIA, but I didn't know what it was. Then I started doing volunteer work at the Insight office, and someone invited me to attend an MSIA seminar at the Light Loft in New York City. I agreed to go, but the person who invited me didn't show up—so I found myself at the seminar in a room full of strangers.

I sat down on a hard, carpeted bench, but I noticed that many people were getting comfortable on the floor. As I watched my first MSIA seminar, I saw that everybody in the room had fallen asleep except me. When it was over, they all woke up, stretched, and said things like, "Oh, that was so great! I got it on the other levels." I didn't know what to make of it all.

The first time I saw J-R in person was when I participated in an Insight Super II in New York. As one of only forty people in the seminar, I had the good fortune of sitting in a circle every day for five days with J-R, John Morton, and Candace Semigran facilitating, and I remember loving J-R so much. It was astonishing how much I loved him! There was a moment when somebody was sharing something that J-R turned to John and said, "That one's for you," so John Morton responded to that person's sharing. Then a little later, when I was sharing something, he said to John, "That one's for me." So that was a happy memory of sharing with J-R, and I just remember him smiling at me with love throughout those five days. It was so beautiful.

At one point, when I was sharing with him, I could feel this energy—almost like inner tubes around me—and they would come from way above my head, through my body, down, down, and into the ground—again and again, one after another. It just kept happening. I told J-R, "I am feeling this energy!" He looked at me and said, "You feel that?" I said, "Yes," and he looked away. That night, I was reading a Discourse or book that talked about the Twaji—the gaze of God. The next day, I asked J-R if that energy I was feeling was the Twaji. He answered, "Yes, that is what it was."

RON BERNSTEIN
Just Been Zapped

About a year after I left college while I was looking for a job, I started searching for some alternative spirituality, something more spiritually focused than traditional Jewish doctrine. Although I had been raised in a Jewish community, it was always missing something for me—what I later identified as the spiritual energy of the heart. I was living in New York at the time—this was in 1983—when my brother invited me to visit him in Florida where he was studying for his law degree. While I was there, I was invited to a birthday party where I got into a discussion about art with an artist named Meredith Miller. After talking about art for a while, I said, "So tell me about this dude J-R," because I had heard his name mentioned at the party but didn't know anything about him.

And that started a seven-hour conversation that lasted until about five o'clock the next morning—just sitting on the couch for seven hours, not even getting up. During that time, I went through a lot of physical stuff—energy coming in. I couldn't explain it, didn't know what it was. It was like, "What's going on here? Tell me more about this." So, there was a lot of conversation and Meredith was very patient with me and just kind of stepped me through all the stuff that was going on. That's how I learned about J-R, through that process. And that's how I met Meredith—and to make that part of the story a little shorter, I think I moved in with her the next day. I said, "Well, I can look for a job anywhere. I don't have to go back to the snow in New York in January. Why don't I hang out here?" And she agreed. Talking to Meredith about J-R during those seven hours was an awakening and it attracted me to learn more about him. I'm thinking, "Hey, this is something better than what I've ever experienced!" At that time, I was twenty-two years old so I was young and open to something new.

A few months later, I took an Insight I seminar with my brother which was fun and I finally got to meet J-R. He scoped me out in a room of a hundred and fifty people and it was obvious not only to me but to two or three people sitting next to me. It was the Twaji—he looked straight at me and smiled, turned away, and then he turned back and looked straight at me again. This was across a crowded room during the Insight seminar. Meredith was sitting next to me, and she said, "You've just been zapped." I said, "Oh, yeah, I felt that." It was like, "Okay, let's step up the energy—you're now connected. I've got my eye on you." I think that was in 1983, the same year I started Discourses.

Shortly after that, I landed a job in San Diego. I drove across the country and went straight into an Insight II in L.A. which was being facilitated by David and Deborah Allen, Liz Bixby, and J-R. That's where I had my first sharing with J-R, during Insight II. I experienced J-R as being very enlightened, and I thought, "He could be a good wayshower—I'll check this out." So, I got into MSIA pretty deep, pretty quick— took Insight I, Insight II, got on Discourses, studied for initiation, got ordained, took PATs I, II, and III. I think I did all that in two years, so it was pretty fast.

SALLY KIRKLAND
His Energy Went through Me
Like a Bolt of Lightning

In 1987, when I was nominated for an Academy Award in the Best Actress category for the film *Anna*, my first thought was,

"Will J-R go as my date?" I was given three tickets to the awards ceremony, so I invited my mother, the film's director, Yurek Boga-yevicz, and John-Roger. J-R said yes, and the excitement began.

A limousine picked us all up and I made sure that J-R would be seated on my right side so I could hold his hand for moral support. J-R was in a tuxedo, I was in a Giorgio Di Sant' Angelo black gown, and off we went. When we got to the red carpet, I couldn't believe the excitement I experienced! I went onto the red carpet with J-R and Yurek and I heard hundreds of fans and photographers yelling "Sally! Sally! Sally!" J-R told me to go and pose by myself, but we also got a lot of pictures of the two of us. I was so proud! Talking to the press, I introduced J-R as my best friend and the founder of the Church of the Movement of Spiritual Inner Awareness. J-R was the perfect date, and I introduced him to everybody I knew. Throughout the ceremony, I held his hand and his energy went through me like a bolt of lightning—it was just incredible! I felt that all my chakras were opened. While I didn't win the Oscar that night, I was very aware that I had gotten the prize of my dreams—having J-R by my side all evening.

I took J-R to the Oscars a lot. One time, I was wearing a gorgeous blue Marc Bouwer gown and when I was talking to the press, J-R said to them, "You know she doesn't have anything on underneath her dress." Omigod, I felt like the sexiest girl in the world! The happiest memories of my life are having J-R as my date on those occasions.

One day, I went to the Metropolitan Museum in New York City to look at the paintings of Christ. In the section of fifteenth-century Italian masters, I found a small painting with Jesus, John the Beloved, and Mary. I looked closer and I couldn't believe my eyes! John the Beloved was J-R—the same curly reddish-brown hair, the same eyes, the same cheeks, the same chin, the same mouth. I kept looking and looking—I thought maybe I was hallucinating! I later wrote J-R a letter asking him if what I saw was true—that he was John the Beloved. He wrote back that it was, and I received my next initiation.

WINDERMERE RANCH

ASHTAR-ATHENA
Windermere Ranch Is on Sacred Land

This is my memory of how MSIA acquired the Windermere Ranch property in Santa Barbara, California. A woman who was almost a hundred years old lived on this land that had never had bloodshed on it. It was a completely holy Indian land, and she wanted it to go to a group of people who would use it appropriately, in a sacred manner. Several people had looked at the property, but they didn't pass muster with her. When she met J R and the staff, she said, "You are the people," and she sold us the land. J-R told the woman that she could live on the land for the rest of her life.

The first thing we did when we bought the property was to drill a water well. We had a vision of building a retreat center there. We had all the drawings, including for a seminar facility where we could have trainings and workshops. However, we couldn't get clearance to use the property for that purpose or permits to build. We did everything we could to get a Conditional Use Permit, but it was not to happen. So, it was on to Plan B. At some point, we began being gifted some beautiful Arabian horses who then lived on the property, and more horses were donated over time. We also dug more wells and created beautiful ponds on the property.

Do you know what Spirit used that property for? When a horrific fire hit the San Marcos Pass, Windermere provided a staging area for firefighters and water to fight the fires. So you see, no matter what happens, God always has a plan.

FACING CHALLENGES

VIRGINIA RIDGEWAY
Know the Loving Inside Yourself

One of the interesting things about the Movement is how it stirs things up in people and the environment. We have definitely gone through periods where there's been a shake-up, and I think it's kind of important that this has happened.

For me, what I used these periods for was to check MSIA out inwardly. During those times, I would look at what was going on and hear all the stories. But what I needed to do every single time was to go inside and see where my alignment was—what was true for me, how the spiritual energy was sitting inside of me. Did it feel corrupt, did it feel like I didn't belong there anymore? It never did. So, I never felt like I needed to participate in the negative stuff that was going on during those times. I think it was stuff that only involved specific individuals and their karma.

It's like any other thing on the planet, with its ups and downs, and ins and outs. The energy here is designed to release karma, and people have the opportunity to learn what they learn. That's kind of what life is about. My general experience is that the people in MSIA are really good people. I don't always like them on a personality level, but I find that there's an intention there to be good people—to understand what Spirit is, and what the loving is, and to share that with others. And that's what I look for in people I spend time with.

Not that they're perfect, because nobody is. We had a funny meeting one time with the MSIA staff when our community in Colorado was going through a period of bickering. I was still the MSIA representative at that time, and I said, "People, I love you all dearly—but I really don't like a lot of you! And I don't want to do this negative bickering, because that's not what we're here for!" Everybody laughed, and they seemed to get it.

We may not like things, we may not like people, we may not like situations, but our responsibility is always to be loving. That's what I got from J-R—that's what he was always teaching. It's not a perfect world. There are no guarantees of anything. But what you're here to do is know the loving inside yourself and live that every day of your life.

LAREN BRIGHT
Experience IS More Powerful than Information

In the early 1980s, about 10 years after MSIA had been incorpo-rated as a 501(c)(3) religious non-profit organization and at a time when it was growing as a worldwide church, my wife and I were at a pool party with a number of friends in L.A. when the host got a phone call. He came back to the gathering looking sort of perplexed and said something was going on with MSIA and J-R. There had been some sort of meeting with key MSIA members and some of J-R's per-sonal staff people, and it looked like there was going to be trouble.

Over the next few days, rumors began to circulate about J-R that need not be described here, other than to say they involved sex, drugs, and money. One day, I had a business meeting with a good friend and client who was also involved with MSIA, and I asked him if he knew what the allegations were. He said he did, and he opened his mouth to tell me. And then he closed his mouth and said he did not want to participate in the negativity of the situation by stating and perpetuating the allegations.

Now, I am a very curious guy, but in that moment, the validity of his choice really hit me. By repeating the allegations, he would be perpetuating them or contributing to the energy around them. I thanked him for taking the position he had taken and decided I had no need to know what was being said. I could go on my own experience of MSIA and J-R, taking a step back to make sure my experiences were real for me and not some sort of manipulation I had been subjected to,

At the time, I was chairman of the MSIA Los Angeles Ministerial Board, a volunteer body supporting the nearly 2000 ministers who had been ordained in MSIA. The MSIA ministry is not one of teaching or preaching, but rather of each person identifying the ministry of their own heart and doing the acts of service to carry it out. As fate—or whatever—would have it, when I got to Prana, MSIA's headquarters that night, there was a letter from an MSIA minister laying out all the allegations. Well, so much for my not wanting to know. I read it entirely and kind of shrugged and shook my head.

At the ministerial board meeting that night, I told the board members that we had received the letter and that I was not going to participate in perpetuating the negativity by talking about it as I was convinced by my own experience that there was no substance to the allegations. I said if they wanted to have the information in their consciousness, they could read the letter themselves.

I think most of the people decided not to bother since this was not an area of the board's concern, but one member, Peter, a good friend of mine and a very pragmatic businessman, did read the letter. He called me the next day very concerned and said if this got out, it would be the end of MSIA. I hung up the phone feeling very disturbed for the first time since the rumors had started.

The concern and discomfort stayed with me, and the next week I went to Prana to prepare for the board meeting. Another one of the board members, Randy, was there and I asked if I could talk to him for a minute. We went outside and sat in the courtyard. I told him what Peter had said and expressed my disturbance. Randy listened, and then he did an extraordinary thing. He didn't address any of what I had said. He didn't try to reassure me or talk me out of my distress. He said, "You know, I remember a time when J-R..." and proceeded to relate several instances when John-Roger had demonstrated to Randy in his personal life that he was who and what he said he was—in one instance, showing up in non-physical form and literally saving Randy's life.

At the end of the few minutes it took Randy to relate his experiences, I was back in balance. And I had learned a very valuable lesson from him: That experience is far more powerful than information because it can awaken experience in others.

Because of my perceived position of being sort of inside but outside the organization structure, i.e., I did not work for the church but was an active volunteer, I started getting calls from people wanting to know what was really going on and expressing their concerns. The interesting thing is that one person would call and say, "I don't care about the drugs or sex stuff, but how could he do that with the money?" and the next would call and say, in effect, "I don't care about the money and sex stuff, but how could he do that with drugs?"

I came to realize that J-R had put himself in a position where different people's issues were challenged. Through it all, I took my lead from Randy and did not try and justify anything or talk people out of their concerns. I advised them to go "inside" themselves and check out their own experience and determine if they had received value from the work J-R was doing. It was up to them to decide how they would relate/respond to the situation.

Over time, J-R was sort of ridiculed in the Doonesbury comic strip (J-R said he was flattered to have been mentioned) and the L.A. Times ran a 2-or 3-part story on J-R and MSIA, the first article appearing on page 1. While I believe the writer tried to present a balanced picture, the articles leaned toward the sensational and, as often happens in newspapers, the negative. There was also an article in a major national magazine featuring the "scandal", instigated by the people accusing J-R.

To me, things reached something of a climax at a meeting of several hundred MSIA students where J-R and his remaining personal staff members answered questions about the allegations. When asked point-blank, J-R simply said he owned it all.

When all was said and done, despite the anger-driven perseverance of the accusers who were clearly on a mission to discredit John-Roger and bring down the church, not a single charge was brought to court. Not one. Did people leave MSIA? Sure; some of them were very longtime students and friends of John-Roger's. Even so, MSIA not only survived, it prospered.

To me, the whole process was akin to shaking the tree so whatever was loose would fall away. Those who left were not bad people. Some have retained their friendships with MSIA folks. It wasn't particularly pleasant, most of all for J-R, I expect. But, as J-R had always said, what doesn't kill you, makes you stronger. He also said a Hebrew phrase, "Baruch Bashan," which means the blessings already are. I can certainly say that many blessings came out of this period – it just took a while before I was able to see them. Nonetheless, Baruch Bashan.

JACKIE PETERSON
Spirit Will Use Anything

It was 1983 and I was very pregnant with my third child. I received a call from a friend who told me that a mutual friend, Wendell Whitmore, had left the Movement. That seemed like such a weird thing that I just couldn't believe it. So, I called Wendell and he confirmed the story. He told me that he had, indeed, left MSIA along with his wife, Susan (whom I considered to be a close personal friend), his family and others. He said that he didn't want to tell stories; his reasons were his own, and we hung up.

I sat on my bed in shock. These people were dedicated. We had spent years learning and "growing up" together and they were just walking away. I started to cry, and once I started, I couldn't stop. I didn't understand what was happening to me. I felt like I was being crushed or torn apart, and I didn't understand. My reaction was so far beyond the conversation that it made absolutely no sense to me. Finally, I gathered myself together and called J-R.

I had had J-R's personal phone number for years but had never called him. He was so busy and I just didn't have anything important enough in my life that it couldn't wait or I couldn't write. In this moment, I felt desperate. This was the one and only time I called, and it was just for me.

J-R answered the phone immediately. It felt like he was sitting there waiting for my call. He was so understanding, so loving, as I burst into tears again. I don't remember a lot about that call except that he told me that this was the start of a long thing and that I had to protect the baby I was carrying. He suggested that I not talk to people about this and let it pass by me. I felt like I was being protected and would be protected. When my husband, Jim, got home from work, I told him about all of it. He instantly understood and became very protective of J-R and our family.

Over the next few months that extended to years, there were many stories that circulated, but I didn't listen to them. I would change the subject. One friend came to dinner and wanted to tell negative stories about J-R, and my husband stopped her and told her we were not interested. She called me the next day and said that if she couldn't say whatever she wanted to us, then we couldn't be friends. I was so sad, but by then I could see that there was great negativity that was attached to these stories, and I didn't want to participate. Actually, I thought that the people who could listen to this junk were stronger than me because I seemed to be so sensitive to it that I would feel down whenever I was around it. So, I protected myself and my family by not participating, not listening.

Some of the people who left MSIA spent a lot of time attacking J-R and MSIA. They would hold meetings to tell stories and actively work to denigrate J-R personally. In 1988, there was a series of articles in the Los Angeles Times. By then, I was working in a large multinational company, and my co-workers were aware that I was part of the Movement. When a particularly long series came out, I decided to read the articles because I knew there would be questions at work. So, I surrounded myself with the Light, sat down, and read every word. I was a bit shocked that the allegations were so minor. I didn't understand what the big news was. J-R never claimed to be perfect. He claimed he made mistakes regularly. He never claimed to be celibate. In fact, I was glad that he may have had relationships in his life. That his supposed relationships may have ended badly wasn't news; it was normal human behavior. I say supposed because there were parts of the stories that I knew from my own personal experience to be incorrect or so twisted from fact to become fiction. I was there when some of the stories took place!

Then I remembered how on that first day, that first phone call, I didn't hear stories, but I was hit so hard by the negativity. That negativity was the real news and it drove the stories. I understood.

Monday morning, as usual, I was the second person to arrive at the office. My closest friend at work was always first. I sat in his guest chair and gave him our usual greeting, "So?"

"So," he responded, "I have one question."

"Go ahead," I told him, bracing myself for questions about the sex, drugs, and rock & roll J-R had been accused of.

He asked, "What's this MSIA service called an aura balance?"

The next summer, I had the opportunity to tell that story to J-R while we were on a family retreat. He threw his head back and laughed. "Spirit will use anything!" he said.

RON BERNSTEIN
A Cleansing That Needed to Happen

When all the negative stuff about J-R and MSIA was stirred up, I paid attention to what was going on and tracked the energy. I watched the people who were shifting their energy because I had some friends who left MSIA during that time. I thought of this as a natural cleansing. I watched it all and said, "I'm going to check it out for myself." I didn't see a whole lot of truth in it, but I did see manipulation going on.

There was a lot of disruption, including negative press in the L.A. Times. There was a narrow-minded atmosphere of, "We don't like it because you're doing something we don't understand, and therefore it must be bad." The whole cult idea was a big thing back in those days, and not just with MSIA but with a lot of other organizations as well. That was in the early eighties and then again in the late eighties.

I do remember one time—I think it was on one of the later PAT IV trips—J-R talked about the energy in that time and how it was a cleansing that needed to happen. It wasn't a bad thing—it just needed to happen. It was part of the process. It wasn't fun when it went on, and it was pretty intense. There were a lot of accusations and negativity. Some people just went their way and never came back.

It didn't really affect me much, because my relationship with the Traveler and the teachings was inner. I wasn't wrapped up in the gossip. If people were sitting and gossiping, I walked out. I know what's in my heart. Everything else is on the physical level and is immaterial.

ROBERT WATERMAN
It Was Reassuring

In the early 1980s, I heard about all the things people were saying about J-R and MSIA, and I checked inside to see if it made any difference—and it didn't make any difference internally. In fact, it was reassuring, which seems like an odd thing to say. It made it more clear that you're not spiritual because of your 10-percent level in the outer world; you're spiritual because of your spiritual level. So that kind of freed me up so I could relax and not be so arrogant about spirituality, because it just seemed to be two parallel tracks—not one controlling the other. Anyway, whatever went on back there—what was true and what wasn't true—was just very liberating to me.

Also, after what I had been through with other spiritual teachers in the past, this was nothing—I wondered why people were so upset. I didn't have the kind of spiritual idealism that a lot of people tripped over when the negativity happened. And the MSIA staff who came through here later seemed in pretty good shape after that—they seemed clearer somehow, I guess because it just cleared a lot of stuff out. I've always had a strong inner sense of being with John-Roger when he was going through these crises—ministering to it in some way internally.

THE NEXT TRAVELER: EXPERIENCING JOHN MORTON'S DEVOTION AND LIGHT

JOHN JURKOFSKY
Devotion

John Morton received the keys to the Mystical Traveler Consciousness in 1988, but I saw his devotion back in the '70s. He and other MSIA staff members came to our house in Pennsylvania one day to offer services. We made a wonderful meal, and we were hoping the staff would have enough time to sit down and enjoy it.

J-R was there with quite a few other people, and everybody sat down to eat—but John excused himself. He went upstairs and did an hour's worth of spiritual exercises while we were down there eating and joking around. I saw right then and there his devotion, and this stayed with me for a long time.

MARY BEARD
Authentic and True to Himself

I first saw John Morton shortly after I became aware of MSIA and John-Roger in the mid-1970s. John was a Northern California kid like I was, and had come into the Movement just a few months before me. He seemed like a normal, though somewhat shy, kind of guy and several of my friends from Sacramento knew him well. We took Insight I together, and he was going through the normal kinds of stuff like the rest of us. However, the choices he made afterward—his clarity of purpose and intention—were mind-blowing to me. He seemed to have a focus and devotion that were nothing short of inspirational.

As he grew in spiritual stature, what I loved about him was that he never put on airs. He always remained authentic and true to himself, and he shared from his "ordinariness" that was so extraordinary. Because he could do what he did, that meant I could do it too, even if at a slower pace. I will always be grateful to John for showing us that the spiritual path—upwards and inwards—begins right where we are now, right where we find ourselves, right in our ordinariness. He has helped me to see the perfection and blessings in where I am right now.

JACKIE PETERSON
He Just Doesn't Get Me

I was in an Insight Training probably in 1979. I believe it was a Service Training for Ministers in MSIA, and we were directed to do a group exercise in a circle of ten. Each of us was to stand and describe our ministry, and as the nine other ministers in the circle heard what they considered a true ministry from the speaker, they were to sit. I was speaking and one by one the ministers sat. All except one. This new guy who I had never met, John Morton. He stood and stood as I went round and round with this very active ministry. I was doing a lot in those days. I was the volunteer head of the MSIA printing department, on the Ministerial Board, raising a child, living and doing the work of living at Prana, etc. I enumerated all these acts of service, and still, John stood. Finally, we were the last two people in the room still standing and a staff member came over to listen in. He turned to John and directed him to sit. I was frustrated, embarrassed, and angry with this new guy. I thought to myself, "He just doesn't get me."

As the years went on, this judgment played out over and over. John and I just didn't click. He became part of J-R's personal staff, and I thought J-R might straighten him out about me. But still, I felt John just didn't get me.

Then right after he received the keys to the Traveler Consciousness, I had a sharing with John. He responded to my question, but it didn't seem to answer what I was asking. At the next seminar, J-R called me up and rephrased my initial question. He confirmed that this was what I had asked, and then he answered it. J-R got it, but again, I was embarrassed and thought to myself, "John just doesn't get me."

More years went by and John stepped up as J-R stepped back. All too soon, we were rarely seeing J-R. It was always John. By now, I had had a few experiences with John that were much better, but still, my belief held.

Somewhere around 2007 or so, I was the facilitator of a PTS class at 2101 and, as the facilitator, asked John if he would come and speak to the class. He said he would, and the setup was complete. I was to introduce John. Often the introduction included a little story of the person's experience with John. As I considered what I might say, it all came back to me, complete with "John just doesn't get me." I took a good look back, and finally (I can be a bit slow sometimes) I saw the Light, literally.

As I introduced John to that class, I told my story of the Insight workshop complete with my admission of my judgment of "John just doesn't get me." This time, I smiled as I said it. The story had a new ending. As I looked directly into John's eyes as he stood at the back of the room, I added, "John listened to all I was doing as my ministry but what he was not hearing, what he was waiting to hear from me was the loving. I kept talking about what I was doing. He was listening for me to put the loving into my ministry, and that is our Traveler."

John came to the front of the room, hugged me, and whispered into my ear, "That's right." Turns out, John got me all along.

ARDYTHE PHILLIPS
My Introduction to MSIA

I participated in Insight I in the mid-1980s in Jacksonville, Florida. While there, I heard rumblings about something called MSIA, but I didn't know much about it. A short time later, I found out that John-Roger was coming to Jacksonville to participate in an MSIA-related workshop led by John Morton. I knew I wanted to see J-R, so I attended the workshop.

At the workshop, I was browsing through books on the products table when it felt like a gentle magnet was guiding my hand toward one particular book by J-R, *Passage Into Spirit*. Of course, I bought that book which I later took with me to my first scheduled service, an aura balance. While I was waiting for someone to take me to a room for the aura balance, I opened the book and read the beautiful dedication. It was apparent that J-R had dedicated the book to someone for whom he had the highest regard. It read:

> *Once in a while, someone comes along who is an inspiration. This is often because of something they have done, something they have added, or even something they are going to do. Of course, this individual qualifies on all of these.*
>
> *There are, however, those rare individuals who add that something special just because of who they are. To this rare individual, I have the utmost pleasure of dedicating this book. Alas, I flounder for words to convey the thanks from this dedicated heart to another just as dedicated. Perhaps it will be sufficient just to say "Thank you."*
>
> *To John Morton*

At the very moment when I finished reading the dedication, a man walked toward me, put his hand out, and said, "Hi, I'm John Morton." This was my introduction to MSIA! Since then, it's been a wonderful, non-ending, lovely journey—for which I will be forever grateful.

CINDY NORTON
He Is the Energy! He Is the Traveler!

When I was in my early forties, there was a lady where I worked who would just not shut up about this Insight thing. She was trying to get everybody in the office to take it. Most of the guys were engineers, and nobody was really interested. Finally, when my husband was away on a business trip, I decided to take Insight just to get her to shut up. Of course, it was absolutely perfect because that particular trip, without going into the details, was the beginning of the end of my marriage. I went to Insight, and it was just what I needed—I kept thinking, "Oh my gosh!" But I was afraid of MSIA.

I remained very reluctant about joining MSIA in the beginning. I took my first Insight in 1984, and I continued taking Insight in '86 or '87 when the second round of negative newspaper articles about MSIA began. I remember my now ex-husband saying that there was something about my guy in the newspaper. I said, "Oh!" He said, "Well, it's not good." He was real happy it was not good because I had tried to get him to take Insight at a time I knew that we were probably going to split up. I had gifted Insight I to him. He went the first night and would not go back even though I was not in the training. For other reasons, I could see that the marriage was not going to last. Originally, I had not wanted it to end, and I was quite upset about what was happening. Yet I got clear that whatever it was that I was involved in through Insight, it was important that I stay in for myself, even when I did not understand it, and when I was very cautious about the cult thing.

I took Insight I three more times, and then I finally continued to Insight II, Insight III, and even USM, the university founded by John-Roger. Somewhere during that time, I got on Discourses and mailed my letter of intention to study toward initiation. Although I had an inner clarity about the importance of this path for me, I was still very unclear about it outwardly. It was like, "I don't know about all of this…"

It didn't help that a couple of times I went to events and watched some participants being pushy so they could get a front seat. I'm thinking, "What is this?" So, I just kept my distance. And yet I could tell that J-R was working with me—or John Morton. I wasn't actually sure what was happening. But I knew something was happening, and I just kept going with that rather than worrying about whether MSIA was a cult, what people were going to think, and all of that. I was feeling a connection that I had never felt before.

In 1991, during my second year of USM, there was an Insight Super II, an all-audit Insight II. I decided as part of the USM process that I was going to take this Super II, and my intention was to know by the end of the Super II whether I was going to be in MSIA or not. Inside, I was getting a sense that everything was for a purpose and a reason, and I was gaining a new understanding of love. I realized that I could have the romantic kind of love—such as when I fell in love with my husband—I could have that and even more all by myself. There was a larger love over it all for which you didn't have to look a certain way, you didn't have to have certain things, you didn't have to be in a marriage or not in a marriage, and if you couldn't have children that was okay too. All of a sudden, I realized that those weren't the barriers to love. They could be barriers, but none of those conditions was necessary to experience love. There was a higher love—a more profound experience that covered it all no matter what the conditions.

John Morton and Candace Semigran were the facilitators of my Super II. J-R was there a couple of times, and there was one point where people like me who had never shared with J-R could share with him. I didn't know what to say or what to ask. I started to ask him about making mistakes. All of a sudden, I was looking at him and I was saying that I didn't know that you could make mistakes. He just grinned at me and then didn't say anything. I'm thinking, "Well…he's not saying anything. What am I supposed to say?" He had this kind of silly grin on his face. I have come to know from my dreams that when J-R gives me that kind of look, it's like he's saying "It's not about the words. If I say anything to you, you're going to just do more words. So, I am going to keep my mouth shut, and I am going to love you through my eyes and not give you a lot of words." Part of me wanted a lot of words, but that is not how J-R works with me. What validates the experience inside of me is an inner knowing. It takes it out of the mental realm, and even out of the emotions. There are times when I want emotional validation; I want the outer experiences. And yet, that is not what my soul needs this time around. It needs to learn that it is above all those things.

I also realized that I needed to make this commitment based entirely on myself, not based on what other people in the Movement are doing, or on what either John or J-R are doing or not doing. I need to own this experience—that J-R and MSIA and John Morton not only mean something to me but that they are pivotal in my soul's journey. It is important for me to own it and do it, even if I am silent about it.

My experience in the Super II with John took me to places and experiences inside myself that I never knew existed. So, it became very clear by the end that, "Yes, I am in this. I don't care what anybody calls it, I don't care what anybody says—because what happens inside of me validates it to a level of who cares what anybody else thinks." It felt very safe, very right, and I didn't feel like I had to justify it. After that Super II, I became an initiate and then a minister—I did the whole nine yards. And I have been grateful from that day forward.

When I got initiated, I was told that John Morton was my Traveler. And I thought, "Well, everybody is always talking about J-R. How come he isn't my Traveler too?" And yet, it was perfect that John was my Traveler because he had been so amazing with me during my Super II. I mean, there really aren't any words for what I experienced. It was like he could see right through me. There was a process, a sharing about my dad, that was so tender—and one of the issues in my life about which I had carried so much grief and shame. John just held for me through the whole process, even to the point where I was so into it with him—not as a personality but with him as Spirit—that when I was done, the issue was totally complete. He was able to do that for me. I grew to respect that and love the fact that he was my Traveler. I quit worrying about whether J-R was my Traveler, or whether I got to see him, or whatever. I learned to be okay with whatever it was.

Not long ago, when I was taking a Travelers Through the Ages class, John's name came up, and one of the participants said, "Well, he's never had initiates or anything!" I just spoke up and said, "Yes, he has. I am one!" The person was just floored. This was someone who had been in the Movement since she was really young and, for whatever reason, never dreamed that somebody other than J-R could have initiates. She said, "Well, how could he? He is not J-R." I replied, "He is the energy! He is the Traveler!"

A couple of times when I wrote to the Traveler, I would write, "Dear John & J-R," and I would get the reply," John is your Traveler." I just gave in to it and let it be what it is—which for me is absolutely perfect. Through the years, I have been very, very happy that John is my Traveler. It has been perfect the way it all happened. There were times when I was taking MSS or DSS classes when John and J-R would arrive together to take sharing, and during those times I considered them both to be my Travelers. John was the one who had led me through all my initiations until a certain point. Then when I wrote in to say, "Can you take me to the next level…," the answer came back, "Only J-R can take you there." So now J-R is my Traveler too. I don't begin to understand how it all works, but it doesn't really matter to me who is my Traveler. I have learned through the Travelers Through the Ages class that some of the past Travelers have been working with me in very powerful ways as well. It is the energy of the Traveler and not the personality that is important.

LAUREN NAPPEN
Peace that passes all understanding

Stepping on the path of Soul Transcendence has been the most magnificent decision I have ever made. It has not always been an easy experience or necessarily an easy path, however, I cannot imagine a life where I didn't have the Traveler's support or love.

I have had many opportunities to be in the presence of John Morton physically that have been powerful moments of pause and then endless potential. I recall going to my first fundraiser, scared half out of my mind, the shyness factor through the roof! Having the tendency to keep my heart close to me, I wasn't sure how I could be open in front of a group of people that I barely knew. And alas, before I knew it, my name came out of the hat and the microphone was in my hand. I mostly remember trembling, as every clever thing I thought I would ask just disappeared!

I finally asked something and I'm pretty sure it was "safe," yet as I stood there listening, I felt like all my protective layers were just falling away. I stood before him for about 20 minutes and only remember one thing - he asked if I was someone who hesitated, or at minimum that is what I heard. I remember feeling confused and then it was over and people were telling me what a wonderful sharing it was! I just remember feeling dazed and confused! For some reason, the energy and judgment I had on the word "hesitation" was huge. I worked with it for months; looking at myself, how I came to decisions, how long it took me to chew on something. Eventually, whatever judgment I had about hesitating or defining myself as shy just fell away and I became more of me, standing quietly and clearly inside my heart.

The next time I was in front of John was a few years later. I was asked to introduce him at the Philadelphia fundraiser, which was such an honor and also very humbling. I had been with MSIA for several years, had taken many classes and retreats, literally diving into my self so I could fly in my soul. Learning to love bigger than I have ever imagined, learning how to let anything that isn't loving go, learning how to simply BE love has been a fabulous journey. That night brought those teachings home all the more!

There was a lot of chaos as everyone assembled in the upper room after dinner. I had a sense of inner trembling as I prepared to call in the Light, and not because I was necessarily scared; I was actually feeling so full of emotion—this incredible sense of loving and openness was flowing through me and overflowing. So powerful, so sweet, so stunning. I noticed John in the back of the room, looking oddly irritated by something, and then I just started speaking ... introducing myself, calling in the Light, and then I began to share my experience of John and how my life had changed because he was in it. After just a few words, I could barely speak, and then our eyes were locked. The rest of the room fell away—everyone disappeared and it was just the Traveler and me. It was a moment of connection, of Twaji, of loving beyond words. It was along the line of the "Peace that passes all understanding." The giving and receiving was so powerful that I can tap right into it just by sharing this—it was that profound. It's one of those moments that gets etched into the heart, a reminder of how simple it all is, even when it feels otherwise.

I love this path and what it stands for. I love the Traveler and how he shows up with every breath. I now know how to love myself and the God within me because of Soul Transcendence and MSIA. God bless us all.

CHAPTER FIVE

A NEW TRAVELER STEPS FORWARD (1988-2000)

In 1988, John-Roger passed the spiritual "keys" to the Mystical Traveler Consciousness to John Morton. The two worked closely together over the following years to continue the educational and experiential process of awakening those choosing back into their spiritual learning. In this chapter, students share stories of welcoming the new Traveler while continuing to receive the blessings of J-R's participation with John in trainings, events, and worldwide travels—and the ever-present inner teachings.

WELCOMING THE NEW TRAVELER

KAREN BERRY POWELL
A Bright White Light Was
Radiating Around John

I was fortunate to attend the celebration commemorating J-R's twenty-five years as the Traveler, which was held in 1988 in Los Angeles. It seemed to me that it was at that celebration when John Morton finished receiving the keys to the Mystical Traveler Consciousness that J-R had begun transferring to him earlier in the year. That night, inside of me, I very clearly heard J-R encourage us to love and support John just as we had done for him.

Shortly after the celebration, I received an aura balance with John. This was during the time when John was still traveling as a member of J-R's staff and doing services. We talked about various things during the aura balance. At one point, he stepped back from me with his arms at his sides and his palms wide open and said, most humbly, "If anyone is speaking the Traveler's language, I want to listen to them."

At that moment, a tremendous aura of warm, bright white light was radiating around John and going straight into my heart. It melted my heart open, and I felt that I was standing in the presence of Jesus. It brings tears to my eyes to think back to this moment. I had never seen or experienced anything like it. He was standing two or three feet away from me and there was no denying the gorgeous, loving emanation of holiness coming out of him.

I knew in that moment that John was who J-R said he was, and I wanted to honor what J-R asked of us. It felt important to give others the opportunity to experience John as I just had. I called PTS and asked if John, in his capacity as the Traveler, would come to El Paso, Texas, and give a workshop. PTS asked what class I would like, and I said, "Whatever John wants to do." Luckily, he agreed to come and facilitate a Spiritual Exercises workshop, for which we had a great turnout. As I said at the time, "Thank you, Johnny!"—for all that you do for us, and for who you are.

ASHTAR-ATHENA
A Soul the Lord Can Count On

I remember the first day John Morton came on staff, and I recognized him as a disciple from the time of Jesus. I have loved him always. I don't think I have ever met anyone who exemplifies a disciple of Christ as purely as John Morton. Many years later, we can see that demonstrated in how he honors and serves his master, John-Roger. John is a Soul of such impeccable humility and purity.

When John Morton received the keys to the Mystical Traveler Consciousness, I breathed such a sigh of relief because I knew they were safe, that you could place great trust with this Soul. Do you know how precious it is to be a Soul that the Lord can count on? To be trustworthy and faithful even unto death? That's John Morton.

KAREY THORNE
A Very Elegant, Simple Gesture

I had a dream that J-R took off a sort of cloak and placed it on John's shoulders. It was a very elegant, simple gesture between the two of them.

The next morning, a friend called to say that J-R had passed the keys to John. So, for me, it was always very clear that John was the Traveler—it was an internal communication.

WIN HAMPTON
He Brought John to Me on the Inner Levels

After J-R had announced he was giving the spiritual keys to John Morton, he brought John to me on the inner levels. He said, "This is my good friend, and he will be working with you now also. I am bringing him to you in this way so you may know the truth of it." After that, I would see John occasionally inside.

Yvonne Mochel: A Deep Place of Gratitude

Kathy Jeffares and I helped create the Travelers Through the Ages class for PTS, which was a wonderful experience. At that time, we thought John-Roger exemplified what a Traveler did. Then when John became the Traveler, we realized that John-Roger's remarkable abilities and gifts came from being such an old Soul, and not necessarily from being the Traveler. When John became the Traveler, we began to see how the Traveler manifests in a unique way through whichever person holds the energy of the Traveler.

When I shared with John during a Living in Grace retreat at Asilomar, I became very aware that I was talking to the Traveler. Whenever I stood in the Traveler's presence, my mind would go blank and I wouldn't be able to think of anything to ask that I needed help with. This happened to me when I stood up to share with John. Instead of asking a question, I was just drawn to that deep place of acknowledging the Traveler—that there's always one on the planet. How they manifest in the physical really doesn't have to do with how they manifest in the spiritual—they are that energy that anchors the highest onto the planet.

When I shared about this, it brought tears to my eyes, and it brought tears to a lot of people. I felt that Spirit came present because I shared from such a deep place of gratitude that the Traveler is always on the planet.

SHERWOOD DUANE
Spirit Stood Me Up

When John became the Traveler, I thought he was really boring. He would talk slow, slow, slow—but the energy would come in. I went to his first seminar in Santa Monica. A lot of the old-timers in MSIA thought the Traveler was J-R, that the Traveler coming through J-R did all those amazing things. And then there was John. It was like, what?

At that first seminar, I was sitting in the back of the room, and Ted Drake was sitting nearby. I was listening to John and I was going, "Well, this is boring." But the energy that was coming in was very strong. Very strong, like, "Whoa!" People were going to sleep, which I did for a very long time with John's seminars. And then the seminar ended with John saying "Baruch Bashan." I came shooting straight up out of my chair. I did not stand up—I was stood up by the Spirit. Ted Drake stood up, too. There were a few other people who stood up. The whole room did not stand up, but I was "stood up" and I've never had that happen before. It was quite an experience.

At that point, I knew all I needed to know about John Morton, regardless of what he did. I knew I was a John Morton man, and that I would support him in his ministry. If he needs somebody to be there, I'm there.

BOB STRIMPEL
An Anchor Point for the Spirit

Years ago, I stood up at an Initiates meeting and asked J-R, "Who's going to give us our initiations when you're gone?" J-R said, "There'll be somebody up here, and you'll say it's a different body but the same energy." That's really true. That's been my experience of John.

One time, around 2002 at a training in upstate New York, John invited me over to the table where he was sitting. We were talking, and all of a sudden, I looked at his eyes, and they were like "whoosh"— they got big or something. And I thought, "What was that?" It was

202 🔅 SOUL TRANSCENDANTS

like a darshan of some kind, and I knew, "Wow, that's the guy!"

I had an inner experience where J-R came to me bathed in purple, and then he morphed into John. I was like, "Okay, I got it." I may doubt myself, but I don't doubt J-R or John. When I listen to John, the energy's here. It's not in the words. It's not in the body. He's an anchor point for the Spirit. And the Spirit just comes present in the room and things start happening.

RACHAEL JAYNE
John Morton, the New Traveler

I still remember John got the keys in 1988. And in 1989, I was on PAT IV and he was there. I found it confusing in terms of there was just stuff with our relationship. And I remember being confused. But he was the Traveler.

I think John was learning how to step into it. God help him—I cannot imagine in my wildest dreams how anybody who has an ego could have followed J-R. With the amount of comparisons I run, I would have just felt like, why even get up in the morning?

I think John, in many ways, was the perfect person to be picked because of his love for J-R and his willingness to do the Ed McMahon to Johnny Carson.

I think it's taken John a while to find his own Travelership. It's really wonderful to see it. In many ways, from my perspective through this pandemic, he has really stepped into it.

Justin, my husband, came into the movement a lot later than I did, and John is his Traveler and was from the beginning. Justin has so much room for John to be John that it has really taught me. Because of my role with Insight Seminars and John being on the Board, I would get my feelings hurt a lot because of the way John would respond to me or some of the things he would say to me. It's just like there was a lot of learning in how John was working in the world and confusion over, "Well, is this John the personality who has it, you know, or is this the Traveler?"

But Justin's helped me so much in that. He has really taught me a lot. It's allowed me to just relax around John.

TRAVELS WITH J-R AND JOHN

RANDY GARVER
A Prayer from the Depth of My Being

I was fortunate to be part of many trips with J-R and John, including ones to South America, the Middle East, Alaska, Canada, China, and Japan.

At one point on the Japan trip, J-R was not feeling well because we were dealing with an energy that was very deep and very heavy. It was almost like we were in swamps and being pulled energetically. We were visiting some Japanese bathhouses one day, and I had forgotten something on the bus. When I went back to get it, I saw J-R just kind of lying there. As I walked past him to the back of the bus, I was praying from the depth of my being that God would help lift whatever this thing was off him. When I left the bus, J-R looked up and said, "Randy, thank you. That really helped me."

Sometimes we forget or don't think that prayer has an effect, but it really does have an effect. I am grateful that I was able to be so close to J-R on those trips.

MARY BEARD
Showing Me How Strong I'd Become

For many years after I met J-R, I felt very fragile. On the outside, I looked normal and in good control of my life, but inside it was as if the boundaries of who I thought I was had burst open.

I felt tender and vulnerable. At workshops and retreats with J-R, I sometimes shared with him. Though he often used harsh words with others while calling them into line, he was always gentle with me and just kept loving me into my next steps. I felt carried in his spiritual arms until I could stand on my own feet and really stand up inside myself.

Years later, in 1988, I had an opportunity to share with J-R again when I was on PAT IV. He lit into me at one point and pulled me up short. Instead of collapsing inside, I rejoiced at his harsh words. I no longer interpreted them as punishment but rather his showing me how strong I'd become. I never thought I could be scolded and find myself smiling and happy about it!

ASHTAR-ATHENA
Anchor the Living Love

When I was with John-Roger on a PAT IV trip, we were in Egypt in the court of the Sphinx at dawn. I was sitting next to J-R, and he started chanting all the different mantras for all the world religions. He said, "We're going to tie them all up together so we can go up as one group." That is what I had been working for my whole life—the vision that I had seen forever. When I was five years old, I gave my life to Jesus, to serve him all the days of my life, and Jesus said, "I want you to help troubled people find God."

That's what we came in to do in the Movement—to establish golden age education, to find some sort of technique that would open hearts, and to anchor the living love on this planet in as many venues and avenues of expression as we possibly could.

RON BERNSTEIN
Course Correction

I remember the first time J-R came up to me and said something to me personally. I was on a PAT IV trip, and a group of us were sitting around some tables in a kibbutz in Israel, talking about something that had come up during a personal sharing. J-R was listening and said, "What goes on in sharings, stays in sharings," and it made me realize that sharings are sacred. I understood that he was correcting me and giving me guidance, which was nice. He was calling me out, but he was also saying, "Let's do some course correction." When he said that, I felt a lot of energy, like a quickening of the heart. I let go of all the mental stuff quickly, because people were saying, "Just let go. Just take it and let it go."

The energy that came in was a good, heavy dose of Light that filled my body with a tingling and laughter, and then a joy came out of it. It was amazing. I don't really know how to explain it, but it's a physical feeling that also goes beyond the physical. There is a heightened energy and a greater level of awareness that comes in—an acuteness that goes with that energy when it comes in. I've had that energy many times since I've been in the Movement. Often there's a guidance that comes with it, like, "Are you on track or are you off track? All right, let's get back on track." It's never a right or wrong sort of thing. It's more about presenting choices, like, "This will provide a better path"—for your life path, or whatever the issue is.

LESSONS LEARNED AT SEMINARS, TRAININGS, OR CLASSES

SUSAN SHYNE
Accepting That You Are Divine

I had been really frightened about sharing with J-R and John Morton during the Doctor of Spiritual Science (DSS) classes. But I kept hearing inside that at some point you've got to do this. You have to stand up, and whatever happens, happens. One day, they said, "Is there anyone in the room who has never shared with J-R?" I remember that I was wearing a wool sweater that day, and I raised my hand. I stood up and I thought I might die. My mind went blank. I'm like a zombie standing up there in a wool sweater, and I couldn't remember what my question was.

While I was trying to say something, I heard J-R say, "Why don't you ask me about feeling unworthy?" So, I followed through on that. And he asked me a question, something like, "Was anybody in your family authoritarian?" I said yes. Then a follow-up question, "Did anyone in your family ever make you feel inadequate?" And the answer was yes. Then there was this whole silent thing, where I was still standing there, and it felt like the world had stopped while they were talking about other things, or John was talking to somebody else in the audience. And all of a sudden, I was so hot with this sweater on that I was burning up and I couldn't take it. I put the microphone down and ripped off the sweater, and J-R said, "Getting a little hot in there, huh?" I was just about sweating by then, so I said yes, and J-R asked me some other questions, and I kept nodding my head yes.

What it came down to was this feeling of unworthiness to be divine. Then J-R put it out to the class, "Who here has ever felt unworthy?" I looked behind me, and everyone in the class had raised their hands—all the hands were up. Then John said, "You ought to look at the stage." I turned back around to look at the stage, and both John and J-R had their hands up, too.

So, the question was, "Why did I feel unworthy?" It tracked back to my father and my family, which set up the whole unworthiness path. An entire book could be written on it, but then the whole issue was being burnt off, right then. Finally, J-R took it back around and said, "Who hasn't felt unworthy? Who hasn't felt unworthy to be one with God—which is really the question? When will you come into your divinity and accept that you are divine?"

MARY NELL JEFFRIES
You Will Be a Healer

I began studying Discourses while living in an intentional community in the Sierras. After living there for fifteen years, I moved to Southern California in 1989 and decided to go back to school to become a physical therapist. At age thirty-seven, I began the arduous task of taking night classes while working full-time. Everyone around me said it was an impossible dream because I didn't have enough education, I was too old, and I was too poor. Trusting God, I dove in anyway.

Physical therapy schools have rigorous requirements and are very competitive, but I kept plugging along. Even so, four years into the process, I was feeling discouraged and decided to take a study break to attend my first live J-R seminar. At the end of the seminar, J-R spent a little time fielding audience questions. He had just announced the seminar's close when out of nowhere a question popped into my mind regarding my recent aura balance. Totally out of character for me, I raised my hand. J-R, who didn't know my physical self from Adam, suddenly said he'd take one more question and called on me. After answering my simple question, he looked at me so lovingly and said, "I called on you because lightning shot out of your hand when you raised it. I am to tell you to keep going. You will be a healer!"

It was life-changing. J-R's message came when I was at a low ebb—emotionally, mentally, and physically drained. I left the seminar with a renewed dedication to my dream. It took eleven years to graduate, but at the age of forty-eight, I became a registered physical therapist.

For the past eighteen years, I have worked in an acute hospital setting as a physical therapist and an MSIA minister, holding the Light for patients who are often coping with depression, life-changing illnesses, and terminal diagnoses. I am so grateful for J-R's inspirational prophecy that I would be a healer, which has clearly been fulfilled after all these years.

SANDI BROWNE
He Can Do That to Me Any Day

John-Roger was always loving to me, but he could also be challenging and confrontive. At a Living in Grace retreat one year, I was standing in line waiting to share with him. He had picked a number of us from among the participants who raised their hands. I was shaking inside as I stood in line, but I kept visualizing my heart open and moving into neutrality. I kept saying inwardly, "Nothing is more important than the loving." My intention was that no matter what he said to me, I was going to keep my heart open and loving.

When it was my turn, I walked up to the microphone and said my name. I am an overweight person and had been in various stages of being overweight and guilt about my size since I was about six years old. Any training in California was particularly challenging for me since the majority of women at these trainings were incredibly cute and sexy—true California girls, including some who were movie stars. Basically, I felt like a fat slug at these trainings when I focused on my weight.

So, I say my name, and J-R looks at me and says, "You sure are fat!" I laugh as I write this, but I sure wasn't laughing then. Instead, I was trying to remember to breathe and trying to keep my heart open. I think I mumbled, "Yes," or something inane like that. I don't remember if we said something else in between or not, but J-R was on a roll. He said, "Well, one thing about masturbating is that you don't have to look good." I smiled, then laughed, and said, "Well, that's true." J-R and I—and the whole group— started laughing. We laughed and laughed. I have no idea what else we said. I had kept my heart open and I was flying. J-R and I just talked for a while, and eventually, I sat down.

Afterward, one of those beautiful gals came up to me and said, "How could he do that to you?" She made some comment about J-R's own roundness, which he was. (He used to sit upfront with his big belly and was not the least bit self-conscious. I just loved it!) This gal was fairly new to MSIA and didn't recognize what J-R's and my interchange had done for my inner consciousness. I just replied, "He can do that to me any day."

After the retreat, I didn't suddenly get slender, but illusions about my weight never had the same hold on me. Now, many years later, whenever that old pattern of self-judgment about weight rears its head, I remember the interchange with J-R and hold my heart open. Each encounter I have had with J-R and John over the years has assisted me to change my consciousness—to become more accepting of myself and more loving.

RACHAEL JAYNE
Relationships

I had a sharing with John-Roger at Living In Grace two years after I'd been divorced from John Morgan. I said, "J-R, I'd like to be in a new relationship." And he looked at me and said, "Are you ready to deeply receive? Because you haven't been."

It took me a moment, and I said, "Yes." From that moment, for about the next 12 hours, I felt like I was going to throw up. It just did not stop. Then J-R asked me about the kind of relationship I wanted. I said, "I don't know, J-R. I just want somebody for my highest good." He said, "Nah. You need to be very specific."

During that sharing, he said something like, "How old are you?" I think I was 53 at the time, and I told him. And he said, "You don't look a day over 37. I said, "Oh J-R, I love you." And he said, "Okay, 36." And we were just playing back and forth. Then I said, "So, does age matter?" And he said, "No. Physical age doesn't matter."

Someone who was at that sharing told Justin to ask me out because he knew Justin really had a thing for me, even though he was significantly younger.

So fast forward past the sharing. I did a very detailed ideal scene on the relationship I wanted. I think I covered 52 points. I was really focused on what experience I wanted to have in it. It was not about he has to have this much money in his bank account and he has to be this tall. I figured God could fill that in. I was just very clear about all the experiences I wanted to have, and how I would receive it—all of that.

Very soon after that sharing, Justin called me on the phone and said, "I really love you. Would you like to hang out with me?" I think we had been in a meeting together, a conference planning meeting. He was in charge of products, and I was in charge of the conference planning meeting at the time. I said, "Yeah. Sure. Sounds like fun." I remember hanging up the phone and going, "Did he mean go out?" And I remember thinking about Mrs. Robinson in the movie The Graduate because Justin is 29 years younger than me. And I thought, No. He doesn't really mean "go out" with me.

But we did end up going out. And I remember just having this awareness that at this point in my life, do I want to be happy or do I want to look good to the rest of society? And the answer was I really want to be happy.

Later, I had had a sharing with J-R at a Super II. He was very clear with me. He said, "Your boys may push back, but it's your time, Rachael. You know, they had theirs. It's your time." And he really encouraged me—because my three sons did push back.

Justin is four years almost to the day older than my oldest son Sean. So of course, they were like, "What mom? You're with somebody our age." And through it all, J-R's words rang inside of me.

With Justin, every single item on my ideal scene matched including I put in "the perfect age for me." I did not put an age down. Every item was in alignment with who Justin is. And still is.

I always thought that J-R's hand was involved in getting us together. I had an opportunity to share with J-R at a Best of Super II at the Ojai Valley Inn; I think it was the last time I ever had a sharing with him. I still remember it. He said, "So where is Justin?" I said, "He is working blah blah blah." He looked at me and said, "You're really happy, aren't you?" And I said, "Yes, J-R, I really am."

NANCY CARTER
Experiencing the Sweet Energy
He Left Behind

There was an earthquake in 1994 that damaged the MSIA property at 2101 Wilshire Boulevard in Santa Monica, which held offices, large classrooms, and some tech operations. As the repair and restoration work was nearing completion, a decision was made to hold a big holiday event in the building. At the time, most of the NOW Productions personnel (people working for the MSIA production company responsible for event broadcasts) were busy with the restoration. Since I was the event producer for NOW, I set about creating a program for the event.

One of the MSIA staff members, who had no idea of my background as an event producer, objected to my participation and offered substitutes of other, good-hearted but less experienced, people to produce the event. The staffer kept up the pressure until it felt like a great deal of negativity. By the day before the event, I was feeling pretty low.

We had scheduled a rehearsal for that evening, and as I was waiting for the participants, J-R walked into the room. I made my way to his side, and he began to ask questions about the event—how it was working out for me, whether the moon would rise, and the price of tea. All that is to say that we had a conversation that lasted twenty or thirty minutes.

By the time J-R left the room, I experienced the sweet energy he left behind. It was the most uplifted I had felt in quite a while. J-R had stayed long enough to clear the energy and prepare the room for all who would attend the event.

This was perhaps the first of many times that I experienced J-R stepping quietly into a situation where there was a disturbance going on. Always by the time he withdrew, healing, peace, and smooth energy would have replaced the disturbance. As I write this, tears of gratitude are in my eyes. How very blessed we are, those of us who had a direct relationship with J-R and experienced his ability to transmute negativity. I consider it part of my ministry to follow J-R's example as best I can and pass along that sweetness to the people around me.

JACKIE PETERSON
It's My Room Now

One year, I was head usher for J-R's Christmas Eve seminar in Santa Monica. It was my job to open the doors and make sure the room was filled and ready for J-R. Taking a deep breath, I centered and grounded myself, asked for the Light, and opened the double doors. The crowd flowed past me and immediately filled the three hundred or so chairs in the main seminar room. It was the most sacred eve of the year, and everyone wanted to be in the room with J-R. But the room was just not big enough to fit everyone. For about thirty minutes, my team and I checked for empty chairs, hoping we could let in a few more jubilant participants.

The line in front of the door gradually thinned as latecomers realized they would have to watch the seminar on video in one of the overflow rooms. Those rooms were rapidly filling with people who were enjoying each other's company. Christmas carols filled the air as an informal choir sang above the chatter of voices. Everyone was excited and filled with joy.

However, I still considered it my personal mission to make sure there was not a single empty seat in the main seminar room. When the sit-down music started, I continued to search, even as my team of ushers took their seats. J-R then walked to the front and took his seat. Noticing a few hopeful faces at the door, I continued to search for just one more empty seat, checking and rechecking.

Then my attention was drawn to the front of the room and I found myself looking right into J-R's eyes. In my head, I heard him simply say, "It's my room now." I looked and noticed that my aura was completely filling the room. Instantly, I sucked it in. Then I was given a gift. I was allowed to see J-R roll out the Mystical Traveler Consciousness of love like waves, one following the other, gently filling the room. The loving in those waves of the lightest, purest purple and blue and golden-white light was magnificent. I was filled with awe as I came present and experienced the joy of Christmas in a single moment.

My experience that night is an example of being connected to J-R through the inner master, which is how J-R often worked with us. Not a word had been spoken outwardly.

STORY FROM MSIA STAFF MEMBER – LIVING AND WORKING WITH J-R

MARK HARRADINE
Is This Guy the Real Deal?

When I was fifteen, I took a Teen Insight seminar in Sydney, Australia, and afterward, I got highly involved in assisting at all the Insight seminars. I was also training to be a professional tennis player at that time.

A friend I was training with invited me to an MSIA seminar, thinking it might help me deal with a rough time I was having with a relationship I was getting out of. At first, I said, "No, I'm not really interested in spirituality or anything like that." But I didn't want to go home either, so eventually, I decided to go to the seminar. At some point, they put on the seminar tape, and it put me right to sleep. I hadn't been getting any sleep during that time, so I said, "Give me every tape you've got because I need to get some sleep." I would listen to those tapes every night, and it would help me go to sleep. Eventually, I started listening to the information, and I thought, "This is the biggest lot of nonsense I've ever heard—but in a strange way, it's the only thing that's ever made any sense to me."

A few years later—sometime around 1994—I finally met J-R in Sydney at a meeting of about two hundred people. He was sitting down, and I went up behind him and tapped him on the shoulder to get his attention. He just turned around immediately, looked me straight in the eyes, and said, "Do you do drugs?" I started to answer, "No, I don't," but he continued, "No, that's not it... Your ex-girlfriend did drugs, and that energy has lodged on your back."

Well, I had recently broken up with my girlfriend because she smoked weed, which I didn't like. J-R said, "Would you like me to clear it?" And I said, "Sure." So, he ran his hand down my spine gently and found this big knot of energy in my back, and he said, "That's where it's lodged." And he did some muscle test-ing—which I had no idea what that was—winked his eyes a few times, pulled his ears, and said, "You're clear. Would you like to sit next to me, or go back to your seat?" I said, "I think I'll go back to my seat, thanks." I was definitely flipped out—but in a good way, not a bad way.

What I took from that was, "This man is the most on-purpose human I've ever met in my life. He sees negativity and clears it, and that's what he does—he's not operating where most people exist, on the social plane." I mean, he's got some wonderful social graces, but that's not where he's operating from. And more than anything, I was attracted to how on-purpose he was. I loved that, and it became an inspiration for me.

Later, as I was watching J-R on a videotape, I suddenly real-ized, "That's my life, that's my life—I have to go do that. I have to work with this man." But it was strange because I still had no interest in spirituality, which I thought was just for weird hippies. When I went to MSIA events in Australia, for example, I didn't relate to the people at the events. But I knew there was a real inner calling, so I plotted my way to get to the States. My friend Steve Ferrick suggested that a good way to get to the States was to sign up for a wilderness training with Terry Tillman, which I did. Terry lived in Mandeville Canyon, California, and I stayed the first night at his house. While I was there, he took me up and showed me J-R's house, which was also in Mandeville Canyon, and I thought, "I have to live here." It was strange because I'd never been clear about these kinds of things in my life before. It was almost like another voice, saying, "This is where you have to be."

So, after the wilderness training, I got a scholarship to attend a college in Ventura, California, and I went to everything I could that J-R was doing locally while I was in school. A year and a half later, I moved down to Los Angeles and volunteered for NOW Productions—whose offices/studios were located in J-R's basement—so I could be around J-R. I would go up there two or three times a week for about a year, and Phil Danza would have me erase old videotapes and take out the trash. I think that's such a metaphor for me getting to J-R—it's like, "Erase old tapes and take out the trash."

During that time, I may have seen J-R once leaving the house in a car and giving me a light wave. But I didn't care—it was like, I was there. And every time I'd go to a seminar, I'd say, "Oh, I'm going to come and live and work with you." And he'd say, "We'll see, we'll see." One night, I knew things were getting closer, so I called him and said, "I'm coming to the house." And he said, "I'll meet you there. I'll be there later." That night, we must have chatted until about four in the morning, and he said, "Where are you staying the night?" I said, "Here." And he said, "Well, there's a place on the floor for you," and he showed me to a bed. So, I had a bed for that night, which was Nathaniel Sharratt's bed, who was away in Chicago doing MSIA services. This was my bed for a couple of days, and when Nat came back, I didn't have a bed, so I'd sleep on the couch or on the floor.

During the first six months, it was really bizarre living there, especially since my intention was to be of service to J-R in a particular way. I was a personal trainer, so part of my deal was to get him moving physically, and I also wanted to support his organizations and help him lift them in the direction he saw Spirit taking them. But for the first six months, he would say, "Sit on it—sit on the couch and watch TV. You've had a hard life." And it nearly drove me insane, because I was young—I was twenty-four and full of energy. Before I got there, I had been working out four or five hours a day, so I was very fit. I said, "Watch TV, sit on a couch—are you serious? I'm here to work my ass off. Give me something to do!"

When you're living with J-R, there are no rules, there's no structure, there's no nothing—and you just have to find your own way. It's like being in space in terms of there being nothing to stand on. You don't even know if you're going to stay there that night or not. And it was always that way. So, I didn't know if I was there on staff or not, or what was involved with any of that—but eventually, it came around to my being part of the staff. Okay, so I'd ask, "What do I do?" And he'd say, "Do as you please, 'cause you're going to anyway." It was always like that.

Despite this lack of structure, my experience of living with J-R—being so close to him for four years of my life—was the most magical thing I could think of. It made life magical in the greatest sense of magic, putting color to the world and making life rich. More than anything, I learned that the divine spark is within— which is the Soul. As the Traveler, J-R was awakening that in us in such a way that we could catch it and grow in that consciousness. My experience is that he gave me access and keys to the Kingdom of Heaven here on Earth. I'm certainly not in it the majority of the time, but I know I have access, and I know what I need to do to get in. That's the greatest gift anyone could ever receive. And my focus is to share that gift—to be of service to people and expand everything that he's shown me.

I think John-Roger has the greatest consciousness that's ever been set upon this planet. For me to have been so close to him for so many years, it feels as if it was preordained. There's no way I could have gotten to him if there wasn't some divine plan playing itself out because I just wasn't smart enough to look in that direction.

One of the main reasons I wanted to live with J-R was to find out if he was legitimate. I wasn't going to be on Discourses and just kind of be a disciple. I had no interest in that. I wanted to know how he lived, took a shit, put his shirt on. You know, is this guy the real deal? Is he living these teachings? Or are these just nice ideas. And I learned that there's absolutely no question that he was the real deal and that he was living the truth. That can come with a lot of disguises, too—there's all kinds of human flaws in there. But the Spirit was so strong that he made it look seamless.

We would often go on night rides, and there was one time just J-R and I went for a long drive out past his old stomping ground of

Rosemead High School, and farther out in that direction. We kept going and going to where there was nothingness. I said, "What... what are we doing here?" He said, "I've got to remove an earthquake. An earthquake's going to happen." And I'm thinking, "Oh God, here we go with bullshit—you know, tell me another one." Then he said, "I've gotta take off for a moment. I need you to hold the keys of the Traveler." I'm like, "Well, I'm here to serve, whatever that means." Well, this thing hit me, and all I can say is, it just felt like I had a real sense of let's call it universal consciousness. There was no time—it was just all connected. It was really quite something—that's the best I can describe it. I certainly didn't feel very present in my body. So, he said, "I've got to move this earthquake." So, he does whatever he does, and we get back in the car and start driving.

Well, of course, I'm looking for earthquakes the next day. You know, "Where'd you move it to?" He says, "I'm going to move it to Europe; they'll be fine." I kid you not, the next day—and this could be looked up somehow, someway—there was an earthquake in Italy. And to confirm that there was an earthquake the next day, and that it was over in Europe, and that this really happened—it was like, "Oh man, who can do that?" So, that was one experience I had with J-R that just really rocked me. It showed me the power of the Traveler when he decides to use it, and I guess for some reason, I needed to experience that.

Another incident that stands out was my last initiation that I got from him, which was a cool one because I had a lot of recognition during the initiation. We were in the upper room in Israel, and it was a transcendent moment where it felt like the whole roof had come off. I was seeing things that went on back in the time of Jesus that were amazing. When you're around J-R, you can be transported in consciousness into the future, into the past—it's a built-in time machine, spiritually.

His ability to read the Akashic records and do all that work of clearing was always combined with being practical. Practical spirituality is really what he's about. There's a lot of hocus-pocus that we could have gotten into, but he would never do that. He wouldn't go looking into the psychic worlds for the fun of it—

simply to exercise that ability—because you can just create karma there. But we would certainly go there to clear things when it was necessary. J-R has always taught simplicity and practicality, and how to live here as a spiritual being.

At that time in my life, I was interested in the world and world politics, so I asked him one time, "Why don't you be president of the United States?" He just looked at me, and he says, "Why would you want to demote me?" And I thought to myself, "Whoa!"—because that's considered probably the most powerful position in the world. He says, "As far as I'm concerned, it's a jail."

One thing J-R would often say is, "I wish my thoughts would leave me alone." And I remember saying to him, "I wish my wants would leave me alone." Then I asked, "J-R, what do you want? Don't you have all these wants?" I knew he really didn't want for much, because anything he really wanted, he would manifest and someone would deliver it to him—he's pretty swift. But he said to me, "Mark, you think you've got a lot of wants. Imagine wanting six billion plus Souls to go home." And I just went, "Whoa." That kind of tired me out—imagine wanting six billion plus Souls on the planet to go home. And the truth is, that's probably a small part of his wants, because, as the Preceptor Consciousness, he's playing on so many levels. I felt like he took Jsu (Garcia, another staff member) and me into a lot of those Preceptor places, which were really remarkable. I mean, that's real high country—to have that level of consciousness working in so many universes. There's so much that the Preceptor is aligning and continues to align, expand, and grow on so many levels.

What J-R has shown me is that, in a strange way, this life is heaven, that heaven is right here. It's just a state of being, a consciousness. I find it challenging in the world to live there all the time, but J-R certainly demonstrated living there a lot—even all of the time. I don't think he was ever out of it. The only thing that would get him was when he got really sick, he'd get irritated sometimes with the sickness and the pain. He was in tremendous pain, and how to manage the pain was tough on him. So, we—us staff guys—would do our best to support whatever he needed.

There are many J-R quotes from seminars that are well known, but there were also many quotes for staff that we used to talk about. He had some sayings for us that would absolutely leave me in hysterics. And no matter how angry J-R could get, there was no real anger that would come at you. Usually, when someone gets angry at you, you can feel their rage. I never felt that with him. Always the loving was behind it, so no matter what he said in words, the frequency would never hit me. Those little sayings he would have for us could become absolutely hysterical. The one to always watch out for, though, was, "Do as you please because you are going to anyway." That meant hell's about to show up. So, if you say, "Hey, J-R, I'd like to go do such and such," and you get told, "Do as you please, because you are going to anyway." That's when you know to be wary—that you'd better watch out.

My experience with being with J-R was that he's a lot of fun. He's funny—I mean, hilarious—and the greatest noise for me in the whole world is J-R's belly laugh. If I'm having a bad day and I think about that, it turns into a great day. Just to hear him really wail is just so much joy, it's really quite something. The other thing is his immense power. He has tremendous brute strength, physically. I would wrestle with him, and he could pin me and put me in a hold when I was twenty-five and strong, and he was in his sixties. He just kicked my ass. But there was immense power in his beingness. Everywhere we went I always felt completely safe.

I always felt like he had Jsu around for the humor. I think of Jsu as the court jester. Jsu really doesn't have a lot of filters, so J-R's interactions with him would sometimes get really hilarious. They were like two ten-year-olds who would just play together, and it was really sweet to watch the love they had for each other, the joy and the playfulness. They would start doing such stupid stuff that it was hilarious, and we could laugh for eons.

Every day with J-R was hilarious. But part of that, too, is that he could be extremely funny and witty in one moment and then real serious and blow up at you in another moment. Things could switch like that around him real fast. When I first started living with him, he said, "Hey, man, living with me is like living with a volcano, and it's going off most of the time. It gets really hot."

And that's really true about him. There was no real solid ground to walk on around J-R. The Spirit was demanding of him and it was demanding of us. He's following Spirit, and we were following him. But even with the uncertainty of it all, living with J-R always brought me joy.

I can't think of a life without J-R. I just don't know what it would be like. J-R showed me not just the world—he showed me universes. When you know J-R, you're no longer a civilian. You know who you are, and it forever changes your life. It showed me that anything is possible, and it showed me the road map for life—what life is about—that this level is important because it's all one. You take care of yourself first, so you can help take care of others. But the spiritual magic he possesses and shares—and what I see in the initiates today—just puts you on a different playing field from most people. The key thing is the magic and the infinite possibility of what's taking place because we're co-creators with God. And we can paint our own paintings here, which is our life—the actions we take in our life.

There are so many teachings in so many areas that he's tapped into in that multi-dimensional consciousness, and that's why I think he's this greatest consciousness that's ever lived. And I think what he's done in this lifetime, in this body, is plant seeds for the future. I think he protected himself and the teachings while he was alive by avoiding too much notoriety. He's not that well known, relative to who he is. Most people would say, "How come I haven't heard of J-R? He can't be that great if I haven't heard of him." I think he's done that in a real divine way. I think he has protected the source of the teachings while in the body and left it up to us to continue the work.

STORIES FROM MSIA COMMUNITIES OUTSIDE OF CALIFORNIA: LIFE IMPACT

DONNA COOK
Like Two Old Friends

I was fortunate to meet John-Roger personally on one occasion, and it was a life-changing event for me. It was the spring of 1992, and I had been ordained as an MSIA minister in Washington, DC, just a few years earlier. At that time, J-R and his staff traveled from California to the East Coast once a year, doing seminars in Washington, Philadelphia, and New York. This was always an exciting time for our MSIA community in Washington because seeing John-Roger and hearing him speak at a live seminar was a rare and special treat.

When we heard the dates for the East Coast tour, my husband, Don, decided we should invite J-R to our home for lunch while he was in town. I laughed and said, "Why don't you invite the Pope while you're at it!" But Don insisted we had nothing to lose, and "he might just come," so we sent an invitation to J-R through his secretary, Betsy Alexander. When J-R wrote back that he accepted our invitation, Don and I were ecstatic. I could hardly believe it! J-R was coming to our home. This was such an extraordinary opportunity.

We spent the next few weeks in preparation and anticipation. When the day finally arrived, I watched out the front window as John Morton and other staff members got out of their cars and strolled up the sidewalk to our home. I was impressed with how slowly and deliberately each of them walked, appearing so peaceful and present in each moment. I stood on the porch and greeted each one with a hug and a warm welcome. Then I saw John-Roger, the last to appear. He was wearing dark sunglasses, and as he approached, with no one else around us, I suddenly became nervous. Time stood still, and I started babbling trivial facts about the town we lived in. I felt like I couldn't control what seemed like mindless chatter.

J-R just stood there, silently looking at me, until I finally stopped babbling. After a moment, I softly said to him, "I can't see your eyes." He lowered his dark sunglasses and gazed into my eyes with a smile on his face. I immediately felt tremendous loving and upliftment. With our eyes locked, we shared a lingering smile, and then J-R broke into a grin as I escorted him into the house.

In the East, they have a word for this, called the Twaji, which is a spiritual transmission that passes through the eyes of an enlightened one. I don't know if what I experienced was the Twaji, but from that moment on, I felt relaxed in J-R's presence. He and I conversed freely, like two old friends, for the rest of the day. After a pleasant lunch, J-R joined Don and me for a tour of our house, where we talked and laughed together. I knew I had been blessed by the Traveler, and my heart was opened to his unconditional loving. It is now twenty-five years later, and the memory of that close encounter still opens my heart and fills me with gratitude.

PAULA JENKINS
The Same Information and Blessings

I was introduced to MSIA in 1994 when I was living in Steamboat Springs, Colorado. I wrote to J-R shortly thereafter to ask him to work with me towards Soul Transcendence, and a year later I was ordained as a minister.

I was disappointed when I first learned that J-R was gradually stepping down. However, I was pleased that John Morton had been chosen to be the next Traveler, even though I didn't know much about him. Although John's audiotapes were starting to come out, I still preferred the J-R tapes.

While attending an MSIA ministers meeting in Albuquerque, New Mexico—where I had moved in 1997—I had an unusual experience that I've never forgotten. At the meeting, we decided to listen to the newest John Morton audiotape. I wasn't too happy with this decision, because I was more interested in listening to J-R's tapes. However, we soon settled down, chanted for a while, and then played the tape. As I heard John's voice, I remembered the teaching that there are no mistakes. If this is what I was meant to listen to, there must be a message here for me.

After the tape ended, the meeting was opened up for comments from the group. When my turn came, I said, "I was surprised by this tape, because It's always been my experience that seminar tapes are either only J-R or only John Morton, never both of them on the same tape." I noticed everyone looking at me curiously, and someone asked, "What are you talking about? What did you hear?" I casually answered that the tape started out with John Morton's message to us, then J-R talked for about twenty minutes on a variety of topics, and then the tape ended with John Morton.

The funny thing is that it turned out the tape was 100 percent John Morton, and it was about forty minutes long. Everyone with me in the room heard the same tape, and they all kept asking me, "Are you sure you heard J-R?" I said, "No question in my mind. I heard J-R for about twenty minutes, and then when I mentally came back into the room, I heard John Morton summing things up." To this day, I still can't say exactly what J-R talked about on that tape.

The lesson for me that day was that I could rely on John-Morton as the Traveler in the same way that I relied on J-R. The experience confirmed that I would receive the same information and blessings from the Traveler whether I listened to John Morton or J-R—the Traveler speaks through them both.

SUSAN JACOBY FRYE
Participate in Things That Give Me Joy

I was about twenty-eight when I took a train from Philadelphia up to New York City for my first Insight training. J-R was one of the facilitators. It was a very impactful training, and I felt like I came awake in it. I came awake to the experience that what I had kind of sensed could be happening in life—how I had sensed that people could be together was actually true. When I hugged J-R at the end of the training, I had an inner experience that I hadn't anticipated at all—there was a fragrance… It was a very awakening experience. So, that's how I met him. And there was something that was touched beyond words about his presence and his loving. I later went to an MSIA showing of *Brother Sun, Sister Moon* in Philadelphia, and I remember being in the lobby and noticing people hugging in a way I hadn't seen before—it was almost like "Wow, this kind of loving can really be manifested on the planet!" So, I studied in MSIA and was eventually ordained.

I was pregnant when I was ordained, and my first husband and I split up during that time, so it was a very intense, deep time for me. The guiding light that helped me through that period was the sense of home, the sense of love, and the sense of knowing that I had through studying with J-R. This was the center that has carried me ever since through everything I've been through. It's like I was shown the essence of beauty, love, and knowing—the essence of life, where we connect.

Later, I moved to California. I remember sitting in many seminars, and J-R's face would just be like home. And there would be the knowing of that back and forth, and I would feel like I was looking at myself, and know that he was looking. There would be a oneness, and everybody in the room was part of that. So, I just felt blessed, at home, and very aware of the privilege of being in this time and this place now.

When I first heard J-R say, "Not one soul will be lost," it absolutely rang true for me. Many of the teachings in the Discourses were like the nectar of truth when I read them. And my understanding would change over time. Sometimes I would come back later and find, "Oh, this is a little different." But I have been guided and helped by the basic teaching that earth is a school, and we're here to love and wake up in the loving that we are—that everybody is doing this, and that when we look in someone's eyes there's that life connection that we all share. Everybody is on this path in their own perfect way. It's helped me when I take responsibility for my life and see that the things I've been given that are challenging in my life are perfect.

For example, years after I moved to California, I got cancer, and it was pretty serious cancer. It was awakening in the sense of, "Okay, you're not exempt from the things that everybody goes through, and this is one of them." So, that was a powerful experience for me to learn from. I also learned to pay attention to what works for me and what gets me past my unconscious or my resistance. I discovered that for me, it's joy—participating in the things that bring me joy.

I was going through the most intense cancer treatment available at the time. My doctors were considering a bone marrow transplant but instead opted for chemotherapy and radiation. Each time I went into a radiation treatment, J-R and Jesus were with me, and I would say, "I meet the energy of this radiation with love." I did it as a prayer.

In the middle of the treatments, I had a chance to go to New England to visit my daughter at college during the winter. Because of my blood counts, I was supposed to rest and not travel. But I was determined to go, so I went with my sister. It was snowing—and it was also joyful. I had no hair, but I wore a cap, and we danced contra dances and went sledding. I had a wonderful time!

When I came back to California, my blood count levels weren't worse—they were better. So even though my doctors had warned, "The stress of travel might knock you back," it was the opposite. I learned through that experience that it is nurturing and healing to participate in the things that give me joy.

Part of what the cancer was about was learning how to more deeply nurture myself. That's one of J-R's teachings that's been very important to me: "Take care of yourself, so you can help take care of others." Also, "Fill yourself up and let it overflow to others." The first time I had chemotherapy I arrived with a lei of flowers around my neck, as if to say, "I'm going to have fun with this, no matter what." It wasn't always fun in that chemo chair, but I could always go inside and find the joy, the kernel of joy. It was like a part of me was testing, "Can I find this even now?" And I discovered that the Traveler is always there inside me.

SUELY PENHA RODRIGUES
Forgive and Ask for Forgiveness

I am Brazilian, and I had my first inner experience of J-R when I was living in Brazil in 1982—even though I had no conscious knowledge of J-R or of MSIA as an organization. (That didn't show up until eleven years later after I had moved to Chile—which is when I heard about MSIA and signed up for Discourses.)

Although I didn't know about J-R physically during those early years, I began to more vividly experience his guidance in my dreams as well as when I was awake. This inner guidance prompted my decision to move with my family to Santiago, Chile, in 1989 for work. J-R's guidance was invaluable to me as I made crucial decisions for myself as a single mother. I had two children under the age of ten, and I was also supporting my own mother, who was helping me raise the kids.

I felt J-R's presence helping me in many ways, from practical decisions about how to manage our life in Chile to coaching me through specific healing exercises. For example, during this time I was diagnosed with a generalized infection, which became quite serious. I was unable to function and was confined to bed while receiving the care of three doctors, who were puzzled by my condition. I went from dealing with one infection to another as I felt my life slipping away.

Feeling close to death, I started reaching out to God and more deeply surrendering in my prayers. One night, I was guided through a process of forgiveness. I was asked to "forgive and ask for forgiveness" while I watched a long line of people with whom I needed to clear something—one at a time. I completed this forgiveness process during the night with each of the people in the line, and at the break of dawn, I finally had the strength to get out of bed to meet my two children. They looked at me as if they were staring at a ghost since I had been lying in bed for the past three months. That process of forgiveness healed me completely. In a few days, I recovered my lost energies and went back to my normal life.

In 1993, four years after moving to Chile, I overheard someone's conversation about Insight Seminars. One of my team members at the office had missed a business meeting because of being in a training. When I was told about this particular training, it immediately resonated with me. I knew this was exactly what I was looking for, and I proceeded to do further research. One week later, I took Insight I, followed by Insight II and III, and I assisted at every subsequent Insight seminar that year.

In January 1994, I registered for the first Insight IV in Santiago, Chile, when Alex Padilla was the Insight director for Latin America. At that time, being on Discourses was an Insight IV prerequisite, so I decided to subscribe to Discourses. When I finally had the Discourses in my hand, I was certain that I was in contact with my Inner Master. Then when I saw John-Roger's photo, I recognized that he was the one who had been talking to me for the past eleven years.

My Quest in Insight IV was to bring Insight Seminars to Brazil. I was able to enroll numerous people at a reduced tuition of $100, which Alex had suggested to get the ball rolling in our country. The first Insight Seminar I organized took place in Campinas, São Paulo, Brazil, in 1996—two years later.

When J-R came to Rio de Janeiro in April 1997, I had my first physical contact with him through an unforgettable hug, which was wonderful. And although my most intense contact with J-R always happened spiritually, the familiarity I experienced through this hug was a confirmation that we had been connected since 1982.

I'll let you in on a little secret. When I first experienced J-R in 1982, he appeared to me in white Hindu robes and a turban. We walked together in green fields of an intensity I'll never forget. He remained with me all night, but the only message imprinted in my memory that comes up for me to share is when he said, "The one you seek as your companion is not here on this planet."

INSPIRING MOMENTS

GABRIEL JOHN MORGAN
You Need to Do This

To say I'm familiar with the teachings of MSIA is an understatement. I grew up in a household where getting caught eating onions was like getting caught having sex for the first time as a teenager. In my perception of spirituality, the teachings of John-Roger are not only what I've been brought up to believe, they are the only teachings and practices that make sense to me. Ultimately, the only true experiences I've ever had correlate with the teachings of John-Roger, and to me, experience is everything in spiritual practice.

The first memory I have of John-Roger was at Windermere, a ranch-like property in the Santa Ynez Mountains above Santa Barbara, California when I was in my father's arms. J-R is my godfather, and he was talking about how special a kid I was, saying a lot of mumbo-jumbo about me I didn't understand—but he did it in an encouraging way, which felt good. I would see J-R many more times, and every time I saw him, I felt special—even one time when I misunderstood a joke and got offended. He found me, held me in his arms, and spent ten minutes telling me how special I was and how much I was loved. That's a friend I wanted; someone who would do that.

The first time I really understood that the teachings of John-Roger were for me was in my darkest year on earth, during seventh grade. I was without friends at that time, and I was bullied by the other kids at a private school that taught peace and love (go figure). Verbal abuse became emotional abuse, which became mental abuse, which became physical abuse. At the peak of all this, my parents got divorced, and I had to accept my mother and father dating other people, which hit me hard. Nothing was easy for me that year—no hope was achievable.

I began to abandon my belief in God, and shortly after that, I abandoned my belief in life. I attempted suicide by grabbing my mother's prescriptions and anything I could get my hands on. It didn't work—but it certainly caught my mother's attention, who sent an e-mail to my godfather, J-R. Within an hour, she got a call back. She then called in the Light and handed the phone to me. I don't remember much of that conversation now, but I do remember having hope for the first time in a long time. I only remember J-R telling me one thing, which resonates to this day: "Life's too short to quit early. You've got a long way to go, Gabe." That was the first spark of my spiritual belief. For the first time, I truly believed there was something listening. I had no concept of outer or inner, but I knew something was listening—and I knew that J-R had something to do with it. That was the first spiritual belief I ever had. I came out of that year a different person. In a way, I became a man. I lost my innocence, but I gained a sense of spirituality. Throughout all the muck and mess, I knew something was listening.

Throughout my childhood and adolescence, I would have these random experiences with J-R, my godfather. For example, I never understood the invisible barrier that seemed to keep people who were trying to see him from… well, seeing him. I never found any issue with walking up to him, giving him a hug, and talking to him about random stuff. To me, at the time, he was a friendly guy with a grandfatherly aspect who would say the right thing at the right time.

A great example of this happened when I was eight years old. At the MSIA Conference dinner, I went on stage and performed "Baby, You're a Rich Man" by the Beatles with my dad backing me on guitar. This was the first time I'd ever gone on a big stage and performed anything, to my recollection. Upon finishing, I didn't know what to think. What was going through my mind was, "Okay, I walked up there, I sang, people got loud, I walked offstage, and now I'm sweaty."

My dad had disappeared and I was on my own, kind of petri-fied. The first person to see me after I performed was J-R. He was alone (which wasn't usual for him) and he power-walked right up to me. I thought I was in trouble or something—or maybe my fly was down. When he reached me, he put his hands on both my shoulders and said, "You are damn good at this, kid, and you need to do this." He then walked off as if I was just a stop along the way to something else. I was in shock, but I got it. I have been performing music on stage and in many other settings ever since. I have the wise man who approached me after my first performance to thank for that.

A key part of my spiritual upbringing throughout adolescence was forgiveness. However, I have to admit that I am terrible at forgiving people—I have very strong emotions and an excellent memory. The first nonfiction book to truly have an impact on me was J-R's *Forgiveness: The Key to the Kingdom*, which taught me the value of forgiving and letting go of the pain I held onto for so many years. Many people had tried to convince me to forgive my family, my past enemies in seventh grade, and myself, but J-R's book somehow bypassed the mind and hit me on every level—enough so that I was able to forgive and let go of a huge amount of resentment and grudges.

What really defined me, as a man, was the first time I went to Tanzania, Africa. It was my first chance to live all that I had learned from J-R's teachings. My trip to Tanzania was through Teen Insight, and my experience there was diametrically opposed to what I was used to in the United States. Here we are defined by our posses-sions, our successes, our morals, and our upbringing. There we are defined by who we are as people, how trustworthy we are, and how many people we have in our lives that we can call friends. The purpose of my trip was to be of service to kids and teens—and ser-vice is a key quality of John-Roger's teachings. Growing up, I saw the service J-R provided for many people, both in and out of the Movement. Being in Tanzania taught me how to be the best man I could be, and J-R's teachings were a great support for me.

Over the years, I started to see less of John-Roger. I'd see him at big events, only really to say hi and tell him I love him, as I've always done. What I found interesting was that the less I saw of John-Roger, the more I delved into his teachings. I think this is because I had more capacity to understand the greater picture as I grew older.

One theme in my life—more of a code that I live by—is completion. I always wanted to complete the things I started, and I would never quit until I did. This was something I felt almost obsessive about.

I finally came to a point in my life where I was ready to be a minister and an initiate of the Traveler. I was cleared to be initiated and ordained on the same day—on the morning of the last day of an MSIA conference. I remember showing up to get my initiation and not thinking much about it—feeling calm about it, expecting it to be a routine event. However, something happened during my initiation that was like getting the biggest slap in the face that I could've received in that moment. I felt thrust somewhere else entirely, and whatever I did physically was on autopilot. I don't even remember leaving the room where I was initiated. When I went to the next room to receive my ordination, I don't remember seeing anything more than a fog and an aisle, with a chair in the middle. I sat down—still not really there—and a bunch of stuff happened, and I was still not really there. Then I heard J-R's voice saying, "This is a blessing of completion for you." That's all I remember hearing, and that was all I needed to hear. Listening back to the tape later only provided further confirmation. This blessing hammered in the final nail. It confirmed that this is what I was meant to do. I was home, and I was here to complete this so I could truly go home.

Two years after I was ordained, I received the shocking news that John-Roger had died. I knew J-R wasn't in the greatest of health, but I didn't know the death of the physical body was even close to imminent. I couldn't describe the emotion I was feeling. It was a mixture of sadness, relief, depression, frustration, serenity, calmness, and shock. These feelings would stay with me for the next two months. I cried briefly, but it was never a predominantly sad event for me. I had known J-R wasn't well, and I knew he had been spending most of his time on other levels than the physical for a year or two leading up to his death. Still, the news of your godfather, spiritual teacher, and friend dying doesn't come lightly. I still miss J-R, but only physically. I'm very much in his company in Spirit when I leave my body. It has been John-Roger's teachings that have given my life a direction and a purpose, and it will be John-Roger's teachings that bring me back home.

CHAPTER SIX

THE PHYSICAL AND SPIRITUAL WORLDS (2001-2018)

These stories highlight the practical nature of the Traveler's teachings in this physical world, as well as the profound process of Souls transitioning from the physical into the spiritual worlds. J-R's passing into Spirit in October 2014 evoked powerful emotions—sadness that he is no longer among us physically, gratitude that he is still present with us spiritually, and joy for him that he is now free of the physical body.

At this time, both old and new students in MSIA expressed a deep gratitude and love for John Morton as he continued to anchor the Mystical Traveler Consciousness and spread the Traveler's teachings across the planet.

PRACTICAL SPIRITUALITY

ANNIE PETERS
Repurposing Energy

In my consulting business, I specialize in developing systems and policies to reduce, reuse, repurpose, and recycle waste materials. This is a field that didn't even exist when I was growing up, so I've gotten to be a bit of a pioneer, and it's been so enjoyable. I used to think that I should have a job involved with healing—doing something like what MSIA staff do—but then I realized that when I follow J-R's teachings to validate my experiences inwardly, anything I do is God's work.

J-R has often described what he does when he lifts karma from his students as being the garbage man taking out the garbage—and I feel a deep affinity with that. I even told him once at the end of a sharing, "Well, I work with garbage, J-R," and he just chuckled. But that spirit of completing karma and wrapping things up is what we do in MSIA when we work toward fulfilling our responsibilities.

When you throw something physical away, you think you're completing it, and yet that item may still have value. It may have worth. By ensuring your unwanted discards are repaired, reused, recycled, composted, and/or repurposed when you part with them, you are moving things to their next highest level and respecting the positive potential inherent in the material world. You are also conserving energy in the universe by lessening the energy it takes to make new stuff. The care you show towards your trash is a spiritual practice. Just like I try to take my sorrows, misunderstandings, or hurts and transform them through self-forgiveness, that unwanted negative energy gets repurposed by the profound act of God's forgiveness. And there's no loss of energy in the universe. I was listening to a J-R seminar today where he talks about that. So, while garbage and trash is the most mundane, most basic stuff you can deal with, recycling and repurposing garbage is a beautiful metaphor for what we're all here to do on this path.

JOYCE EVANS
Replace the Roof and Move On

I was living in Aspen, Colorado, in 1979 when I first heard about J-R. I was in a relationship that was not particularly satisfying to me, and my work was not stable. I felt very unsettled inside. There was a woman at the gym where I worked out who kept talking to me about Discourses. Paying $100 for Discourses was out of the question because I was barely hanging on financially. However, I did manage to come up with the money to take an Insight seminar, and it was through Insight that I got into the Movement. In the Insight seminar, my heart opened in a way I had not expected. As a result, I decided to take a PTS class called "The Traveler in Your Dreams." I couldn't resist the value of what I was learning, and I soon found the money to subscribe to Discourses. I never looked back.

In those days, Discourses were mailed out monthly. I saw right away that whatever the topic of the Discourse I was reading manifested in my life. I couldn't wait for my Discourse to see what kind of experience I was going to have. I loved the mystery of it all, and I loved the little MSIA community in Aspen. When I received my first Discourses, I had the opportunity to declare my intention to study them toward receiving initiation. My MSIA friends were very clear with me: "Write the letter to J-R about initiation."

I was attracted to the idea of initiation but didn't know what it meant. I didn't know what I would be getting into, other than I was deeply attracted to it. This was all so magical and mysterious to me, and I loved it. But eventually, I took their advice and wrote my intention to receive initiation.

Then there was ordination. It took me a while to decide to request ordination. I didn't think I was spiritual enough to get ordained. I thought I had to have some grand ministry in order to get ordained. But then what I kept thinking about was marrying couples. I kept seeing myself officiating at weddings. It just seemed so sacred to me. Within six months of getting ordained, sure enough, I started officiating at weddings. It wasn't something I pursued, but rather it came to me. I still love working with couples, writing ceremonies, and officiating at weddings.

A few years ago, I was deeply challenged. My husband made a poor business decision, and we were faced with huge legal bills, a collapsing economy, losing our business, and his going to prison for a couple of months. I had no idea how I was going to pay our mortgage and manage our living expenses—never mind my embarrassment about my husband going to jail. I had to completely surrender, accept our situation, and trust in the Lord.

During that time, I found strength in the teachings of MSIA. Individuals in the MSIA community came forward with such loving compassion and money. I was given enough money so that I could manage what I needed to handle. I realized then that a deeper prayer was being answered through this crisis in my life— that I would be able to handle whatever I needed to handle in the world. Growing up, I had been afraid of the world. Now I realized that I had just faced everything I never wanted to face and I had survived—and even thrived, spiritually. I believe that all challenges are actually prayers being answered.

A couple of years ago, we moved to a small town in Arizona and bought a fixer-upper house. If something could go wrong with it, it did. I remember when we learned that we needed to replace the roof, which was quite expensive. We hadn't budgeted for this, so we were upset and supremely bummed.

I decided to go over to the house to do some painting, and while I was painting, I turned on a J-R seminar tape to listen to. The first thing I heard J-R say was, "If you have to replace the roof, replace the roof. Do what you have to do and move on." I stopped everything and started laughing. I told my husband about it, and we were both blown away by the perfect timing of J-R's statement. Our feelings of despair were totally replaced by aware-ness that the Traveler was guiding us. We happily replaced the roof—which was a good thing, because the monsoon season that summer brought record-breaking rains.

I love J-R and the teachings. I love that sacred feeling I get when I listen to a Soul Awareness Teaching (SAT) recording, read a Discourse, do my S.E.'s, and avail myself of events such as Living in Grace. I believe that it's my deep desire to go home to God in this lifetime that truly keeps me engaged. The teachings are very alive in me. I see what happens when I send the Light to someone or a situation—how the Light touches people in the most mag-nificent ways. I have had out-of-body experiences, and I know that what J-R talks about in Discourses and on SATs is true. MSIA is the single most important thing in my life, and I am deeply grateful that I found the Traveler (or he found me) when I was as young as I was.

RACHAEL JAYNE
Marijuana

I remember being in J-R's office and Sean and Jeff were there with me, and J-R said, "One of you has marijuana in your aura," and they both said, "Probably me because it's around me at school." Neither of them had smoked it. I said to J-R, "Well, how do they protect themselves?" And J-R said, "They don't need to protect themselves. The light of God will protect them as long as they don't reach out and do it themselves."

RANDY GARVER
Be Careful What You Ask For

One year, I went to a Founders Dinner which was a fundraiser for Windermere Ranch, held in Santa Barbara. Each person there had the chance to ask J-R a question. The session went late into the night. When it was finally my turn, I said, "J-R, I don't have a question, but I would really like to be more consciously aware of Spirit." He responded, "We'll look into it." And that was that.

I got home from the event about 4:30 in the morning. I went to sleep and had a dream that was later characterized as going through the eye of the needle, or what's called the "terror of God." This is a separator between the lower realms and the higher realms of Light. It strips you of your illusions and your negativity because, by definition, you can't be in that place with that burden. In my dream, I was in that place, and it was a remarkable experience. I couldn't even see because it was so bright. When I came back into the body, a lot of "stuff" had been stripped clean from me.

Afterward, it literally took me three or four years to assimilate and reintegrate myself back here in this world. I had to hire people to do things like drive me to work and help me clear the negativity after meetings because I couldn't close it off. I was so open—it was like a gentle breeze kind of feeling. The experience taught me that a lot of illusions and karma are here to support us in being in this physical world. To not have them is like being without a filter. This was a big lesson about being careful what you ask for, and understanding that there's a certain kind of grace in not knowing. There's a balancing act between longing for that higher experience and being here on the planet.

SOULS TRANSITIONING: PROFOUND LESSONS AND EXPERIENCES

JUDITH JOHNSON
Souls Having Human Experiences

After studying in MSIA for about twenty-five years, I had the following inner experience:

> *I was sitting in a circle of chairs, meeting with my spiritual support team—among whom were J-R, John Morton, and Jesus. There was an empty chair for a guest, and my father had taken up residence in the guest chair. I was practically spitting with rage as I demanded that he leave immediately. I insisted that he had no right to be there, as he had never given me one ounce of support or love my whole life.*
>
> *Then Jesus walked over beside me and put his arm around my shoulder, like a wise older brother. He suggested a different approach to the situation: "Why not hear what your father has to say for himself, since he has shown up? Then, if you still want to throw him out, you can." That gave me pause. "After all," I thought to myself, "this is Jesus."*
>
> *Slightly less enraged, I glared down at my father and demanded he justify his presence there. I was stunned to see a tear fall out of his eye and run down his face. I had never seen my father cry. Then he uttered words I will never forget: "That was my assignment. I was never to show you any love." It was as though sheets of ice and glass within me—which had*

held all my judgments and anger against this man—shattered into a zillion pieces, falling away from me. I was aware—truly aware—that my Soul was speaking to my father's Soul. I was overcome with profound gratitude for this being who had willingly taken on this role in service to my highest good. That was a kind of love beyond any I had ever known before.

That inner event changed me and continues to change me. From that moment on, I have been emotionally free in relationship to my memory of my father, who had died several years before that event. I have also noticed how, often, I seek to rise above the minutiae of mental concepts and emotional reactions to people and events in my life and to be aware of myself and others as souls having human experiences. Although this level of awareness eludes me most of the time, I know that inner event really happened, and I no longer get hooked emotionally as fully as I used to. Whenever I start to derail over the trials and tribulations of life, I remind myself that I am a Soul, and I look for the wisdom and upliftment available to me in whatever is going on.

I have also come to see an exquisite perfection in my father's apparent rejection of me. In seeking his approval and love, I had been turning outside myself to find those experiences—even though I always knew there was a deeper kind of love that I was trying to reconnect to. Had my yearning been satisfied by the love of my earthly father, I might never have pursued the quest that eventually led me to MSIA. When I first connected to MSIA, I felt myself breathe a sigh of relief and gratitude, and heard an inner voice proclaim, "I'm home!"

KATHLEEN FLEMING
The Teachings Working with Me and through Me

Just about a year ago, my son called with a devastating message. He said that his son—who was twenty years old, just short of his twenty-first birthday—had committed suicide. It's still hard to talk about. At that time, I was getting close to being totally disabled, and I didn't think I could manage the one-hour drive up to his house. So, my son said, "No, Mom. Just say a prayer for us." I said, "Okay."

I crawled into bed early that night, knowing that whatever I could do for my grandson, it would happen after I went to bed. As I lay down, I was thinking that I would work with him however it showed up that night. My grandson was about six-foot-two, with long blonde shaggy hair and geeky eyeglasses that were always on the end of his nose. He had not filled out yet, so he was still very gangly.

I remember very clearly having the experience of putting my hand over his heart and just wrapping him with love. I was awake off and on all night doing that. I remember that. Every time I would awaken or be conscious, my grandson was still there. At some point during the night, I felt such a sense of peace with him that it brought me peace.

That's one of the times when I really felt the teachings of the Traveler working with me and through me—however exactly that was going on. I mean, my grandson was as clear as if he were with me right here and now. And to just be able to help him at that time—to know that whatever he needed I could help him with—that was really important to me.

I shared this with my son and his wife, and his wife's mother, who all found comfort from it. I don't know how much of this is "initiation stuff" and how much is "ministerial stuff," but there's something really solid about being in MSIA and working with the Traveler and just doing whatever I can every day to somehow spread that in the world. That's just who I am now.

MARIE GERHART
Shipping Out with the Traveler

When my father was passing, it was an emotional time for me and my family. My brother and I were going to the hospital to be with him, and I was feeling desperate. As I was going in for the visit, I called on the MSIA ministerial body for support so I could get through this smoothly. I felt the ministerial energy come in, and it was so sweet and supportive inwardly. I believe it even extended to my brother and to my father so that his passing was smooth and quiet and very nice.

At one point, my dad was saying, "I'm going to be shipping out tonight." I tried to clarify what he meant by asking some questions, but it was, "No, no, I'm going to be shipping out. You have to bring me some warm clothes because it's really cold out at sea." He had been a Marine in World War II. I said, "Well, maybe I'll go, too," and he responded, "Oh, no—you're not discharged yet. The captain said I could go, though."

Later, I asked J-R who he was referring to, and J-R said that John Morton was the captain of that ship. And I felt that was very beautiful that the Traveler was taking care of him. My father passed quietly in his sleep that night. He had been on Discourses for five years earlier in his life. It's a wonderful blessing that the Traveler works with Discourse subscribers and their families. It makes everything go so smoothly. You know that you still have love in your heart, so you don't feel completely bereft.

YVONNE MOCHEL
Full of Joy Just to Be

My friend Ken Jones was on quite a journey around his passing—he demonstrated a high consciousness. Before he left, he couldn't walk or do much of anything. He knew his body was invaded with stuff that wasn't going to change, and yet people were still taking care of him and feeding him well. He said, "You know, I can't move out of this place, but I am the happiest man. I am so happy to be here on this planet." It was an honest outpouring of his heart. His physical body was not available to him, yet he was so grateful to be right where he was—even to be in a body that didn't work—so full of joy just to be.

I remember sitting in his room the day before he passed. I was one of those who participated in the Circle of Light ministry to hold the Light for him. And we were friends. We had been planning to retire together, so we had even checked out places that Gale Honeycutt and Kenny and Carol and I would all like to retire to—so we had a wonderful connection. And I'm there, and I got to experience the place he was in—that being in a physical body is such a privilege. And that was a big challenge for me—coming into the understanding that man is spiritual, not material. I didn't understand that at all. I didn't have experiences of it. And he gave me the most full experience—of what a privilege it is. And here's a person who can't move.

Since then, I've read stories of people whose circumstances have brought them to a place where they literally cannot move, and yet they are so filled with joy. Not being able to move a physical body does not interfere with the joy they have at being physically present.

That's one of those things I'll never forget. It's with me in a place that I treasure as a great gift. And I'm so grateful that we did that. I think it's one of the nicest things J-R provided—a way for us to chant and hold for people as they leave the physical body. I hope when I leave the planet, I'll have the opportunity to have a Circle of Light around me.

J-R'S FINAL YEARS AND
PASSING INTO SPIRIT

INELY CESNA
An Evening of Magic

The first time I met J-R in person was at the Evening of Magic 2010, a beautiful fundraising event for the University of Santa Monica (USM), from which I had recently graduated with a Master's degree in Spiritual Psychology.

At this event, Philip Barr—who had been my physician for the past four years—asked me if I would like to meet J-R. I hesitated at first because I didn't know what to say to J-R. Phil insisted, however, saying that he rarely introduced anyone to J-R in this way, but he had a feeling that I would enjoy the encounter. I finally agreed, and we walked over to J-R's table. Phil tapped him on the shoulder and said, "I would like to introduce Nick to you." (Nick was my nickname). J-R looked at me over his shoulder and shook my hand without saying a word. I simply said, "It's very nice meeting you. Thank you." The encounter took maybe a minute or two.

As we walked back to our table, I asked, "What's going on with J-R's eyes?" Phil said something to the effect that J-R couldn't see well with one of his eyes. However, J-R's eyes dazzled me from that moment on and kept appearing in my mind constantly. Unbeknownst to me, in that brief encounter, I had been face-to-face with the Twaji, which reappeared in my mind's eye numerous times.

I then decided to learn more about J-R's teachings, and two months later began reading the Discourses. A year later, at the

Evening of Magic 2011, I encountered J-R again. This time I was open to allowing my experience to be whatever it would be, and I was also willing to "marry" J-R as my spiritual teacher. I was wearing a beautiful white cocktail dress, which had been my wedding dress several years earlier. As I waited in line to see J-R, I felt an intensity building up inside me. I was shaking and crying with the feeling of seeing someone I had not seen in a long time. When I reached J-R, I hugged him as if he were my father alive again. This was a hug that had been waiting for a long time—perhaps many lifetimes—to manifest on that magical evening. I will always keep this memorable event sacred in my heart—there are no words to fully express it.

MARYA FOLEY
Endure to the End

One of the last experiences I had with J-R on the physical level was in September 2011 on a trip to Scotland where we were celebrating his birthday. I was one of the first people chosen to share at the celebration, and I didn't have time to think through what I wanted to say—in particular, I forgot to say "Happy Birthday" to J-R. John Morton was the one responding to people's sharings, but J-R was sitting right there.

When I sat down, I started grieving that I hadn't said "Happy Birthday" to him. I said to myself, "Stop, it doesn't matter. He gets that you love him." But I couldn't let it go. This sadness that I hadn't spoken with J-R directly kept welling up inside me. This went on and on, even into the next day.

At the very end of the seminar on the next day, I was sitting at a table near the exit when J-R came over to me. He couldn't really walk on his own. His staff members were hanging on to him by the arms, and he led them over to me and said, "Can I have a hug?" I stood up and said, "I didn't say Happy Birthday to you." I knew he had been hearing me the whole time. I knew that he knew I was suffering from not having said what I wanted to say to him. And he said, "It's okay, Honey. It's all right. I hear you, I hear you."

And that's the way he loved us; he knew what we were feeling. It was another example of him ministering to me and me needing to give my love to him. It was so fulfilling. He was always giving us an extra ounce and an extra piece of his loving. So, I hold it very dear that he heard my heart and gave me that gesture of his loving.

Near the end of his life, although frail and barely able to walk, he continued on with so much courage and dignity. He kept working right through to the end. Just when you'd think he's not alive anymore, he would lean forward and scream something like, "Wake up!" This happened at one seminar I attended. He demonstrated to us how to have courage in old age and infirmity and to just keep on going. Endure to the end.

J-R continues to be very inspiring to me. The bottom line is that I think he demonstrated loving to each and every one of us every day—all the time.

CAROL COLE
The Last Seminar

I had this experience in October 2014, just before J-R passed away:

It was in the night travels, and we were all gathered together in a huge room— all of us, the MSIA family. And J-R—you know how he always sits in the back—he was in the back of the room. He was the J-R of 2014, but as he got up and started walking toward the front of the room, he got younger and younger and became the J-R of 1979, when I first met him. He stood in the front of the room and shared with the group his gratitude for each and every one of us. He thanked us for being part of his journey. His gratitude was so amazing.

Then he said, "I'm going to give you the last seminar, and I'll give you everything you need." I don't remember anything that was said at that point, but I do remember his love and gratitude for us. I knew that he would be passing over soon because of that whole process of him getting younger as he walked down the aisle.

It's amazing because he's so present now. It validates that we have always existed and that we always will. And we're here in a physical body to do the work of God, Spirit, Christ, the Traveler—all of that. And for me, there's never been a question. It's always been, "Yes, whatever it takes, I'll do it."

RACHAEL JAYNE
Radiating Love

I'm one of those people who really had a hard time with J-R leaving—which is surprising because I hadn't relied on him physically for a very long time. But I felt the loss of him here, his presence, whatever that powerful presence is. Do I still find him inside? Absolutely—stronger than ever. When I start talking about him, he is right here with me. But for a while, I was really aware that he was no longer here physically. And I don't think that was a popular point of view. A lot of people were saying, "Oh, he's stronger inside of me than ever." But he was already strong inside of me. I wasn't looking for more of that—I lived that way. For the longest time, even for major decisions, I didn't need to write J-R because I could just check inside and the J-R inside of me would guide me.

I deeply felt the loss of his physical presence, and I had to come to terms with whether I was willing to stay here—part of me was like, "I don't want to be here without him." I really had that very strongly, to the point where my husband was saying, "Are you going to step in front of a truck?" I mean, he was worried because I loved J-R at a level that was so powerful for me. I had talked to J-R about this once during an aura balance, where I was sobbing about how close I am to him. He said, "You know, it's like we're blood relatives. We go way back, Rachael—but it's going to be much more powerful if you find me on the inner than anything we could ever have here physically." And I know that's true. That's why, for years when there'd be an entourage around J-R, I would never have traded my inner relationship with him for that kind of closeness on the outer—it just pales in comparison. And it's not like I didn't get closeness with J-R, but it was that I valued the inner relationship so much more. That's been as strong as ever—but I had a very hard time adjusting to not having him physically on the planet.

I facilitate Insight Seminars, and something happened in an Insight II that was so interesting. Even though the seminar has modules with certain learning goals, the way you get there is different with every Seminar. There's a part of the Insight II where I don't usually share my own personal process. Yet this time, I heard inwardly a few hours before that I needed to present something personal to the participants—specifically, to share about my journey since J-R left and how hard it was for me.

We were at a point in the Seminar where I had everyone dancing and then we told jokes. The group was loosening up, and it was really a great place. Then one of the participants began sharing, and another participant said she was uncomfortable with what he was saying. I remember thinking, "J-R, what do I do now?" Instead of creating a safe space, it was as if we had just taken ten steps back. What I heard inwardly was, "Now you need to share the thing I was telling you to share." So, I said, "Okay, guys, we're going to change it up now. You're going to have another opportunity to unburden yourself."

I described what we were going to do and then said, "I'll start." I was very vulnerable, very transparent, very real as I shared how hard it was for me when J-R died. Not only did this energetically change the direction of the Seminar, but it also brought forward a coming together of the group that was phenomenal. At the end of my very tender sharing, the entire group in unison said, "Thank you for sharing." And that became what they did after everybody's sharing—which had never happened in this particular part of Insight II. It was amazing—it created so much safety.

The next day, a participant I considered to be the most resistant and unconscious—and really fighting for her limitations—had a breakthrough. Very quickly, she had come up with an affirmation that ended with something like "and radiating love." I asked her what it meant to her. She responded, "I just want to live my life like the way people talked about J-R." Somehow, whatever happened in my sharing, something that I was nervous about sharing—it very directly impacted her. So once again, I was reminded how present J-R is with the process if I just listen and trust—to me, that was a miracle. It was a miracle, first, that this particular girl got an affirmation so quickly and, second, that it was driven by the energy of what J-R is—which is radiating love.

JOE MILLAR
No Words to Say
What It Means to Know You

I met John-Roger in 1973 when I was twenty-eight years old—the best thing that ever happened to me. His love and his teachings have shown me the way ever since. I thank God for him.

OCTOBER 22, 2014
for John-Roger

Even though you've often told us
not to waste our time weeping
everyone's shedding tears today,
salt water washing everyone's face
while you are traveling
away from this body,
body we've touched and gazed upon
which came to earth near the coal mines
of Rains, Utah, USA—
body with reddish Welsh hair,
dark blue eyes that seemed to change color,
larger and more luminous
in the pictures from Israel,
body with delicate freckled hands

wearing the black ring
Sai Baba gave you
healing and blessing the planet.

No words to say
what it means to know you,
to feel you close by
in the company of horses
in the fullness of trust,
or walking beside the sea.
Whatever we were thinking
you already knew it,
whatever dark deeds
you had already done them
and now this day has finally arrived
you've waited for so long
and we keep hearing your voice in the dawn.

Though it's another ordinary day on earth
filled with the autumn wind,
the boats all rocking,
the church and the steeple,
open the doors and see all the people:
the waitresses and electricians,
the garbage men and the Magi kings,
the constellations far overhead
invisible in the daylight
tracking their vibrant rings.

MATTHEW VANFOSSAN
John, I Love You!

The first time a companion of mine mentioned "the Traveler," I felt the same amazing energy I had experienced earlier in USM classes with Ron and Mary Hulnick. It was a moment of that same magic from the classes—a soothing pressure on my forehead, a gentle warmth through my body, a sense of indescribable freedom and joy. Soon it passed—but I wanted to know how to get more of it. My companion directed me to the MSIA website to learn more about the Traveler, and there I learned that the first year of Discourses cost $50. That's where I stopped. "No thanks," I thought, "I didn't just spend thousands of dollars on a master's degree in spiritual psychology to waste my time subscribing to monthly booklets from a church. I'll keep my fifty bucks."

Weeks later, remembering the energy I had experienced when I first heard about the Traveler, I made up my mind to go back to the MSIA website and order Discourses—especially since I had learned that I could get my money back if I didn't like them. The Discourses came as an e-mail attachment. I opened the first one and hit the key for my computer to start reading it aloud. As I listened to the first paragraph, I felt a wash of that same energy—*the Traveler*, they called it. It was the strongest I'd ever felt. "My God," I thought, "this is incredible!" I continued listening. The actual content was not nearly as spectacular, I thought. But the energy...

Two months into my Discourses, I headed to Santa Barbara for a picnic at Windermere Ranch, where John Morton was scheduled to speak. My first John Morton seminar had been at the USM building before I subscribed to Discourses. I had been unimpressed. John didn't say anything I hadn't already heard from Ron and Mary at USM. When my wife and I arrived at the Windermere picnic, John was already speaking.

As we got closer to him, I started getting really excited—I could sense the presence of something amazing. "That's Jesus Christ!" I said to myself. That made absolutely no sense to me, but I was so moved that I knew I had to share with John. I pulled away from my wife. "What are you doing?" she asked, horrified (after all, I'm blind and she was the person guiding my steps). But I was determined. I bumped into someone who guided me to the line of people waiting to share. As I took the microphone, I said, "John, I...I love you!" And then I felt really embarrassed. "I'm like a teenage girl at a rock concert," I thought. But even though I felt stupid, the compulsion to stand and profess my love to this stranger didn't leave me. I just stood there listening as he asked me about my blindness.

That was a few years ago. The urge to serve this energy, this man, and this phenomenon that somehow relates to Jesus Christ, has remained strong in me.

LEE CLAUSEN
The Christ Has Blossomed in Me

One day during the Living in Grace retreat at Asilomar, California, in 2015, I was sitting in the back of the room when John Morton was speaking, and I felt like he was talking directly to me. He said, "I want you to work out what it is you want, then write it down using no more than 150 words." He was addressing the whole group, but I knew he was talking to me in particular. Then he said, "Take three minutes every day and read over what you wrote down. Three minutes. That's not much. The rest of the day, you can do whatever you want."

So, I did this. I don't know what John called it, but I call it a "big affirmation" since it has 150 words. Since I've done this, the Christ has blossomed in me, because what I wrote has to do with owning the Christ.

The first few times I said this affirmation, I would say it for about three or four days in a row, and then I would just get hammered by negativity. And I knew it was from saying the affirmation. So, I'd lay off it for three or four days, and then I'd do it for a couple more days and get hammered again with the negativity. I told John about this in a letter, because I was resisting doing it. He wrote back, "Lee, I'm sending you the Light," which was a great comfort to me.

I have it memorized now and I usually say it every day, at least three times in succession.

"I'm living in loving through the spiritual heart of the Christ. I'm walking as the Christ and seeing the Christ in others. I'm seeing my life and all my experiences through the eyes of the inner master. I am forgiving all. I'm forgiving everything, past, present, and future. I am cooperating with what is now and knowing that

God's plan is perfect. I am present in my loving for all things, living in perfect health, wealth, and happiness. I walk on holy ground. I only speak words of loving and encouragement. I am a river of forgiveness and loving to everyone that I meet, and to every situation, circumstance, and environment that I enter into. I am discovering God in all things, knowing that Christ is present in me, in everyone, in everything, and in every moment. And in this Christ, Lee, I am well pleased."

VAL ALOE
I'm John, Your Travel Companion

I have been working with a transformational coach who is also an MSIA minister since January 2017. After one of our sessions, I mentioned to her that I had a feeling that God was calling me. In response to my sharing this, she gave me the link to the MSIA website and invited me to take a look at Discourses to see if that was something that interested me. It was only a few hours later that I ordered them! I had been seeking a closer experience with God for decades, and I felt compelled to get those Discourses right away.

As soon as I began reading the first Discourse, I sent an email to John Morton expressing my interest in becoming an initiate. A week or so later as I was doing my spiritual exercises, I felt someone coming from my left, holding my hand, and saying, "I'm John, your travel companion." At that very moment, my phone, which was next to me, vibrated. I opened my eyes, and what do I see on the screen? An email from John Morton himself lovingly welcoming me to MSIA. It was a nice surprise to hear from John Morton seconds after "John" held my hand in my spiritual exercises!

A few months after this experience, I can only say that my life is filled with joy, gratitude, and trust. I have never felt this supported, knowing—and really experiencing—that God has my back. I'm looking forward to progressing in this amazing journey of love and Light.

HEARTFELT SHARINGS FROM THE MSIA FAMILY AROUND THE WORLD

MARINA BUSTAMANTE (SPAIN)
Onward and Upward, Always

I started reading Discourses and attending MSIA home seminars in 2004 in Spain. MSIA was already established in Spain at that time, but I didn't find out about it until after I participated in Insight. My first MSIA seminar was a joyful experience. Not only had I found a very effective meditation method, but I felt a communion in sharing with other souls. I realized that MSIA was what I had always been looking for and that J-R's teachings were exactly what I wanted.

I met J-R and John Morton at an MSIA event in Madrid soon after I became a student of the Traveler. I say I met J-R, although I only saw him sitting at the back of the room.

It wasn't until years later, at a Living in Grace retreat in Chile in 2013, that I had the opportunity to share with the Traveler. My experience during this sharing was one of great expansion and movement inside of me. It really had an impact. Something inside me changed as I experienced many things being freed up—I felt renewed and was filled with joy and happiness. I returned to Madrid with a different perspective, knowing that something big had taken place.

For me, being a student of the Traveler means having found the path back home—something I had been seeking for a long time. I also know that I have been walking hand in hand with the Traveler for many lifetimes without being aware of it. Something in me recognized J-R—not his physical appearance, but spiritually. The Traveler's teachings have radically changed my way of life—I am now committed to continuing the path onward and upward, always.

J-R's passing left me with a longing for his physical presence, even though I had seldom seen him with my physical eyes, although I often saw him inwardly. My relationship with him is now stronger during spiritual exercises, and he makes me laugh as much as he used to before his passing.

Because John Morton had received the keys to the Traveler Consciousness before I joined the Movement, I met John as the Traveler and J-R as the Preceptor, which was perfect for me.

MARCELA COSTA (BRAZIL)
I Felt So Connected

I'm thirty-one years old and I've been in the Movement for six years. I did Insight I, II, and III about eight years ago, and my "buddy" from an Insight reunion gave me my first Discourses. She is seventy years old and my best friend.

Later, while I was working in a shipyard in China, I saw many pictures and videos from MSIA Conferences and Peace Awareness Trainings (PATs), and I decided I wanted to participate in them—to do it all. Every day I asked God to let me leave the ship before the PATs started in L.A., for the highest good—and then my work contract suddenly ended just a month before the PATs! Because I wanted to "do it all," I decided to stay at Prana, MSIA's headquarters, attend the MSIA Conference, and then do all three PATs.

This was my first trip to the U.S., and when I arrived at Prana, things started to happen. I was so moved that I cried when I saw the Peace Pole there. I could not sleep more than two hours a night—the only place I could get some rest was in the solarium, a room Prana residents and guests use for doing spiritual exercises, where I snored. At the Conference, I was blown away by how many people were there from all over the world. I assisted at one event, and I don't know how I did it because I had hardly slept at all. I decided it was the work of Spirit because I felt so connected.

I used to have a wish to meet J-R and lay my head in his lap, but unfortunately, I never got to meet him physically. However, I did have a strong experience with J-R: I was in the store at Conference, sitting on the floor and watching PTS's Doctor of Spiritual Science (DSS) graduation. I felt that somebody was staring at me and pulling me to look in a certain direction toward a wall of pictures of J-R, one in particular. Then J-R's picture spoke to me: "Marcela, you must do the DSS." I started to laugh (how weird this must look—a crazy girl talking to a picture), and I responded, "Yes, J-R, but take it easy—I need to do the MSS first" (the Master of Spiritual Science).

After Conference, I participated in all three PATs, and when I got back to Brazil things were different. I had this huge energy inside of me and a greater devotion to God. Since then, I have committed myself to taking the Masters and Doctorate of Spiritual Sciences classes and to making the Traveler's teachings more available in Brazil.

KATJA RUSANEN (SPAIN)
Starting a New Journey

I had just returned to Barcelona, Spain, in the fall of 2013 from a holiday in Santa Monica, California, but I was feeling restless. I felt a growing yearning inside me to continue learning after having received my Spiritual Life Coach certificate a year earlier.

One evening, as I pondered what I wanted to study, I typed "Spiritual Psychology Master" into Google search. The first link I opened was the University of Santa Monica website. When I looked at the page—without even reading the content or talking to anyone—I knew I had found my next step. An additional bonus, of course, was the fact that it was located in Santa Monica where I had just spent my holiday. I wondered if I had actually been scouting the place without knowing it during my recent trip there. This made it easier for me to leave the old continent behind and start a new journey.

When I walked into the USM building for the first time in October 2014, my eyes got misty, and it was a challenge to let in the enormous love I felt. At the same time, I felt uplifted by the Light. I knew I had arrived at the right place, but I had no idea what kind of learning journey I had signed on for. Over the course of my studies, I soon discovered that there were many branches of the tree that John-Roger planted—just as there are many paths home. For example, I saw a USM class announcement about an upcoming Insight I seminar. Even though I was on a tight student budget, the reduced fee offered through the Founder's Special made me say yes to the seminar, and I later took Insight II and Insight III.

Then it happened that I was a Christmas orphan in December 2015, and I saw an invitation to MSIA's family Christmas Eve seminar. I felt called to go there, even though I was a bit uneasy because I wasn't part of MSIA. However, I overcame my doubts and joined in. It turned out to be a beautiful celebration, and John Morton's presentation opened doors in my heart to welcome the Christ Mass. That was the day I gave myself a Christmas present of Discourses—and what a present it has been!

My heart is full of gratitude for the transformation that has already taken place in my life, and my journey continues onward and upward as John-Roger's teachings keep guiding me home.

Ana María Corvalán (Chile): Keys That Illuminate My Path

After having spent three months working at the World Bank in Washington, I returned to my family in Chile in 1981 and signed up for a seminar offered by Carlos Warter that was related to the teachings of MSIA. Discovering this path during that seminar was a very valuable experience for me. Then, in October of 1982, J-R came to Chile, and I met him and attended two seminars that he gave. Meeting J-R validated the profound connection I felt to the Movement. His presence, message, and charisma provided an answer to something I had been searching for all my life. There was clearly a "Before" and an "After" in my spiritual growth relative to when I experienced the wisdom of the Traveler.

During this visit by J-R and his staff to Chile, I was ordained as a minister in MSIA. Receiving my ministerial blessing was the beginning of the most relevant spiritual experience in my life, initiating a long and deep expansion in my consciousness that is centered in my heart. Studying with J-R, I have learned Soul traveling and experienced the knowing that I am transcendent—as well as enjoying a sense of humor that helps me see life with a smile, with no constraints or judgments.

Starting the study of Soul Awareness Discourses opened up the path to my true self and to the appreciation for the perfection inside of me. It was the beginning of a life centered in my heart and not my mind. In 1985, I asked the Traveler to initiate me into the Sound Current, which was the start of a new challenge: how to reach higher levels of consciousness. I have always felt supported, guided, and loved by the Traveler on this journey.

Today, after years of being the Traveler's disciple and participating in events like Insight seminars, PAT trainings, and PTS classes, I feel blessed and living in grace. My life has a clear purpose, and I can see from a higher perspective. Forgiveness, acceptance, and compassion, along with unconditional loving, are keys that illuminate my path.

During all this time—although there have been ups and downs in the administrative area of MSIA, both in Los Angeles and Chile, I have kept my spiritual conviction that I am a disciple of the Traveler and that the outside form is not important. I know that the essence of the teachings is pure and everlasting.

I was very happy when J-R gave the keys to the Traveler Consciousness to John Morton because now my spiritual master was not only J-R but John Morton as well. Each one gives me their wonderful energy, and I am doubly blessed. For me, J-R's passing was a natural process filled with love and gratitude. His presence in my life is not conditioned by a physical form—it comes from his essence, which is always present.

There have been profound changes in my personal life that I attribute to being a disciple of the Traveler. I learned how to let go of my self-image, of the importance of my role on this planet. From identifying as a well-known professional in the international field of education—in which my ego was the protagonist—I now identify simply as a woman filled with love, gratitude, and compassion—dedicated to service wherever I am.

INSPIRING THOUGHTS

YVONNE MOCHEL
The Bridge to the New Age

There is a place for everything, and everything is just the way it should be. I'm very grateful that I have been in the Movement since the early days to watch it grow and change in perfect ways.

We were part of the change from one dispensation to another, and J-R was the beginning of this change. We were all so excited about being part of this dispensation, saying, "The new age, this is wonderful!" But J-R said, "Well, you know, being the bridge you do get walked on." And we were like, "Oh, yeah, that too…" We were so excited to go over the bridge we were forgetting that a bridge is there to be walked on. I have a great peace about it now—I feel as if I was at the beginning of the beginning.

I say to people in MSIA in the years to come, the energy that is the Traveler is always with us. You may think, "If only I had been there then, it would be so different." But when J-R left the physical body, it was as though he was with us in even fuller ways. That energy is always with us. The gift of what he brought and continues to bring—there really are no words to describe it.

CHAPTER SEVEN

CELEBRATING AND REJOICING

As this book is being published, it has been fifty-two years since John-Roger offered that first home seminar in Santa Barbara and thirty-two years since John Morton accepted the keys to the Mystical Traveler Consciousness. This chapter is a loving tribute to both of them by a longtime friend and student, Rama Fox. We invite you to partake of the blessings that come to life in these heartfelt and profound sharings.

RAMA FOX

One Traveler Manifest
Through Many Forms

An Open Letter to John Morton *(8/6/2015)*
by Rama Fox-Cheever

Dearest John,

I'm writing this as an "Open Letter" because I got inwardly to do so, as possibly some others may gain something valuable in reading it. However, whether or not anyone else ever sees it, this message comes from my heart to you, John.

Last month, when you and Leigh came to the Travelers Through the Ages class here in Santa Barbara, I experienced something similar to what I'd long ago experienced with John-Roger. I came into MSIA in Miami during the latter part of 1969. J-R seminars were held in my home, and in early 1970, he physically came to stay with me, doing services and holding seminars—as he continued to do in my home for many years. As he sat with us, there was a sweet, sacred intimacy only those of us who have sat with him closely can understand. You, of all people, know well what I'm attempting to express.

For those of us sitting with you in our home in Santa Barbara last month, what permeated the class was the oneness of heart and soul, the loving tenderness and fellowship, the deep honoring of who you are, and the profound consciousness you so beautifully and humbly share. As I sat there, I was transported back in time—as if I had double vision—seeing both J-R of then and you, now. And inwardly I heard J-R suggesting

I share an experience regarding you and the Traveler Consciousness that I'd had in a prior Travelers Through the Ages class. So, I shared it, as follows:

You were sharing at another Travelers Through the Ages class in Los Angeles that I was taking a couple of years ago. As I sat there trying hard to stay present with what you were saying, a force greater than my desire to stay present started to show me another scene entirely. Initially, it appeared something like a transparency overlay of another dimension, while the physical level was still visible. At first, I wondered if it was my imagination until over my right shoulder I heard J-R's voice say as strongly as if he were beside me physically, "Look at what you're being shown in Spirit. Let go of the physical." So, I did... and the physical room began to disappear.

As I watched, I saw you, John, standing what in the physical would be about ninety feet away. A depth of deep blue light that I'd never seen physically was laced with deep purple light and permeated the surroundings—except around you—which radiated golden-white light. You weren't looking at me but appeared to be looking into the depths of being. Right above and behind you stood J-R ... and immediately behind and lifting slightly above him was a continuous stream of Travelers, one after another—each appearing slightly above the one below—much like jewels strung on a single necklace, all connected as one, extending and lifting into infinity. The entire line radiated a golden-white light.

As I beheld this manifestation of all the Travelers working together as one—all one with you—I began to notice a sound that grew more audible as I listened. It was the combined voices of angels, singing as one, a song that permeated all creation.

While I listened, still beholding you and the line of Travelers, all one, my vision began to also see legions of angels appearing to be sitting in a kind of cosmic stadium, tiers upon tiers stretching beyond view—voices of Light and loving—all as one. And I heard J-R say over my right shoulder (although I could still see him standing behind and above you), "You are now seeing that the Traveler Consciousness is one consciousness—flowing through many vessels throughout time—standing in unified, continuous support of the one who holds the physical keys." J-R then said some other things that are personal to me. Tears were pouring down my face as I quietly sat in a corner of the class circle, as the scene gently evaporated. I later wrote to J-R about this and he confirmed it.

Those of us who have taken the Travelers Through the Ages class have been blessed to experience ways of awakening to the Traveler Consciousness that are not available anywhere else of which I know. Although one may not necessarily experience a vision per se, a deep clarity and understanding almost assuredly occurs. It's almost as if this class is one of the best kept "secrets" of MSIA. Personally, I encourage everyone in the Movement to do themselves a favor and take this class. And for those who may have taken the class a long time ago, they may discover—as I have—that as their consciousness has grown over time, so has their ability to hear, see … and receive of the blessings.

During the last MSIA Conference of the Christ, as you shared during two meetings, I saw you step into what I don't know how to describe—but can only say I recognized as a deeper manifestation of your work as the Traveler … which included a profound message that those with the eyes to see and the ears to hear could consciously recognize. And whether or not it was recognized there and then by different individuals, the action was definitely taking place.

As you know, I love J-R. He is the heart of my heart. He has lifted, opened, and freed my consciousness beyond what I could ever have imagined. And I am so deeply grateful that in his incredible wisdom, foresight, and loving he handed the Traveler keys to you—knowing and trusting that you will manifest the Traveler Consciousness on into the future, continuing as a living Traveler to grow the awareness of MSIA. Your work in the world keeps the door to MSIA and J-R freshly open and inviting.

My heart also calls me to acknowledge Leigh and the extraordinary value of loving support, wisdom, and grace she *exquisitely brings and shares with us all. I can't imagine a more perfect wife and partner for you and your work, John. She is a splendid, shining Light … and we in MSIA are so blessed to have her with us.*

I stand in profound honoring of you, John, as my Traveler in this world … and I thank you with all my heart.

Your sister and supporter in heart and soul,
Rama (Fox-Cheever)

The Purple Rose
by Rama Fox-Cheever

I came into a very young MSIA in the fall of 1969 when I was living in Miami, Florida. A dozen or so of us would get together weekly and listen to cassette tapes lovingly sent to us from California by Reuben Perez, who taped J-R's Santa Barbara talks. In early 1970, J-R came to Miami on his first trip to work with the Miami MSIA family. And we certainly had become a family—with many of us to this day still remaining very close and living now in Los Angeles.

As I recall, it was during that first visit when I heard J-R casually mention the "purple rose" in connection to MSIA. He didn't elaborate about it, as it was just one item in other information he was sharing—and I didn't have the awareness at that time to ask for clarification. Actually, back then if we'd questioned J-R about every new thing he brought up, he'd never have gotten through a single seminar. We were relative babies, and he was spoon-feeding us timeless wisdoms.

It is well known that throughout the ages, there have been countless icons and symbols found on ancient ruins, tablets, and writings. So, when J-R mentioned the purple rose, I thought he was merely referencing an especially lovely and figurative symbol that might be relevant to MSIA.

However, quite a few of us were seeing purple light flashes that J-R often spoke of as an indication of the presence of the Mystical Traveler—even when J-R wasn't physically present himself. Also, when J-R was physically present, many of us frequently saw a vast purple aura radiating from him—which we also experienced when we were with him in our dreams. A purple rose, therefore, seemed an ideal symbol for MSIA, and various renditions of purple roses were abundant in the creations of MSIA artists—from tooled leather handbags to oil paintings.

A while later, when a historical building was purchased in Los Angeles for MSIA offices and residences, it seemed perfectly fitting that it be called PRANA, an acronym for *Purple Rose Ashram of the New Age*. Although the name was later changed to Peace Awareness Labyrinth and Gardens, many of us still lovingly referred to it as "Prana"—which also means "breath of life" in Sanskrit.

Fast forward to 1982. During a meditation, without any clue that something extraordinary was about to occur, I was suddenly awestruck to see an actual purple rose suspended in space before me! It was no figurative symbol. I intuitively knew it was the "Purple Rose" about which J-R had spoken.

J-R recently gave me the go-ahead to share what I saw back then. Even though it is beyond my ability to do it justice, I'll do my best to convey my experience in words. Perhaps as you read this, the Preceptor will aid your higher self in recognizing and resonating with what we all intuitively know.

As anyone who's had a direct experience of higher reality knows, there's nothing else quite like the experience. It is charged with meaning and intensity, completely eclipsing the common perceptions of everyday life. And it is self-validating—there is no question whatsoever that it is an experience of divinity. One enters a state of intuitive knowing that transcends mental thoughts and intellectual reasoning.

It was as if my eyes were suddenly opened into a new dimension. There, suspended before me, I saw an amazingly vivid, enormous, and breathtakingly beautiful "rose" made of living purple light containing all the shades of purple—from the deepest hue to magenta and ultraviolet. It was a continuously moving, radiant, mystical, and exquisite flower-like manifestation. To some who might see it, this beautiful revelation could look like a gigantic and eternal living lotus.

The "flower" appeared to me to be constructed of an infinite number of "petals," or elongated ellipses, consisting of flowing, ultra-radiantly alive purple light. Each petal/ellipse joined the others in the central core of the flower. As each petal flowed toward the central core, its color was absorbed into diamond-white brilliance. Each petal's perimeter was vivid purple light, some of the perimeters flowing clockwise and others flowing counterclockwise—like multiple infinity symbols in motion. (If you trace an infinity symbol—which looks like a horizontal version of an elongated number eight—in the air, it may give this more clarity.) The point where the loops of the infinity symbols join in the center corresponds to the core of the flower.

It was crystal clear to me that each petal was (and is) an entire universe. And there was a constant opening and unfolding of the petals from the core, even as the petals themselves were moving. This movement was many things—including life Itself, and all that goes on in each universe. Where all the petals met—the core—is where infinity, the eternal now, is undiluted. It appeared to me that the central core is where one moves in and out of any given universe. And deep within that infinite center is the seat of the Preceptor—the Light of all universes. As you might imagine, I was transfixed and spellbound.

Again, my words cannot even begin to do this justice. And although it is not clear to me how I know it, this is not even the Whole, but only a living aspect of the Whole. Perhaps the purpose of my consciously seeing the purple rose was so that I could one day share it with you... and J-R will take it from there.

APPENDIX

Infinity
by Rama Fox-Cheever

As the years went by since my 1982 inner sighting of the purple rose described in Chapter 7, I only thought about the purple rose occasionally. I didn't really know what to do with the awareness, which rested more or less in the wings of my consciousness.

Knowing that purple is associated with the Traveler, however, I have always paid attention to information about purple. I noted with interest, for example, that any colors beyond purple in the visible spectrum—which consists of red, orange, yellow, green, blue, and purple (or violet)—are invisible to the human eye. Purple has the shortest wavelength of all the colors, which means it has the highest frequency and energy.

Several years ago, I discovered that I could buy strings of LED Christmas lights that emit a purple light reminiscent of some of the light emitted from the purple rose I saw inwardly. I have put them on my Christmas tree each year, and many a night when I have my tree up, I gaze at those lights… as Spirit stirs my soul.

Something else was given to me in early 2012 that gave me chills, moved my heart, and brought me to tears. It is said that things come to us when we're ready—so we (you who are reading this and I, who received the information) are apparently *ready*. An email arrived in my computer with a link to video images from the Hubble telescope—into the "ultra-deep field" of this universe. What I saw was mind-bogglingly transportive.

The back-story goes that the scientists responsible for this viewing were fascinated by a very small speck in the universe near the Big Dipper that appeared to be completely empty—devoid of stars, planets, galaxies… anything. They wanted to use the powerful resources of the Hubble telescope to focus on this small speck to determine whether it was as empty as it appeared. In 1996, they took the calculated and very costly risk of utilizing their allotted time with Hubble to focus into what could have turned out to be nothing. From our perspective on earth, this seemingly empty speck appeared to be no bigger than a grain of sand held away from the body at arm's length. (To visualize how small that is, extend your arm and pretend to hold a grain of sand in your fingers—then imagine it up in the night sky.)

Over the course of ten full days of viewing, the Hubble telescope revealed three thousand more galaxies, each with hundreds of billions of stars! It was considered by some at the time to be the most profound and humbling set of images in human history.

Eight years later, in 2004, the scientists decided to view another seemingly empty sliver of sky, this time near the constellation Orion. Over the course of eleven days, the Hubble telescope revealed ten thousand more galaxies! This became known as "the ultra-deep field"—an image representing the farthest that science has ever seen into the universe. It's currently estimated that there are over one hundred billion galaxies in the universe, each with hundreds of billions of stars.

Astronomers suspected that what they saw in this Ultra-Deep Field was the edge of the universe, which is continually expanding and growing. This raises the question, "What is beyond the edge of the universe, and what is it growing into?" It is reported that scientists have no idea what makes up 95 percent of the universe.

As I observed what unfolded before me while I was watching this amazing video, I consciously experienced J-R, as Preceptor, utilizing this video to show me a minuscule slice of the unimaginable vastness of God's physical body, just in *this* universe alone. I recall hearing from deep within me, "Oh, my God—I am looking deeply into a tiny part of *myself. Our-Self.* It is all beautiful—in the greater reality, there is nothing that is not beautiful. The perception of non-beauty is an illusion—a reflection of what I do not yet know how to love."

And this is only the physical level—many, if not most, of us don't even see the other levels—and it is only this universe.

Astronomers now acknowledge that there is more than just one universe. Some even speculate that there may be an infinite number of universes. [Long before there was a Hubble Telescope, many times J-R referred to "Universes without end."]

You can watch this remarkable video of the Hubble Ultra-Deep Field at www.flixxy.com/hubble-ultra-deep-field-3d.htm. You might even invite J-R to be with you as you watch.

Watching the Ultra-Deep Field video, the Purple Rose once again appeared center-stage in my awareness, this time as a distant vision from far away—universes, constantly moving, united in the core of white Light. My experience of the Purple Rose was expansive, awakening, and blissful—just as before, there is no way I can capture it in words.

According to J-R in his book, The Path to Mastership, "Buddha said, 'I am the Light of Asia.' Christ said, 'I am the Light of the world.' The Traveler says, 'I am the Light of the universe.' And the Preceptor says, 'I am the Light of all universes.' This is not a spiritual promise. It is reality. It is present now."

One of the astonishing things I have been shown is that the Preceptor (which reportedly is only embodied every 25,000 to 26,000 years – and is with us now through our beloved John-Roger) is for the first time allowing us to view a tiny part of the edge of this universe. It seems to me that our Preceptor is utilizing Hubble to bring this opportunity for awareness to all souls embodied here.

That I am allowed to share this so openly adds to my comprehension that something very special is happening. In the past few years, many of us have witnessed a change in J-R. At times, looking into his eyes has been like looking into infinity—endlessly deep, vast, and still. Full of loving and Light.

A couple of years ago I started to realize that perhaps what many of us were seeing that seemed different about J-R was actually the Preceptor subtly manifesting physically. For whatever reason, I believe that our beloved Preceptor is giving us a gift—an infinitesimal glimpse of the Whole. In no way do I understand this—but I know it, and I see it.

घू

If you were inspired by the stories you read in this book and you would like more information about John-Roger, John Morton, or the teachings of Soul Transcendence, please contact:

MSIA (Movement of Spiritual Inner Awareness)
3500 West Adams Blvd.
Los Angeles, California 90018

323-737-4055
order@msia.org
www.msia.org

www.ingramcontent.com/pod-product-compliance
Lightning Source LLC
Chambersburg PA
CBHW020439130626
46549CB00001B/213